EVERYMAN, I will go with thee,
and be thy guide,
In thy most need to go by thy side

WILLIAM BLAKE

Selected Poems

Edited, with an introduction and notes, by
P. H. Butter
*Emeritus Professor of English Language and Literature,
University of Glasgow*

Dent: London and Melbourne
EVERYMAN'S LIBRARY

© J.M. Dent & Sons Ltd, 1982
All rights reserved

Made in Great Britain by
Guernsey Press Co. Ltd, Guernsey, C.I. for
J.M. Dent & Sons Ltd
Aldine House, 33 Welbeck Street, London W1M 8LX

First published in Everyman Paperback 1982
Reprinted 1986

This book if bound as a paperback is
subject to the condition that it may
not be issued on loan or otherwise
except in its original binding

British Library Cataloguing in Publication Data

Blake, William, 1757–1827
   William Blake: selected poems.
   I. Title   II. Butter, P.H.
   821'.7   PR4142

ISBN 0 460 01125 1 Pbk

Contents

Songs of Experience

Blake's Life

1757   Born 28 November, son of James Blake a hosier, near Golden Square in central London.

1768–72   Attended Henry Pars's drawing school in Strand.

1772–9   Apprenticed to James Basire, engraver. In 1773 engraved his earliest known picture, 'Joseph of Arimathea' after Michelangelo. Made drawings of monuments in Westminster Abbey.

1779   Student at the Royal Academy, where Sir Joshua Reynolds was President. Exhibited there for the first time in 1780. Made living as engraver, especially for the bookseller Joseph Johnson. Friendship with other artists – John Flaxman (b. 1755, sculptor and Swedenborgian), Thomas Stothard, James Barry, and later Henry Fuseli (b. 1741, Swiss, returned to London in 1780) and George Cumberland.

1780   Saw Gordon riots, including the burning of Newgate prison.

1782   Married Catherine Boucher (b. 1762), daughter of a market-gardener in Battersea. Until 1790 they lived in central London. She helped in printing and colouring his works. They had no children.

1783   *Poetical Sketches* printed at expense of Flaxman and Rev. A.S. Mathew, the copies being given to Blake for private distribution. At Mathew's house met artists, writers, etc., some of whom are satirized in *An Island in the Moon* (written *c*. 1784–5, not published by Blake); sang his songs to his own tunes.

1784   Father died. Set up print shop with another Basire apprentice James Parker; unsuccessful.

1787   Favourite brother Robert (b. 1767), who had been living with the Blakes as a pupil, died of consumption.

1788   First works in illuminated printing produced, but not issued—*All Religions Are One* and *There Is No Natural Religion*.

1789   *Tiriel* written and illustrated, but not engraved. *Songs of Innocence* and *Thel* engraved. Attended meeting of Swedenborgian Society; wrote annotations in copy of Swedenborg's *Wisdom of Angels Concerning Divine Love and Divine Wisdom*. Did not long associate with the Society; annotations in *Wisdom of Angels Concerning Divine Providence* (*c.* 1790) more critical; but continued to use ideas from Swedenborg.

1790   Moved to 13 Hercules Buildings, Lambeth. Early Lambeth years were fertile and relatively prosperous ones. Blake was illustrating works of others (e.g. Wollstonecraft's *Original Stories from Real Life* (1791), Stedman's *Narrative of a Five Years' Expedition* (worked on 1792, published 1796)), producing own pictures and drawings, and writing *Songs of Experience* and shorter prophetic books.

1791   *The French Revolution* printed by Johnson, but not published. Met prominent radicals such as Godwin, Wollstonecraft, Paine, Priestley, Holcroft who gathered at Johnson's shop and weekly dinners.

1793   *Marriage of Heaven and Hell*, *Visions of the Daughters of Albion*, *America*, *Songs of Experience*, *The Gates of Paradise* (later expanded) advertised for sale in Blake's *Prospectus*.

1794   *Songs of Innocence and of Experience* first issued in one volume. *Europe* and *Book of Urizen* engraved.

1795   *Song of Los*, *Book of Ahania* and *Book of Los* engraved.

1796–7   Made 537 drawings for edition of Edward Young's *Night Thoughts*, of which 43 were included in the first of four projected volumes in 1797, after which the project was abandoned. About this time began first long poem, *Vala* later *The Four Zoas*, which he continued to work on for about ten years, but never published. His career as engraver was damaged by the failure of *Night Thoughts*; but he was supported by friend and patron Thomas Butts, who bought pictures and drawings regularly from about 1799, especially watercolours on biblical subjects.

c. 1797 Made 116 illustrations to the poems of Thomas Gray for Mrs Flaxman.

1800 Moved to cottage near Felpham on Sussex coast, to be near new patron, Thomas Hayley, a minor poet. During next three years worked on various projects for Hayley, on illustrations to Milton's *Comus*, on *Vala* and *Milton*; learned to read Greek, Latin and Hebrew.

1803 Fracas with drunken soldier in his garden led to trial for sedition (Jan 1804), in which he was acquitted. Returned to London, to South Molton Street near Oxford Street. Worldly fortunes at low ebb—few commissions; but wrote in 1804 of being 'again enlightened with the light I enjoyed in my youth'.

1804 Title pages of *Milton* and *Jerusalem* dated this year, but the poems did not reach their final states until later—*Milton* by about 1808, *Jerusalem* by 1820.

1805 Made designs for Blair's *The Grave*, expecting commission for the more lucrative engraving; but engraving given to the more fashionable Schiavonetti.

1809 Exhibited his 'Canterbury Pilgrims' and other paintings, with *Descriptive Catalogue*, in final, unsuccessful bid for public recognition; works ridiculed by Hunt brothers in their periodical, *The Examiner*. Continued to do some engravings (e.g. of Flaxman's designs for *Hesiod* (1817) and for Wedgwood's china catalogues (1815–17)), and to work on his own paintings, especially illustrations to *Milton*, and poems.

c. 1818 *The Everlasting Gospel* drafted in Notebook, not

published. *For the Sexes: The Gates of Paradise*, enlarged version of work engraved in 1793, engraved.

1820   Designed and engraved 17 woodcuts for an edition of Virgil's *Pastorals*; about this time engraved *The Laocoön*, *On Homer's Poetry* and *On Virgil*; made first complete copy of *Jerusalem*.

1821   Illustrations to the *Book of Job* made for young painter friend, John Linnell; engraved and published 1826. Moved to lodgings in 3 Fountain Court, Strand.

1822   *The Ghost of Abel* engraved.

1824   Met young painter, Samuel Palmer; was the inspirer of a group of young artists, the 'Ancients', who came to 'the house of the interpreter' to hear him talk. Was commissioned by Linnell to make illustrations to Dante's *Divine Comedy*; by his death had made 102 drawings, of which 7 engraved. During same period drew 29 illustrations to Bunyan's *Pilgrim's Progress*.

1827   Died 12 August.

Introduction

'Would to God that all the Lord's people were prophets.' Blake was more confidently a prophet than any other major English poet. What is a prophet? Not one who foretells the future. 'A Prophet is a Seer, not an Arbitrary Dictator.' He sees behind the 'marks of woe' on the faces of the Londoners he passes, behind the wars and other evils of his time, to the attitudes which cause such things. He says, 'If you go on So, the result is So', not that 'such a thing shall happen let you do what you will'.[1] But Blake was not the kind of prophet who sees just present evils and the wrath to come, but one who saw 'Visions of Eternity', one whose 'senses discovered the infinite in everything'. Old, poor and shabbily dressed he surprised a young girl at a party by saying to her, 'May God make this world to you, my child, as beautiful as it has been to me';[2] and, according to his friend George Richmond, 'Just before he died His Countenance became fair—His eyes brighten'd and He burst out in Singing of the things he Saw in Heaven.'[3] Marks of woe in every face, this beautiful world, things in heaven—these visions are not easy to reconcile. His shorter works are showings of the contrary visions, his longer ones attempts to relate them in a comprehensive myth.

The prophet is also a spokesman, one who speaks or believes he speaks for God or some other higher power. Blake claimed in a letter in 1803 to have completed 'the Grandest Poem that this World Contains . . . I may praise it, since I dare not pretend to be any other than the Secretary; the Authors are in Eternity.'[4] His belief in inspiration contributed to that 'terrifying' honesty which T.S. Eliot saw in him, to keeping him uncompromisingly true to his vision in spite of poverty and neglect. But should the relationship of the conscious 'I' to the deeper self through which inspiration flows be only that of secretary to author? He wrote in another letter: 'I have written this Poem from immediate Dictation, twelve or sometimes twenty or thirty lines at a time, without Premeditation & even against my Will, . . . & an immense Poem Exists . . . all produc'd without Labour or Study.'[5] Poets' manuscripts do not suggest that good poems, especially long ones, are written like this. Sometimes a short poem may be 'given' and need no revision; but more commonly the manuscripts show labour and study combining with inspiration through successive drafts to the perfected whole. Blake's own manuscripts show revision and evidence of self-criticism. Only the best of the poems drafted in his notebook were chosen for inclusion in published volumes; The Four Zoas, after strenuous efforts to make it include his growing vision, was finally abandoned; he knew that the prophet must be also a 'maker', a blacksmith labouring at his furnaces to shape 'the stubborn structure of the Language'.[6] Fortunately the secretary often answered back to the authors—but not often enough. In parts of the prophetic books the authors' eloquence is allowed to flow too hastily; even then the writing is fascinating, original, and not, as was once thought, mad or unintelligible. At the best, in most of the lyrics and the best passages in the prophetic books, the poet, the maker, works with the prophet, the seer and spokesman, to give form to vision.

In his earliest volume Poetical Sketches, written according to the Advertisement between the ages of twelve and twenty, it is chiefly the brilliant young poet that we see. Naturally there are signs of immaturity and derivativeness; but the best poems have a startling freshness and originality, especially in the handling of metre. The poet already has the skill to sing his own song, using, not just imitating, contemporary and Elizabethan modes, images, ideas. And already there is freshness of vision too, and interest in strange states of feeling. 'Mad Song', for instance, obviously relates to Shakespeare's King Lear and other sources, but makes its own, quite distinct effect by its shifting rhythms and strength of feeling. The personification of spring in 'To Spring' is felt not just as a literary device as in most such eighteenth-century poems. Putting the two poems together we see themes emerging which we shall

find often again. The land, and we all, long for the renewal
offered by the divine lover who comes in each dawn, in each
spring; but madly we turn away, preferring the night, feeling
the light as 'frantic pain'. Similarly 'Song: "How Sweet I
roam'd" ' is not just an exercise in traditional mythology, but
an exploration of the paradoxes of love and of poetry, which
offer both 'golden pleasures' and a 'golden cage'. Still, in these
early poems it is the apprentice, occasionally the master, poet
or maker who predominates, enjoying the play with words,
sounds, structures. Later the prophet, the man with a message,
increasingly takes over. The best combination of the two is in
Songs of Innocence and of Experience.

In the *Songs* the models are no longer artistic Elizabethan
and eighteenth-century lyrics, but popular songs—hymns,
ballads, moral songs for children. Appropriately for popular
song the language, especially in *Innocence*, is simple and repeti-
tive; the lines and the syntactical units mostly short; the rhymes
emphatic. An apparently—and really—childlike vision is con-
veyed, in ways which subtly subvert the moral models and
suggest nuances of meaning. The rhythms are varied, combin-
ing different kinds of feet—iambs, trochees and anapaests. The
speakers are cleverly handled so as to open up varying perspec-
tives and questions. Even when the poems are not obviously
dramatic, as many are, they reveal particular states of being and
ways of seeing, which the author is not saying are the whole
truth.

Songs of Innocence are 'happy songs/Every child may joy to
hear'; but they are not sentimental, because they contain
awareness of sorrow also. Early versions of some of them are
found in the satirical *Island in the Moon*, written by 1785. That
context gives them a slightly ironic undertone. 'Holy Thurs-
day' is spoken by a complacent character Obtuse Angle, and
'Nurse's Song', spoken by a Mrs Nannicantipot, is soon fol-
lowed by a very different description of children playing—one
bowling a ball into a turd and cleaning it with a handkerchief,
another giving the speaker a black eye. We should not carry
forward the *Island in the Moon* context into *Songs of Innocence*,

which provides a context of its own. In some of the poems the happiness is unshadowed; we should not grub for complexities between all the lines. But taken as a whole the sequence shows the darkness as well as the light which shines within it and overcomes it. Even if we forget, as we should, Obtuse Angle and suppress knowledge of the actual condition of charity children in the eighteenth century, 'Holy Thursday' makes a slightly ambivalent effect. We see with the speaker the radiance of the children, but ask whether he does not too easily accept the conditions in which they are shown—marching in ranks, in uniform, to give thanks for charity. The radiance overcomes the surroundings, but the natural images associated with the children ('Thames waters', 'flowers of London town') implicitly protest against the restrictions in which they are placed. 'Nurse's Song' is more simply a song of innocence. The rhythms as well as the words convey a sense of joy, and of harmony between children, protective elder and the natural surroundings. The nurse's fear of 'the dews of night' is quickly dismissed, and leaves only a slight trace in the mind, a hint of danger, of the possible transitoriness of innocence.

This hint is a little stronger in a similar poem 'The Ecchoing Green'. Here again we have children's play echoed by the natural surroundings. We should not make too much of the coming dark. The emphasis continues to the end to be on peace, protection, natural rhythm; the children go home only when they 'Like birds in their nest/Are ready for rest'. To the eye of innocence, youth and age, day and night are parts of an accepted order. Yet there are hints of sadness—in mention of 'care' which old John laughs away, in the ending of 'our sports', in the transition from the 'ecchoing' to the 'darkening' green, in the rhythm of the last lines. On the edge of these poems, held at bay so that we may contemplate the radiance, is the knowledge of other states of being. In some poems the darkness is brought into the centre, though it is still overcome by the light. In 'The Chimney Sweeper' innocence is seen not in any pretty pastoral landscape, but among the soot. The lives of the boys are coffins from which they escape only in fantasy.

In 'The Little Black Boy' the boy can expect nothing in this life but rejection from the white boy he admires. The children are, some of them, in a worldly sense deprived children, their capacity for happiness all the more poignant for that. The protective elders share their joy, but also in some poems weep for them; and in turn the mother, as well as the children, is wept for by Jesus ('Cradle Song'), who combines the roles of child and protector. The first poem in the series demands happy songs; the last (in the final arrangement), 'On Another's Sorrow', defines the nature of the happiness and of the innocence which the whole series has displayed. Behind all the children and lambs has been Jesus, who 'gives his joy to all' by becoming 'a man of woe'. Innocence not only shines in the midst of woe, as in the chimney-sweeping boys, but in its highest form positively accepts and transforms it.

The 'innocent' poems imply a knowledge of experience, and the 'experienced' poems do not extinguish the vision of innocence. One should not think of Blake seeing wonderful visions in youth and then growing up to reject them as illusory when he found what the world is really like. When he published *Songs of Innocence* he was over thirty, had written the satirical *Island in the Moon* and the sombre *Tiriel*, and had seen plenty of ugliness and suffering in the central London where he lived. Conversely, in *Songs of Experience*, completed five years later, his bard still believes in the possibility that 'fallen, fallen light' might be renewed, though he is now more concerned with the state of those who turn away from the light. The two sets of poems are showings of contrary states, contrary ways of seeing. The different speakers' visions are all true in that they represent ways in which people actually experience the world; none is the whole truth. There are 'whisp'rings in the dale' as well as laughing on the hill, reactions of envy as well as of peace in adults looking at children. But the second nurse does not correct the illusions of the first; indeed it is she who is the more deluded, her vision that is the narrower. The 'mind-forg'd manacles' (forged largely by their own minds) of the experienced speakers confine them in small worlds.

Blake understates what he shows by writing of 'the Two Contrary States of the Human Soul'. Innocence is a relatively simple state, but experience is varied. 'The Tyger' suggests a different state from that of the second nurse. Though dangerous and the contrary of the lamb, the tiger is felt as beautiful ('burning bright'). We wonder at the strength and energy in him and in his creator; and question why the universe should contain tigers and lambs, and the contrary things these represent. The poem consists of questions, and answers should not be read back into it from later poems; but the emotional effect is not that we want to destroy the tiger and have a world only of lambs, but rather that we want to have both the energy of the tiger and the innocence of the lamb in a world in which the one would not destroy the other. The state of the second nurse, on the other hand, though we sympathize with her, is not a positive one at all. Her envy damages the children and brings nothing but bitterness to herself, and we would be glad to see it eliminated. To use Blake's later distinction, 'experience' contains both 'contraries' (to be redeemed) and 'negations' (to be destroyed). But he is not in these poems creating a mythology nor a system of ideas to reconcile the different ways of seeing. We see each vision as it passes, conveyed in most of the poems with wonderful concision by rhythm and image. We should see what we are shown and apprehend the states of being suggested without too hastily imposing our own, or Blake's later, judgments. For instance, most recent commentators say that 'Ah! Sun-flower' implicitly condemns yearning after another world, failure to achieve fulfilment in this one. This is to impose a judgment from outside the poem, which is delicately poised between aspiration after a golden clime beyond time and questioning of the validity of such aspiration. Perhaps the traveller's journey *is* done only in a realm beyond time? Perhaps the pale virgin and pining youth could have fulfilled their aspirations here? In so far as *Songs of Experience* incline, not by statement but suggestion, towards the latter view they are more optimistic than the earlier group. They are influenced by having been written in the early enthusiastic years of the French Revolution. In them the cries of chimney sweepers, soldiers, harlots, menace church, palace and established morality, calling not for removal to 'new worlds', as in 'Night' in *Innocence*, but for the transformation of this one.

A lyric can display a single state, or contrast more than one ('The Clod and the Pebble') or even show a transition from one to another ('The Little Girl Lost' and 'The Little Girl Found'); but a larger form is needed to explore the meaning of these states, how they came into existence and how they are related. A poet's means of exploring is by creating a myth rather than a philosophical system, and Blake was already beginning to do this at the same time as he was writing his songs. *Thel* and *Visions of the Daughters of Albion* are closely related to the *Songs* in that they show innocent speakers and states of experience and ask whether, and why, the state of experience must be entered. In speaking of innocent speakers in *Thel* I am thinking of lily, cloud, worm and clod of clay rather than of Thel herself. Unlike the innocent speakers in *Songs* Thel is timid, self-conscious and self-centred; it is the lily, etc., who see the world as a realm of creative interchange and accepted self-giving. They invite her to enter, and when she does she finds something quite different from what she has been told of—a state of strife in which natural impulses are thwarted and corrupted. Is she to be blamed for fleeing back from this 'grave' into her escapist paradise? Most commentators say that she is, but the poem does not contain any clear answers to the problems it raises. It beautifully creates by its wavering rhythms and images different worlds, different ways of seeing, and ends with questions rather than answers. Oothoon in *Visions* is an innocent, and braver than Thel. She plucks the flower of sexual experience, speeds across the waves to her lover, and, raped by the violent Bromion and rejected by the tearful Theotormon, finds herself imprisoned in a cave, where she nevertheless continues to assert that 'every thing that lives is holy'. Again the effect is ambivalent. Oothoon's action at the beginning seems generous, and yet it leads to nothing but evil for her. Reading neo-Platonically we would say that she is mistaken to pluck the flower, that her story shows the soul, seduced by desire, descending into the cave of this world; but yet do we not feel that her generosity was right, whatever the consequences?

That *Visions* presents a paradoxical situation and leaves us in uncertainty about why, and whether, the soul must descend into the cave or 'pit' of this world does not reduce its force as a poem; for it, no more than *Thel*, claims to answer these questions. A greater difficulty, recurrent in Blake, arises from its treatment of morality, law, good and evil. For here Oothoon—and her eloquence is such that we are drawn towards feeling that Blake is speaking through her—does seem to be preaching a doctrine. She asks, 'are not different joys/ Holy, eternal, infinite? and each joy is a Love'.[7] She seems to be arguing for complete anarchism, for the free fulfilment of *all* desires. Does this include, as logically it should, the desires of the slave-owner and rapist Bromion and of the 'fat fed hireling . . . who buys whole corn fields into wastes'?[8] Oothoon does not confront this question honestly, and nor does Blake. Later he will suggest a possible answer in his doctrine of the annihilation of the selfhood. If the selfhood were annihilated, all desires could be fulfilled because they would not be selfish. But in the meantime? Blake is too impatient to consider this question. He flies towards apocalypse, and does not ask how government or ordinary social life is to be carried on in an imperfect world. Such difficulties do not trouble us when reading the *Songs* nor large parts of the prophetic books. When Blake shows his visions and the various states of the human soul we see and experience with him without asking the wrong kind of question. But increasingly in the prophetic books he becomes a teacher as well as a seer; and when we are taught rather than shown we rightly question.

Visions openly introduces a political dimension into Blake's writing. Bromion is among other things an American slave-owner, and Oothoon denounces the tithe system, the enclosure movement, etc. as well as standing for the oppressed women of England and for women in general. The political

element, always present to some extent, is especially promi-
nent in the work of the early 1790s when Blake, like other
radicals, was greatly excited by the French Revolution. The
beginner will not be able to pick up all the particular references,
and should turn for help to D.V. Erdman's *Prophet Against
Empire*, but will feel at once the force of the denunciations of
war, empire, slavery, industrialism and of the attitudes behind
them. The world of the prophetic books is not some remote
place and time, but here and now. We walk with Los, the
eternal prophet, through London, and see the children playing
among the filth, the 'dens of despair' in a lunatic asylum, and
the youth of England in sorrowful drudgery in the factories,
and at the same time see through his eyes that the ordinary
people in streets and factories are 'myriads of eternity'.[9] The
political element grounds the myth in history. But even in the
most political poems it is always something beyond political
change, though including it, that Blake is after. At the end of
America, for instance, the fires of Orc, the force behind the
revolutionaries in America and France, consume not just old
political, social and moral systems, but 'the five gates' of our
mortal senses. We are to be released from the restrictions of the
senses as we now experience them into new ways of seeing.
Blake was not interested in achieving some limited improve-
ments by the art of the possible. To be content with that would
seem to him a surrender to the God of this world. Man's desires
are infinite, and himself infinite. It was inevitable therefore that
Blake should go on from the history-grounded 'continent'
poems (*America, Europe*, 'Africa' and 'Asia' in *Song of Los*) to
construct a cosmic myth to show man's infinite potential, why
he does not achieve it and how he might. This was not a move
away from reality, but into that reality which is closest to
us—in our own heads; nor was contemporary or past history
left behind. No one interpretation of a passage in Blake is *the*
meaning. There are at least three ways of reading the prophetic
books, which can in theory be distinguished, but which in
practice must most of the time be combined.

(1) They embody a cosmic myth about the fall and salvation

of man, in Blake's terms about the sleep of Albion, universal man, and his waking to eternal life. Awake, man sees (for eternity is now) 'the infinite in all things, sees God', sees the human and the divine as one and as containing, not contained by, the universe. This idea is represented in the illustrations to *Jerusalem* by showing sun, moon and stars as parts of Albion's body. He falls into self-division when 'the starry heavens are fled from the mighty limbs of Albion', when he sees things as 'the outward Creation'. This is in accordance with a long tradition of mystical thought and experience, and is not mad or even, taking a wide enough perspective, eccentric, though it is strange to most of us in the modern West. What may make those who have some inkling of this experience still hesitate to embrace it is the feeling that we do not want to lose the sense of 'otherness' which alone makes possible relationship and love. Blake meets this difficulty in the words of the Divine Family:[10]

> We live as One Man; for contracting our infinite senses
> We behold multitude; or expanding, we behold as one,
> As One Man all the Universal Family . . .

Seeing contrary truths he states them boldly, not worrying much about how they are to be reconciled. He asserts equally oneness and 'multitude'; insists on individuality, freedom, that there cannot be one law for the lion and the patient ox, at the same time as showing all identities as members of one body. As the myth of cosmic man develops in *Jerusalem*, a balancing emphasis is placed on 'Minute Particulars'. 'He who wishes to see a Vision, a perfect Whole/Must see it in its Minute Particulars.'[11] This, at any rate, is the theory. In practice he only occasionally takes much interest in creating in words the minute particulars, in conveying a sense of delight in individually distinctive beauty. He expands our eyes so that we see 'Mountain, hill, earth & sea' (already generalized) as 'Men' and then as 'One Man'[12] rather than, like Hopkins, making earth's dapple proclaim God's glory. At times he does seem to want to make 'this world' as beautiful to us as it has been to him; describes with tenderness the lark and the wild thyme—

messengers of Los and still a little bird and flower. But often he seems implacably hostile to the natural world. Error or Creation must be burned up in order that Truth or Eternity may appear. 'It is Burnt up the Moment Men cease to behold it. I assert for My Self that I do not behold the outward Creation & that to me it is hindrance & not Action.'[13] 'Natural Objects always did & now do weaken, deaden & obliterate Imagination in Me.'[14] One can try to reconcile these positions by stressing the word 'outward': things are hindrance when seen as outward, beautiful and infinite when seen imaginatively. But there seems too much discontinuity between the ways of seeing. Either we are shown the infinite in all things or the seductive Vala, awakening into eternity or imprisonment in nightmare; not simple beauty which may be enjoyed for itself and sometimes lead towards larger vision. But Blake's extremes, put together, are more enlightening than moderation.

(2) The poems depict the divisions within all of us. All the 'Giant Forms'—Urizen, Los, Orc and the rest of them—are in us; in their contentions, changes, reconciliations we see our inner life. In the early books the main contenders are Orc, the fiery boy, human energy and emotion breaking out against the restrictions of Urizen, the starry king, imposer of limits. The force of the poetry seems all on the side of Orc, and we may at first think that they are simply enemies and hope with Oothoon, and doubtless in some moods Blake himself, that Urizen should be destroyed, 'accursed from the earth'. But soon we see that they are not simply good and evil. Orc's fires are destructive as well as cleansing; Urizen is deluded rather than simply wicked. Their fights are self-destructive, and do not lead to liberation. They are curiously alike as well as opposed; the one turns into the other. Later the main contenders are Los and Urizen; and again the emotional force seems at times to be all on one side, on the side of Los, of imagination against reason, of the living form of art against the 'mathematic form' of abstract systems. But again it is at times subtly and movingly shown how they are both damaged in their divided state, that their fights are self-destructive and that the conclusion

must be wholeness rather than the elimination of either. One of the climaxes in *The Four Zoas* is when Los finds 'his Enemy Urizen . . . In his hands' and 'wonder'd that he felt love & not hate'.[15] Similarly the quarrels, reconciliations, mutual dependence even when quarrelling, between the Zoas and their Emanations at times vividly depict the relationships both between the male and female within us and between men and women. At the best, complex psychological states are shown by the creation of beings who are much more than mere names standing for imagination, reason, etc. These are not properly speaking characters, as in a novel; they represent our unstable, fluid inner lives, and cannot be fixed. But they most successfully embody what they represent when they are most human, nearest to being characters in a drama rather than just symbols. Urizen is always an impressive, sometimes a moving, presence—a formidable autocrat, but also a pathetic old man watching painfully as his mistaken but in general well-meant plans go awry. In the passage in this selection from Night VI of *The Four Zoas* he wanders through his 'ruin'd world', seeking vainly to establish relationships with his 'children', whom he has alienated by his own divisive attitudes. Such passages make real to us that he represents something in all of us, *is* all of us as we are sometimes, that he is not just something outside that we must destroy. All wars are civil wars. Similarly Los becomes a moving individual as well as a representative of the imagination. He is the 'eternal prophet', and also anyone in whom imagination is active and often Blake himself. He is the chief hero of the Blakean myth, but is subject to temptation and to error as he struggles with his own Spectre (an aspect of himself) as well as against external opponents. He is a heroic, tragic, at times a comic figure, as he lugubriously puts his left sandal on his head[16] or tries to overcome his irritation against his friend Albion. Blake's sanity is seen in the way he can treat the 'characters' closest to himself humorously—Mr Quid the Cynic in *An Island in the Moon*, the narrator in *Marriage of Heaven and Hell*, Los. He is the least solemn of the Romantic prophets, much less so than Wordsworth. His proneness, however, to accept too quickly the first words of his authors is seen in this aspect of his work also. Only some of the 'Giant Forms' are imaginative creations; some are little more than names.

(3) The prophetic books show the divisions in society, especially in Blake's own time but also in history in general. On this level Orc is revolutionary energy breaking out in the American and French revolutions, and Urizen represents the rulers, regimes, codes of morality, etc. against which revolution was directed. Revolution turns out to be, as the word suggests, a turning of the wheel back to where it was before. The days of liberation are followed in 1793 by the Terror; Robespierre leads to Napoleon; Orc becomes Urizen; there is no breaking out of the cycle. Blake's perception of this cycle did not cause him, however, like some radicals of his time, to retreat into cautious conservatism. After about 1795 he wrote less, and less optimistically, about politics, but the implications of his vision remained as radical as ever.

The fall of universal man, the divisions within each man and between men are all aspects of a single situation. So Blake's own myth, other myths, characters from the Bible and from contemporary and past history can all quite relevantly be brought together. Los walks through London; Milton descends into Blake's garden; Orc is Prometheus and Isaac, etc. Such combinations are among the chief things which make Blake's work so fascinating and full of original insights. In showing how individual and social ills are connected—he might prefer to say are identical—he anticipated many of the discoveries of modern psychology. The sudden transitions are also the cause of his having been thought mad and of his still being difficult for new, and even experienced, readers. To some extent the difficulty has to be accepted as the consequence of such wide-ranging vision; but sometimes one feels it is due to lack of concern for the reader and even for art. It is not that one expects him to make things easy for us by explaining; indeed the trouble in the later works is that there is too much exposition and not enough embodying of meaning in incident, character, rhythm, imaginative language. At the beginning he wrote songs which 'every child may joy to hear' and in which every adult can find subtleties of meaning. Later his writing, on the surface more difficult, is sometimes, because more assertive, less suited to convey nuances and more repetitive. At times the teacher takes over from the seer and maker, and, since the class will not listen, has to go on repeating the lesson. But not for long. Los revives his fires, sees new visions, shows again his mastery of rhythm in the varied handling of the long line.

Particular stories are infinitely various, the situation underlying all stories single, though complex. Blake was interested, in spite of what he said about minute particulars, in the underlying situation rather than particular stories or characters, in the infinite in all things rather than in all things as manifesting the infinite in endlessly different ways. So he tends to return again and again to the same thoughts, images, words. But this limitation can be exaggerated if one jumbles all his works together and abstracts from them a single system of ideas. One should read each poem as a poem, and then one sees that his vision and the mythology embodying it are always growing. He is the greatest, most continuously inventive of Romantic myth-makers. At first he explores the contrary states of innocence and experience, and asks whether and why experience must be entered. Must Thel descend into her grave plot, Oothoon be imprisoned in a cave? In the early Lambeth books the hope of liberation seems to be in Orc as he struggles against the repressive father Urizen, and in 'an improvement of sensual enjoyment'. But the confrontation of Orc and Urizen turns out to be a cycle from which there is no release; and it is seen that sensual enjoyment may subject one to the possessive mother, Vala or Enitharmon, a more insidious imprisoner even than Urizen. Los becomes the chief hope. In *The Four Zoas* the fragmentation of man is shown more subtly than in the mainly one-to-one confrontations in the earlier books—in the Zoas, their Emanations, Spectres and other creations. No sooner has the elaborate four Zoas mythology been devised than it begins to be overlaid by another way of expressing inner division—the separation from Albion of his Sons and Daughters. Los must create a system so as not to be enslaved by another man's, and must create new systems so as not to be enslaved by his own. New and old are mixed, confusingly but excitingly. Finally, in *Milton* and *Jerusalem*, error is embodied mainly in Satan, the Selfhood, that in all of us which makes us think of ourselves as separate pebbles; and the means of liberation are the annihilation of Selfhood and the forgiveness of sins. The young man thinks he must fight against the father and the mother seen as external obstacles; the mature man knows that the struggle is within the self.

1982   P.H. Butter

1 Anno. Watson (K. 392).
2 *Blake Records* 274–5.
3 *Blake Records* 347.
4 Letter to Butts, 6 July 1803.
5 Letter to Butts, 25 April 1803.
6 *J*. 40:59.
7 *V.D.A.* 5:5–6.
8 *V.D.A.* 5:14–15.
9 *J*. 31:14–27, 65:12–28.
10 *J*. 38:17–19.
11 *J*. 91:21–2.
12 'To My Friend Butts' 32–51.
13 *Vision of the Last Judgment* (K. 612).
14 Anno. Wordsworth (K. 783).
15 *F.Z.* VII(a):496–7.
16 *M*. 8:11.

For key to abbreviations, see p. 195

Note on the Text and on This Selection

Apart from *Poetical Sketches* and *The French Revolution* the works of Blake published in his lifetime were produced by himself. He etched text and designs on to copper plates, printed them on fine paper and coloured each page by hand, sometimes with the help of his wife. Each copy is a unique work of art, expressing in its form as well as its content Blake's preference for living over 'mathematic' form. The text on the plates does not vary much from copy to copy; indeed it is a disadvantage of this method that the text, once etched, cannot easily be altered, except that lines may be deleted on the plate or masked so as not to be printed or a line may be added at the beginning or end. But the colouring varies from copy to copy; and, when Blake made up new copies for customers, he could and did insert, omit and rearrange plates. These changes cause less difficulty for the reader than might be expected since the prophetic books, especially the later ones, are not so much narratives or arguments as showings of visions, which can meaningfully be arranged in more than one way. In this edition the ordering and numbering of the plates are in accordance with the consensus of modern editors as to what Blake's final intentions were. The lines in the lyrics and poems from MSS are numbered for each poem; in the engraved prophetic books the lines are numbered for each plate, and the plates are numbered as in Keynes's *Complete Writings*; in *The Four Zoas* numbering is by Nights, as in *Complete Writings*, and page and line numberings as in Erdman's *Poetry and Prose of William Blake* are given in the notes.

The main problem for the editor is what to do about Blake's eccentric spelling, use of capitals, and punctuation. My principle, following Plowman and Keynes, has been to reproduce the spelling (except for a few habitual mis-spellings such as 'percieve') and capitalization, and to modernize the punctuation. In the Notebooks and other MSS there is little or no punctuation; so the punctuation, if any, of poems from these is necessarily editorial. In the works published by Blake there is punctuation of what is, to modern eyes, a very odd kind, not conforming consistently to any clear system. Furthermore it is not possible to reproduce the punctuation in type with any confidence of accuracy. Some of the marks could be commas, full stops or exclamation marks. When one is confident that they are dots rather than commas, to represent them, as one has to in type, by full stops is misleading; they mark some kind of pause, are not always full stops in our sense. Nothing short of a facsimile accurately represents even Blake's text, let alone his total illuminated page. Everyman will probably be content at the start to accept the intrusion of editorial punctuation, but should go on as soon as possible to facsimiles and become his own editor. The disadvantage of modernized punctuation is that it may destroy meaningful ambiguities. Blake's punctuation, or lack of it, often leaves open more than one way of reading a sentence, sometimes producing a complexity of possible meanings, sometimes mere uncertainty.

I have taken as my base text Max Plowman's edition of Blake's *Poems and Prophecies*, and have amended it, mainly the punctuation, after consulting the editions of Keynes, Erdman, Bentley, Stevenson (text by Erdman) and Johnson and Grant mentioned in the bibliography. For the extracts from *The Four Zoas*, not in Plowman, I have used Bentley's facsimile and consulted his and Erdman's transcriptions.

The first principle for a selector is to respect his author. The works which Blake chose to publish by his laborious method alone have his complete authority. So I have included, as well as *Songs of Innocence and Experience*, most of the shorter prophetic books and large extracts from *Milton* and *Jerusalem*. The only engraved poems omitted are ones Blake took little trouble in illustrating—*Song of Los*, *Book of Los* and *Ghost of Abel*. The most important unengraved work is *The Four Zoas*, on which he worked for many years and which contains some of his greatest writing. I have included some passages, but it is impossible in a selection of this size to give an idea of it as a whole, as I have tried to do as far as possible for *Milton* and *Jerusalem*. *Poetical Sketches* was printed for Blake before he had devised his own method, and cannot be said to have been decisively endorsed nor rejected by him. The poems in the 'Pickering' MS have more authority than the other MS poems in that they were written out in fair copy, and the poems in letters to Butts have great charm and interest, showing how myth and everyday events were mingled in Blake's experience. For the rest, though everything he wrote is salty and bears his thumbprint, one must not put rejected drafts, fragments and explosions of passing feeling on a level with the published works. Blake showed good sense in his exclusions.

This edition does not show Blake as a visual artist. His is a composite art; and one must go on to 'read' the whole page, designs and words. But there is some advantage in starting with the words, provided one does not stop there. The Notebook suggests that Blake wrote the words first, and later added the designs. Words are more resistant than pictures to allowing one to impose one's own notions upon them.

Any editor and annotator of Blake is indebted to many predecessors. I am indebted at least to all those whose works are cited in the bibliography—among editors especially to G.E. Bentley, D.V. Erdman and Sir Geoffrey Keynes; among annotators to W.H. Stevenson; among interpreters to D.V. Erdman (*Prophet Against Empire*) and Kathleen Raine (*Blake and Tradition*).

Select Bibliography

Works of Blake

(i) FACSIMILES. The illuminated books have been reproduced by the Trianon Press for the Blake Trust (excellent, expensive), and in one volume in black and white in *The Illuminated Blake* (O.U.P., 1975) with annotation by D.V. Erdman (good value). Other, relatively inexpensive, reproductions include: *Songs of Innocence and Experience* (O.U.P., 1967), *Marriage of Heaven and Hell* (O.U.P., 1975), *Book of Urizen* and *Milton* (Thames and Hudson, 1978). Plates from the illuminated books are reproduced also in some of the volumes listed below in (iii). A facsimile of *The Notebook of William Blake* has been edited by Erdman (O.U.P., 1973); and of *Vala* or *The Four Zoas* by G.E. Bentley (O.U.P., 1963).

(ii) EDITIONS OF THE TEXTS. William Blake, *Poems and Prophecies*, ed. Plowman (Dent, 1927) contains nearly all the poetry except *The Four Zoas* at a modest price; *The Poetry and Prose of William Blake*, ed. Erdman, commentary by Harold Bloom (Doubleday, 1965 and later improved editions) is the preferred edition of most scholars because it reproduces the original as far as is possible in type; *The Complete Writings of William Blake*, ed. Keynes (O.U.P., 1966 and later improved editions), with original spelling and modernized punctuation, is excellent value and the standard edition for most readers; *The Poems of William Blake*, ed. Stevenson, text by Erdman (Longman, 1971) is the most fully modernized and annotated edition of the complete poems; William Blake, *The Complete Poems*, ed. Ostriker (Penguin, 1977) is an unmodernized text with annotation; William Blake's *Writings*, ed. Bentley (2 vols., O.U.P., 1978) is expensive, useful to consult for the full bibliographical information; *Blake's Poetry and Designs*, ed. Johnson and Grant (Norton, 1979) is a large selection of poetry and prose with some designs, annotation and critical extracts. The letters can be found in Keynes's *Complete Writings* and, with other documents and annotation, in *The Letters of William Blake*, ed. Keynes (3rd enlarged edition, O.U.P., 1980).

(iii) BLAKE AS A VISUAL ARTIST. The best place to see Blake's pictures is the Tate Gallery, London. Relatively inexpensive books are: *William Blake: Poet, Printer, Prophet* (Methuen, 1965), a small selection from the illuminated books with commentary by Keynes; *The Drawings of William Blake*, introduction and commentary by Keynes (Dover, 1970); Milton Klonsky, *William Blake: The Seer and His Visions* (Orbis, 1977). A larger selection is *William Blake*, ed. Payley (Phaidon, 1978). Comprehensive and excellent are: *The Graphic Works of William Blake*, ed. D. Bindman (Thames and Hudson, 1978); *The Paintings and Drawings of William Blake*, ed. M. Butlin (2 vols., Yale, 1981). Books reproducing particular series of designs include: *The Illustrations of William Blake for Thornton's Virgil*, introduction by Keynes (Nonesuch Press, 1937); Blake's *Grave*, introduction and commentary by S.F. Damon (Brown University Press, 1963); *William Blake's Water-Colour Designs for the Poems of Thomas Gray* (Trianon Press, 1972) (splendid and expensive; the designs can be seen in scaled-down form in a volume of the same title derived from the above and with commentary by Keynes (Eyre Methuen, 1972) and with fuller commentary in Irene Taylor, *Blake's Illustrations to the Poems of Gray* (Princeton, 1971)); Bo Lindberg, *William Blake's Illustrations to the Book of Job* (Åbo Akademi, 1973) supersedes for those who can get it *Blake's Job*, commentary by Andrew Wright (O.U.P., 1972); *William Blake: Illustrations of Dante* (Trianon Press, 1979) and, with full commentary, A.S. Roe, *Blake's Illustrations to the Divine Comedy* (Princeton, 1953); Pamela Dunbar, *William Blake's Illustrations to the Poetry of Milton* (O.U.P., 1980) contains black and white reproductions with full commentary; *William Blake's Designs for Young's Night Thoughts* (4 vols., O.U.P., I and II 1980) will contain all the designs with commentary, and those published in 1797 can be obtained inexpensively in *Night Thoughts* by Edward Young, illustrated by Blake, edited by R. Essick and J. La Belle (Dover, 1975).

Secondary Works

(i) REFERENCE. S.F. Damon, *A Blake Dictionary* (Brown University Press, 1967); *A Concordance to the Writings of William Blake*, edited by D.V. Erdman and others (Cornell, 1967), is the best help of all, enables one to work out the meanings of the symbols better than by looking them up in the *Dictionary*; G.E. Bentley, *Blake Books* (O.U.P., 1977) lists Blake's works, books he owned, works about him.

(ii) BIOGRAPHY. A. Gilchrist, *Life of William Blake* 1863, edited by R. Todd (Everyman, rev. ed. 1945, reissued 1982); M. Wilson, *The Life of William Blake* 1927, revised by Keynes (O.U.P., 1971); G.E.

Bentley, *Blake Records* (O.U.P., 1969) contains the original materials for the life of Blake.

(iii) CRITICISM. Books on the shorter poems: J. Holloway, *Blake: The Lyric Poetry* (Arnold, 1968); H. Adams, *William Blake: A Reading of the Shorter Poems* (University of Washington Press, 1963). E.D. Hirsch in *Innocence and Experience* (Yale, 1964) is also interesting on the lyrics, and begins to lead one into the later poems. Bernard Blackstone, *English Blake* (Cambridge, 1949) and M.K. Nurmi, *William Blake* (Hutchinson, 1979) are good general introductions, and H. Bloom, *Blake's Apocalypse* (revised edition, Cornell, 1970) surveys the prophetic books.

J.M. Murry, *William Blake* (Cape, 1933) is still a lively introduction to Blake's ideas, as is K. Raine, *Blake and the New Age* (Allen and Unwin, 1979). They lead on to more difficult books such as S.F. Damon, *William Blake: His Philosophy and Symbols* (Houghton Mifflin, 1924); M.O. Percival, *William Blake's Circle of Destiny* (Columbia, 1938); N. Frye, *Fearful Symmetry* (Princeton, 1947); M.D. Paley, *Energy and the Imagination* (O.U.P., 1970); D. Ault, *Visionary Physics: Blake's Response to Newton* (University of Chicago Press, 1974). Stimulating on Blake's intellectual background are D. Hirst, *Hidden Riches: Traditional Symbolism from the Renaissance to Blake* (Eyre and Spottiswoode, 1964); A.L. Morton, *The Everlasting Gospel: A Study of the Sources of William Blake* (Lawrence and Wishart, 1958); K. Raine, *Blake and Tradition* (2 vols., Princeton, 1968). J. Bronowski in *William Blake and the Age of Revolution* (Routledge, 1965; revised form of *William Blake: A Man without a Mask*, Secker, 1944) is lively on Blake's relation to his own time, but less learned than D.V. Erdman in *Blake: Prophet Against Empire* (Princeton, revised edition 1969).

Blake as an artist can be studied in the introductory *The Art of William Blake* by A. Blunt (Columbia, 1959) and the more exhaustive *Blake as an Artist* by D. Bindman (Phaidon, 1977); and the poet and artist are well put together in *Blake's Composite Art* by W.J.T. Mitchell (Princeton, 1978).

Books not specifically on Blake containing discussion of him include: D.G. James, *The Romantic Comedy* (O.U.P., 1948); N. Frye, *Fables of Identity* (Harcourt Brace, 1963); H. Bloom, *Ringers in the Tower* (University of Chicago Press, 1971); D. Donoghue, *Thieves of Fire* (Faber, 1973).

(iv) ESSAYS. Collections suitable for the beginner are: *William Blake: Songs of Innocence and Experience: A Casebook*, ed. Bottrall

(Macmillan, 1970) and *A Collection of Critical Essays*, ed. Frye in the Twentieth Century Views series (Prentice-Hall, 1966). *The Divine Vision*, ed. Pinto (Gollancz, 1957) includes K. Raine's essay on 'The Little Girl Lost and Found and The Lapsed Soul' and other good essays. *William Blake: Essays in Honour of Sir Geoffrey Keynes*, ed. Paley and Phillips (O.U.P., 1973) ranges widely and includes 'Justifying one's valuation of Blake' by F.R. Leavis. *William Blake: The Critical Heritage*, ed. Bentley (Routledge, 1975) is an anthology of criticism from all periods. There are a few good essays in *The English Romantic Poets*, ed. Abrams (2nd edition, O.U.P., 1975).

Notable particular essays include: W.B. Yeats, 'William Blake and the Imagination' and 'William Blake and his Illustrations to the Divine Comedy' in *Essays and Introductions* (Macmillan, 1961; originally in *Ideas of Good and Evil*, 1903); T.S. Eliot, 'William Blake' in *Selected Essays* (Faber, 1951; originally in *The Sacred Wood*, 1920).

1986 Supplement

William Blake, *An Island in the Moon*, ed. M. Phillips (Cambridge, 1986).

Critical books recommended for the beginner: H. Glen, *Vision and Disenchantment: Blake's Songs and Wordsworth's Lyrical Ballads* (Cambridge, 1983); J. Holloway, *Blake* (Open University, 1984); E. Larrissy, *William Blake* (Blackwell, 1985). More specialized studies: N. Hilton, *Literal Imagination: Blake's Vision of Words* (University of California Press, 1983); M.D. Paley, *The Continuing City: William Blake's Jerusalem* (O.U.P., 1983); L. Tannenbaum, *Biblical Tradition in Blake's Early Prophecies: The Great Code of Art* (Princeton, 1982).

FROM *POETICAL SKETCHES*

To Spring

O thou with dewy locks, who lookest down
Thro' the clear windows of the morning, turn
Thine angel eyes upon our western isle,
Which in full choir hails thy approach, O Spring!

The hills tell each other, and the list'ning   5
Vallies hear; all our longing eyes are turned
Up to thy bright pavilions: issue forth,
And let thy holy feet visit our clime.

Come o'er the eastern hills, and let our winds
Kiss thy perfumed garments; let us taste   10
Thy morn and evening breath; scatter thy pearls
Upon our love-sick land that mourns for thee.

O deck her forth with thy fair fingers; pour
Thy soft kisses on her bosom; and put
Thy golden crown upon her languish'd head,   15
Whose modest tresses were bound up for thee!

To Winter

'O Winter! bar thine adamantine doors:
The north is thine; there hast thou built thy dark
Deep-founded habitation. Shake not thy roofs,
Nor bend thy pillars with thine iron car.'

He hears me not, but o'er the yawning deep   5
Rides heavy; his storms are unchain'd, sheathed
In ribbed steel; I dare not lift mine eyes,
For he hath rear'd his sceptre o'er the world.

Lo! now the direful monster, whose skin clings
To his strong bones, strides o'er the groaning rocks: 10
He withers all in silence, and his hand
Unclothes the earth, and freezes up frail life.

He takes his seat upon the cliffs; the mariner
Cries in vain. Poor little wretch! that deal'st
With storms; till heaven smiles, and the monster   15
Is driv'n yelling to his caves beneath mount Hecla.

To The Evening Star

Thou fair-hair'd angel of the evening,
Now, whilst the sun rests on the mountains, light
Thy bright torch of love; thy radiant crown
Put on, and smile upon our evening bed!
Smile on our loves, and while thou drawest the   5
Blue curtains of the sky, scatter thy silver dew
On every flower that shuts its sweet eyes
In timely sleep. Let thy west wind sleep on
The lake; speak silence with thy glimmering eyes,
And wash the dusk with silver. Soon, full soon,   10
Dost thou withdraw; then the wolf rages wide,
And the lion glares thro' the dun forest:
The fleeces of our flocks are cover'd with
Thy sacred dew: protect them with thine influence.

Song

How sweet I roam'd from field to field
    And tasted all the summer's pride,
Till I the prince of love beheld
    Who in the sunny beams did glide!

He shew'd me lilies for my hair,   5
  And blushing roses for my brow;
He led me through his gardens fair,
  Where all his golden pleasures grow.

With sweet May dews my wings were wet,
  And Phœbus fir'd my vocal rage;   10
He caught me in his silken net,
  And shut me in his golden cage.

He loves to sit and hear me sing,
  Then, laughing, sports and plays with me;
Then stretches out my golden wing,   15
  And mocks my loss of liberty.

Song

My silks and fine array,
  My smiles and languish'd air,
By love are driv'n away;
  And mournful lean Despair
Brings me yew to deck my grave: 5
Such end true lovers have.

His face is fair as heav'n
  When springing buds unfold;
O why to him was't giv'n,
  Whose heart is wintry cold?   10
His breast is love's all worship'd tomb,
Where all love's pilgrims come.

Bring me an axe and spade,
  Bring me a winding sheet;
When I my grave have made   15
  Let winds and tempests beat:
Then down I'll lie, as cold as clay.
True love doth pass away!

Song

Love and harmony combine,
And around our souls intwine,
While thy branches mix with mine,
And our roots together join.

Joys upon our branches sit,   5
Chirping loud and singing sweet;
Like gentle streams beneath our feet
Innocence and virtue meet.

Thou the golden fruit dost bear,
I am clad in flowers fair;   10
Thy sweet boughs perfume the air,
And the turtle buildeth there.

There she sits and feeds her young,
Sweet I hear her mournful song;
And thy lovely leaves among,   15
There is love: I hear his tongue.

There his charming nest doth lay,
There he sleeps the night away;
There he sports along the day,
And doth among our branches play.   20

Song

I love the jocund dance,
  The softly-breathing song,
Where innocent eyes do glance,
  And where lisps the maiden's tongue.

I love the laughing vale,   5
  I love the echoing hill,
Where mirth does never fail,
  And the jolly swain laughs his fill.

I love the pleasant cot,
    I love the innocent bow'r,   10
Where white and brown is our lot,
    Or fruit in the mid-day hour.

I love the oaken seat
    Beneath the oaken tree,
Where all the old villagers meet,   15
    And laugh our sports to see.

I love our neighbours all,
    But, Kitty, I better love thee;
And love them I ever shall;
    But thou art all to me.   20

Song

Memory, hither come,
    And tune your merry notes;
And, while upon the wind
    Your music floats,
I'll pore upon the stream,   5
Where sighing lovers dream,
And fish for fancies as they pass
Within the watery glass.

I'll drink of the clear stream,
    And hear the linnet's song;   10
And there I'll lie and dream
    The day along:
And, when night comes, I'll go
    To places fit for woe,
Walking along the darken'd valley   15
    With silent Melancholy.

Mad Song

The wild winds weep,
  And the night is a-cold;
Come hither, Sleep,
  And my griefs infold:
But lo! the morning peeps   5
  Over the eastern steeps,
And the rustling birds of dawn
The earth do scorn.

Lo! to the vault
  Of paved heaven,   10
With sorrow fraught
  My notes are driven:
They strike the ear of night,
  Make weep the eyes of day;
They make mad the roaring winds,   15
  And with tempests play.

Like a fiend in a cloud
  With howling woe,
After night I do croud,
  And with night will go;   20
I turn my back to the east
From whence comforts have increas'd;
For light doth seize my brain
With frantic pain.

To The Muses

Whether on Ida's shady brow,
Or in the chambers of the East,
The chambers of the sun, that now
From antient melody have ceas'd;

Whether in Heav'n ye wander fair,   5
Or the green corners of the earth,
Or the blue regions of the air
Where the melodious winds have birth;

Whether on chrystal rocks ye rove,
Beneath the bosom of the sea   10
Wand'ring in many a coral grove,
Fair Nine, forsaking Poetry!

How have you left the antient love
That bards of old enjoy'd in you!
The languid strings do scarcely move!   15
The sound is forc'd, the notes are few!

ALL RELIGIONS ARE ONE

The Voice of one crying in the Wilderness

The Argument. As the true method of knowledge is experiment, the true faculty of knowing must be the faculty which experiences. This faculty I treat of.

Principle I. That the Poetic Genius is the true Man, and that the body or outward form of Man is derived from the Poetic Genius. Likewise that the forms of all things are derived from their Genius, which by the Ancients was call'd an Angel & Spirit & Demon.

Principle II. As all men are alike in outward form, So (and with the same infinite variety) all are alike in the Poetic Genius.

Principle III. No man can think, write, or speak from his heart, but he must intend truth. Thus all sects of Philosophy are from the Poetic Genius adapted to the weaknesses of every individual.

Principle IV. As none by travelling over known lands can find out the unknown, So from already acquired knowledge Man could not acquire more; therefore an universal Poetic Genius exists.

Principle V. The Religions of all Nations are derived from each Nation's different reception of the Poetic Genius, which is every where call'd the Spirit of Prophecy.

Principle VI. The Jewish & Christian Testaments are An original derivation from the Poetic Genius. This is necessary from the confined nature of bodily sensation.

Principle VII. As all men are alike (tho' infinitely various), So all Religions, &, as all similars, have one source.

The true Man is the source, he being the Poetic Genius.

THERE IS NO NATURAL RELIGION

(a)

The Argument. Man has no notion of moral fitness but from Education. Naturally he is only a natural organ subject to Sense.

I. Man cannot naturally Perceive but through his natural or bodily organs.

II. Man by his reasoning power can only compare & judge of what he has already perceiv'd.

III. From a perception of only 3 senses or 3 elements none could deduce a fourth or fifth.

IV. None could have other than natural or organic thoughts if he had none but organic perceptions.

V. Man's desires are limited by his perceptions; none can desire what he has not perceiv'd.

VI. The desires & perceptions of man, untaught by anything but organs of sense, must be limited to objects of sense.

(b)

I. Man's perceptions are not bound by organs of perception; he perceives more than sense (tho' ever so acute) can discover.

II. Reason, or the ratio of all we have already known, is not the same that it shall be when we know more.

III. [*This proposition is missing.*]

IV. The bounded is loathed by its possessor. The same dull round, even of a universe, would soon become a mill with complicated wheels.

V. If the many become the same as the few when possess'd, More! More! is the cry of a mistaken soul; less than All cannot satisfy Man.

VI. If any could desire what he is incapable of possessing, despair must be his eternal lot.

VII. The desire of Man being Infinite, the possession is Infinite & himself Infinite.

Conclusion. If it were not for the Poetic or Prophetic Character the Philosophic & Experimental would soon be at the ratio of all things, & stand still, unable to do other than repeat the same dull round over again.

Application. He who sees the Infinite in all things sees God. He who sees the Ratio only sees himself only.

Therefore God becomes as we are, that we may be as he is.

[Handwritten notes:]

Songs of Innocence

(organic)

 per: natural order, purity, unselfishness, harmony, [illegible], contentment, unthinking, accepting, faith, no

Songs of Experience

deceit, selfishness, suffering, worry, conflict, faithlessness, rebellion, corruption.

[Handwritten annotations at top:]
Songs / Poems — they should be heard.

Poems work sequentially, one upon the other
very clear, accessible.

SONGS OF INNOCENCE AND OF EXPERIENCE

Shewing the Two Contrary States
of the Human Soul

SONGS OF INNOCENCE

[Handwritten left margin:]
A garden of Eden?
— there's a serpent

Pastoral, natural, country
pleasant, valleys etc

youth, boy, lamb
all symbols of
innocence.

Celebrating life
through art
music, song, lit.

monosyllabic and
piping rhythm

shepherd very
obedient, does
as he's told

Strange unexplained
and therefore
unsettling, foreboding
sense of loss?

[Handwritten near title:]
Piper = narrator
not Blake · but fictional
person.

Introduction

Piping down the valleys wild,
Piping songs of pleasant glee,
On a cloud I saw a child,
And he laughing said to me:

'Pipe a song about a Lamb.'
So I piped with merry chear.
'Piper, pipe that song again.'
So I piped, he wept to hear.

'Drop thy pipe, thy happy pipe,
Sing thy songs of happy chear.'
So I sung the same again
While he wept with joy to hear.   10

'Piper, sit thee down and write
In a book that all may read.'
So he vanish'd from my sight.
And I pluck'd a hollow reed,   15

And I made a rural pen,
And I stain'd the water clear,
And I wrote my happy songs
Every child may joy to hear.   20

[Handwritten right margin:]
ambiguous? wild in
what way.

or some signal of
innocence.

Possible image
of christ child

Piper having some
mystical experience

ambiguous? Joy or
sorrow

very emotional
response.

books learning
ie experience
knowledge
loss of innocence &
ignorance.
tree of knowledge

Emptiness

unnatural
process
has connotations of
pollution

[Handwritten at bottom:]
Repetition of key words; 'happy' words, setting tone of
poem.
very simple, easy to understand, plot, words, simple
for children. — childlike

The Shepherd

How sweet is the Shepherd's sweet lot!
From the morn to the evening he strays;
He shall follow his sheep all the day,
And his tongue shall be filled with praise.

For he hears the lamb's innocent call,
And he hears the ewe's tender reply;
He is watchful while they are in peace
For they know when their Shepherd is nigh.

The Ecchoing Green

The Sun does arise,
And make happy the skies;
The merry bells ring
To welcome the Spring;
The sky-lark and thrush,
The birds of the bush,
Sing louder around
To the bells' chearful sound,
While our sports shall be seen
On the Ecchoing Green.

Old John with white hair
Does laugh away care,
Sitting under the oak
Among the old folk.
They laugh at our play,
And soon they all say:
'Such, such were the joys
When we all, girls & boys,
In our youth-time were seen
On the Ecchoing Green.'

5

10

15

20

Handwritten annotations appear throughout the margins.

heads towards death?

opposite of first stanza — winding down, rather than building up

opposite imagery no longer positive

Till the little ones weary
No more can be merry;
The sun does descend, — *opposite of first stanza.*
And our sports have an end.

links man to nature they are part of cycle

Round the laps of their mothers   25
Many sisters and brothers,

again image of protection — old of young. Authority figures?

Like birds in their nest, — *"rest" — good refrain,*
Are ready for rest; — *part of natural cycle, but also*
And sport no more seen *death*
On the darkening Green.   30

sun going down — normal but darkening of innocence and pastoral ominous?

Narrator — "child" — piper playing child singing about lamb. Song mentioned in "Introduction"

The Lamb

Full of questions
innocent child wants knowledge.

Little Lamb, who made thee?   *only two answers*
Dost thou know who made thee?   *God or don't kn*
Gave thee life & bid thee feed
By the stream & o'er the mead;

Pastoral, Eden countryside.

Gave thee clothing of delight,   5
Softest clothing, wooly, bright;
Gave thee such a tender voice,
Making all the vales rejoice?
Little Lamb, who made thee?   *refrain, ie sense*
Dost thou know who made thee?   *of urgency thro* 10
                                    repetition

Full of answers
child knows, has learnt, been taught

Little Lamb, I'll tell thee,
Little Lamb, I'll tell thee:
He is called by thy name,
For he calls himself a Lamb. — *christ*

very narrow answer to great questions

He is meek & he is mild,   *like the wording of* 15
He became a little child: *child's prayer.*

needs faith

I a child & thou a lamb,
We are called by his name.

equates himself lamb with god

Little Lamb, God bless thee.   *refrain - sense of*
Little Lamb, God bless thee.   *urgency in* 20

absence of a complicated view, his naivety, ignorance of other things shows he has not got whole picture

lamb totally ignorant — innocence.
child less innocent — has some knowledge.

The Little Black Boy

My mother bore me in the southern wild,
And I am black, but O! my soul is white;
White as an angel is the English child,
But I am black, as if bereav'd of light.

My mother taught me underneath a tree,   5
And sitting down before the heat of day,
She took me on her lap and kissed me,
And pointing to the east began to say:

Look on the rising sun: there God does live,
And gives his light and gives his heat away;   10
And flowers and trees and beasts and men receive
Comfort in morning, joy in the noon day.

'And we are put on earth a little space,
That we may learn to bear the beams of love;
And these black bodies and this sun-burnt face   15
Is but a cloud, and like a shady grove.

'For when our souls have learn'd the heat to bear,
The cloud will vanish; we shall hear his voice,
Saying: "Come out from the grove, my love & care,
And round my golden tent like lambs rejoice." '   20

Thus did my mother say, and kissed me.
And thus I say to little English boy:
When I from black and he from white cloud free,
And round the tent of God like lambs we joy,

I'll shade him from the heat, till he can bear   25
To lean in joy upon our father's knee;
And then I'll stand and stroke his silver hair,
And be like him, and he will then love me.

The Blossom

Merry, Merry Sparrow,
Under leaves so green,
A happy Blossom
Sees you swift as arrow
Seek your cradle narrow
Near my Bosom.

Pretty, Pretty Robin,
Under leaves so green,
A happy Blossom
Hears you sobbing, sobbing,
Pretty, Pretty Robin,
Near my Bosom.

The Chimney Sweeper

When my mother died I was very young,
And my father sold me while yet my tongue
Could scarcely cry ' 'weep! 'weep! 'weep! 'weep!'
So your chimneys I sweep, & in soot I sleep.

There's little Tom Dacre, who cried when his head,
That curl'd like a lamb's back, was shav'd, so I said,
'Hush, Tom, never mind it, for when your head's bare,
You know that the soot cannot spoil your white hair.'

And so he was quiet, & that very night,
As Tom was asleeping he had such a sight,
That thousands of sweepers, Dick, Joe, Ned & Jack,
Were all of them lock'd up in coffins of black.

And by came an Angel who had a bright key,
And he open'd the coffins & set them all free;
Then down a green plain leaping, laughing they run,
And wash in a river and shine in the Sun.

Then naked & white, all their bags left behind,
They rise upon clouds, and sport in the wind;
And the Angel told Tom, if he'd be a good boy,
He'd have God for his father & never want joy.   20

And so Tom awoke; and we rose in the dark,
And got with our bags & our brushes to work.
Tho' the morning was cold, Tom was happy & warm;
So if all do their duty, they need not fear harm.

The Little Boy Lost

'Father, father, where are you going?
O do not walk so fast.
Speak father, speak to your little boy,
Or else I shall be lost.'

The night was dark, no father was there;   5
The child was wet with dew;
The mire was deep, & the child did weep
And away the vapour flew.

The Little Boy Found

The little boy lost in the lonely fen,
Led by the wand'ring light,
Began to cry, but God ever nigh,
Appear'd like his father in white.

He kissed the child & by the hand led   5
And to his mother brought,
Who in sorrow pale, thro' the lonely dale,
Her little boy weeping sought.

Laughing Song

When the green woods laugh with the voice of joy,
And the dimpling stream runs laughing by,
When the air does laugh with our merry wit,
And the green hill laughs with the noise of it,

When the meadows laugh with lively green,   5
And the grasshopper laughs in the merry scene,
When Mary and Susan and Emily
With their sweet round mouths sing 'Ha, Ha, He!'

When the painted birds laugh in the shade
Where our table with cherries and nuts is spread,   10
Come live & be merry and join with me,
To sing the sweet chorus of 'Ha, Ha, He!'

A Cradle Song

Sweet dreams, form a shade
O'er my lovely infant's head,
Sweet dreams of pleasant streams
By happy silent moony beams.

Sweet sleep, with soft down   5
Weave thy brows an infant crown.
Sweet sleep, Angel mild,
Hover o'er my happy child.

Sweet smiles, in the night
Hover over my delight;   10
Sweet smiles, Mother's smiles,
All the livelong night beguiles.

Sweet moans, dovelike sighs,
Chase not slumber from thy eyes.
Sweet moans, sweeter smiles,   15
All the dovelike moans beguiles.

Sleep, sleep, happy child.
All creation slept and smil'd.
Sleep, sleep, happy sleep,
While o'er thee thy mother weep.   20

Sweet babe, in thy face
Holy image I can trace.
Sweet babe, once like thee
Thy maker lay and wept for me,

Wept for me, for thee, for all,   25
When he was an infant small.
Thou his image ever see,
Heavenly face that smiles on thee,

Smiles on thee, on me, on all,
Who became an infant small.   30
Infant smiles are his own smiles;
Heaven & earth to peace beguiles.

The Divine Image

To Mercy, Pity, Peace, and Love
All pray in their distress;
And to these virtues of delight
Return their thankfulness.

For Mercy, Pity, Peace, and Love   5
Is God, our father dear,
And Mercy, Pity, Peace, and Love
Is Man, his child and care.

For Mercy has a human heart,
Pity, a human face,   10
And Love, the human form divine,
And Peace, the human dress.

Handwritten top margin: Love changes place in sequence (others stay in M.P.P seq) does it ascend in importance? (what about last V); if so why Emphasised above other virtues. (ie divine St 3) mun't" StS).

Handwritten left margin: All pray in one form or other and essentially to the one in power therefore we all pray God. All's have some religion - Echumenism

Handwritten left margin: implies people don't

Then every man of every clime
That prays in his distress,
Prays to the human form divine,
Love, Mercy, Pity, Peace.

Handwritten right margin: 19

And all must love the human form
In heathen, turk or jew.
Where Mercy, Love & Pity dwell
There God is dwelling too.

Handwritten right margin: why love, wh one of others? because whe there's love, others natura follow

Handwritten right margin: 20

Handwritten left margin: where is peace? transitory? or in God? or with others; it comes naturally as a consequence?

Handwritten note: like child's learnt prayer? moral; must love one another as we are all in image of God. ie "Divine Image"

Holy Thursday

Handwritten left margin: charity schools held. thanksgiving services on Ascension day. Traditional

Handwritten note: manipulation of charity.

Handwritten right margin: image of innocen cleaness, pur

'Twas on a Holy Thursday, their innocent faces clean,
The children walking two & two, in red & blue & green,
Grey headed beadles walk'd before, with wands as white as snow,
Till into the high dome of Paul's they like Thames' waters flow.

Handwritten left margin: walking in regimented lines, in uniform, conforming

Handwritten notes: lewise, respectable. Image of beadles as wise respectable citizens Almost self-righteous display of own beneficence. London - centre / heart of England. Thames - main artery / life blood. Paul's - main church - bastion of religion

Handwritten right margin: Age a beadle ant childs inno (Thames.

O what a multitude they seem'd, these flowers of London town!
Seated in companies they sit with radiance all their own.
The hum of multitudes was there, but multitudes of lambs,
Thousands of little boys & girls raising their innocent hands.

Handwritten notes: Schools - military term - Army - order - conformity regimentation
containes must obey stand etc?
praying
wholesome, meaningful picture - in S.E. shallow: meaningless

Handwritten right margin: machine do wit this page end

Now like a mighty wind they raise to heaven the voice of song,
Or like harmonious thunderings the seats of heaven among.
Beneath them sit the aged men, wise guardians of the poor;
Then cherish pity, lest you drive an angel from your door.

Handwritten right margin: 1
infront, they are seperate different.

Handwritten note: protector representative of and embodiment of christian characteristics ie charity

Handwritten left margin: multitudes - uniformly - uniform, lines being led, told to pray & sing. no equality, those who command / those who obey.

Handwritten right margin: charity. big prol

Night - [See Echoing Green]

Handwritten left margin: NIGHT - ambiguous time of rest and solace but also, defencelessness, potential for harm, not knowing.

Handwritten note: (possibly pessimistic undertone as in E.G)

The sun descending in the west,
The evening star does shine;
The birds are silent in their nest,
And I must seek for mine.

Handwritten right margin: he's at present out in the world

Handwritten bottom: Piper?

The moon, like a flower   5
In heaven's high bower,
With silent delight
Sits and smiles on the night.

Farewell, green fields and happy groves,
Where flocks have took delight;   10
Where lambs have nibbled, silent moves
The feet of angels bright;
Unseen they pour blessing,
And joy without ceasing,
On each bud and blossom   15
And each sleeping bosom.

They look in every thoughtless nest,
Where birds are cover'd warm;
They visit caves of every beast,
To keep them all from harm;   20
If they see any weeping
That should have been sleeping,
They pour sleep on their head
And sit down by their bed.

When wolves and tygers howl for prey,   25
They pitying stand and weep,
Seeking to drive their thirst away
And keep them from the sheep;
But if they rush dreadful,
The angels, most heedful,   30
Receive each mild spirit,
New worlds to inherit.

And there the lion's ruddy eyes
Shall flow with tears of gold,
And pitying the tender cries,   35
And walking round the fold,
Saying, 'Wrath by his meekness,
And by his health sickness,
Is driven away
From our immortal day.   40

*lion and lamb
innocence and exper...
can coexist in harm...
in heaven.*

'And now beside thee, bleating lamb,
I can lie down and sleep,
Or think on him who bore thy name, ← *Christ*
Graze after thee and weep.
For, wash'd in life's river,   45
My bright mane for ever
Shall shine like the gold,
As I guard o'er the fold.' *why guard? — danger
heaven?*

Rythm, very simple,
*Vagueness! who's commanding.
asking*

Spring   *← Piper?*

*Spontaneous joy at
coming of spring*

Sound the Flute!
Now it's mute.
Birds delight   *B'use of
contraries.*
Day and Night;
Nightingale   5
In the dale,
Lark in Sky,
Merrily,
Merrily, Merrily to welcome in the Year.   *image of
universa...
harmon...*

*No names,
representative,
general.*   → Little Boy   10
Full of joy,
Little Girl
Sweet and small,
Cock does crow,
So do you;   15
Merry voice,
Infant noise,
Merrily, Merrily to welcome in the Year.

Little Lamb
Here I am,   — biddable
Come and lick
My white neck,
Let me pull
Your soft Wool,
Let me kiss   25
Your soft face;
Merrily, Merrily we welcome in the Year.

Nurse's Song

When the voices of children are heard on the green
And laughing is heard on the hill,
My heart is at rest within my breast
And every thing else is still.

Then come home, my children, the sun is gone down 5
And the dews of night arise;
Come, come, leave off play, and let us away
Till the morning appears in the skies.'

'No, no, let us play, for it is yet day
And we cannot go to sleep; 10
Besides, in the sky, the little birds fly
And the hills are all cover'd with sheep.'

'Well, well, go & play till the light fades away
And then go home to bed.'
The little ones leaped & shouted & laugh'd 15
And all the hills ecchoed. —

Marginal handwritten annotations present throughout.

Infant Joy

'I have no name;
I am but two days old.'
What shall I call thee?
'I happy am,
Joy is my name.'
Sweet joy befall thee!

Pretty joy!
Sweet joy but two days old,
Sweet joy I call thee:
Thou dost smile,
I sing the while,
Sweet joy befall thee.   10

A Dream

Once a dream did weave a shade
O'er my Angel-guarded bed,
That an Emmet lost its way
Where on grass methought I lay.

Troubled, wilder'd and forlorn,   5
Dark, benighted, travel-worn,
Over many a tangled spray
All heart-broke I heard her say:

'O my children! do they cry?
Do they hear their father sigh?   10
Now they look abroad to see,
Now return and weep for me.'

Pitying, I drop'd a tear;
But I saw a glow-worm near,
Who replied: What wailing wight   15
Call the watchman of the night?

'I am set to light the ground,
While the beetle goes his round:
Follow now the beetle's hum;
Little wanderer, hie thee home.'   20

On Another's Sorrow

Can I see another's woe,
And not be in sorrow too?
Can I see another's grief,
And not seek for kind relief?

Can I see a falling tear,   5
And not feel my sorrow's share?
Can a father see his child
Weep, nor be with sorrow fill'd?

Can a mother sit and hear
An infant groan, an infant fear?   10
No, no, never can it be,
Never, never can it be!

And can he who smiles on all
Hear the wren with sorrows small,
Hear the small bird's grief & care,   15
Hear the woes that infants bear,

And not sit beside the nest,
Pouring pity in their breast;
And not sit the cradle near,
Weeping tear on infant's tear;   20

And not sit both night & day,
Wiping all our tears away?
O, no, never can it be,
Never, never can it be!

He doth give his joy to all;   25
He becomes an infant small;
He becomes a man of woe;
He doth feel the sorrow too.

Think not thou canst sigh a sigh
And thy maker is not by;   30
Think not thou canst weep a tear
And thy maker is not near.

O, he gives to us his joy
That our grief he may destroy;
Till our grief is fled & gone   35
He doth sit by us and moan.

SONGS OF EXPERIENCE

Introduction

Hear the voice of the Bard!
Who Present, Past, & Future sees,
Whose ears have heard
The Holy Word
That walk'd among the ancient trees,   5

Calling the lapsed Soul,
And weeping in the evening dew,
That might controll
The starry pole,
And fallen, fallen light renew!   10

O Earth, O Earth return!
Arise from out the dewy grass;
Night is worn,
And the morn
Rises from the slumberous mass.   15

'Turn away no more.
Why wilt thou turn away?
The starry floor,
The wat'ry shore,
Is giv'n thee till the break of day.   20

Earth's Answer

Earth rais'd up her head
From the darkness dread & drear.
Her light fled:
Stony dread!
And her locks cover'd with grey despair.   5

'Prison'd on wat'ry shore
Starry Jealousy does keep my den
Cold and hoar
Weeping o'er
I hear the father of the ancient men.   10

'Selfish father of men!
Cruel, jealous, selfish fear!
Can delight,
Chain'd in night,
The virgins of youth and morning bear?   15

'Does spring hide its joy
When buds and blossoms grow?
Does the sower
Sow by night?
Or the plowman in darkness plow?   20

'Break this heavy chain
That does freeze my bones around.
Selfish! vain!
Eternal bane!
That free Love with bondage bound.'   25

[Handwritten marginal annotations surrounding the text:]

boundary?

no answer is given here, but in subsequent poems?

the earth is yours / 'd's gift to man? / light is given?

imagery, description / nightmare world, / reft of God. / natural habitat / earth - Darkness / of experience.

personification of Earth

with not apologetic

Intro - Starry pole / or - ie / alousy/ Singtos, / aising language of / Intro / d or Adam / God

attributed to / (gives as good / it gets) / arts asking God / estions

d created man / spring the / ossom - ie this / ation is God's / ll.

any questions and / clamations, harsh / ness of some lines / questions, reflect / ig, angry, dislocated / surprising answer

God

Earth's Answer - Tough, harsh, uncompromising answer attacks God, bitter

female

- alliteration

no light (see Intro st(2))

- is imprisoned in this dark, horrible state. - jealousy one of the chains

which causes uprising

- symbol of experience

How can youth, purity survive, in this predicament. God demanding too much

← imagery of new life, creation, fertility

innocent, purity

inversion of normal / what should be / lack of harmony

enhanced by non rhyming of 2 lines

- Moral burden, carrying of this knowledge

Earth in terrible predicament, but God is silent - doesn't reply.

God - God's love is free, but price is / is a form of Bondage. / - bitter, sarcastic

because of this moral knowledge - good and evil - Earth / cannot just turn back, be different - God can't expect it / unless God lifts, burden, chain -

The Clod & the Pebble

'Love seeketh not Itself to please,
Nor for itself hath any care,
But for another gives its ease
And builds a Heaven in Hell's despair.'

So sang a little Clod of Clay
Trodden with the cattle's feet;
But a Pebble of the brook
Warbled out these metres meet:

'Love seeketh only Self to please,
To bind another to Its delight;
Joys in another's loss of ease,
And builds a Hell in Heaven's despite.'

Holy Thursday

Is this a holy thing to see
In a rich and fruitful land,
Babes reduc'd to misery,
Fed with cold and usurous hand?

Is that trembling cry a song?
Can it be a song of joy?
And so many children poor?
It is a land of poverty!

And their sun does never shine,
And their fields are bleak & bare,
And their ways are fill'd with thorns;
It is eternal winter there.

For where-e'er the sun does shine,
And where-e'er the rain does fall,
Babe can never hunger there,
Nor poverty the mind appall.

Handwritten annotations:

To what extent is Blake judging – Is he saying there are two views – opposing and necessary?

represent human qualities

opposing views of love from opposites

love is selfless — love can make something good/better, more bearable

Narrator – Bard! — clear, harmony — soft, giving but...

Pebble – hard, ungiving — it's being given a... once, trodden under — implication B supports pebble.

– not level, in harmony.

love is selfish — love means a commitment, confining — reversal of first stanza — makes miserable and corrupt, despite being placed in situation of beauty and happiness

Tone in S I (approving). events taken at face value, accepted. In S.E. questioning (rhetorical), accusing

contrasts

calculated to gain — not attractive as in S.I

(cry!) – connotations of pain, sorrow, therefore not joy? — [in S.I a mighty wind]

categorical – so far B has only suggested change of tone, now didactic – (showing its political teeth)

Much negative language and imagery in contrast to S.I's and "rich and fruitful"

Image of sterility in "rich and fruitful" land. — sophistry — contrast fertility

World could be wonderful, but isn't. If sun would shine, onus not on man (despite man's failure (ie usury!) but on controller of elements. (ie God?).

play on "pall" over coffin? — finality – ending with play on death — sting in tail inevitable outcome of poverty and life in this world *handwritten top margin:* as growing up - her need desire to experience become independent (evitable - right) part of natural process.) Her parents fearful of this ...rence [it contains real danger] but L comes to terms with them, and ...y are seen as benevolent - so therefore do her parents

The Little Girl Lost

handwritten: Bard?

handwritten right: Broadly about Lyca's journey from innocence to experience.

In futurity *vision of future*
I prophetic see *slothfulness (not being awake to*
That the earth from sleep *possibilities of faithfulness to God)*
(Grave the sentence deep) *} echoes of Introduction to SE*

handwritten left: t 2 stanzas different ... others, set apart, not ... of Lyca's story what is ...nection?

handwritten: graved? emphasises certainty

Shall arise and seek
For her maker meek, *Creator → God*   5
And the desart wild *→ land of Experience*
Become a garden mild. *← out of future*

handwritten left: land of experience

handwritten left: t of Eden/Eutopia ... t the world as it stands without (doesn't want God)

---

handwritten left: necdote? ...gical story - which ...rks on 2 levels, literal ... metaphorical ...eration, lyrical qualities ...llad, "story time" → ...e a parable?]

In the southern clime,
Where the summer's prime   10
Never fades away,
Lovely Lyca lay.

handwritten right: ← images of summer/prime re youth, health, potential?

handwritten right: - summers not winters, emphasising the most positive, as poem seems

handwritten left: image:- innocent, vulnerable

Seven summers old
Lovely Lyca told. *- totalled*
She had wander'd long,
Hearing wild birds' song.

handwritten left: connotations freedom and experience, which is natural

handwritten right: (wandered after bird's song recognises something in it, [Experience] which she doesn't have, wants to know more

'Sweet sleep, come to me
Underneath this tree.
Do father, mother, weep,
Where can Lyca sleep?   20

handwritten right: Lyca feels safe, happy, unthreatened, so she can sleep.

handwritten left: background there are ...hority figures, who do not ...nt her to venture into ...ld of experience ...e authority figures ...rude, even though ...y are not there.—

'Lost in desart wild
Is your little child.
How can Lyca sleep
If her mother weep?

handwritten right: metaphor for world of experience.

handwritten left: ...ca worries, that her ...ther is upset, and she ...nat be easy in the ...y she is going if her ...ther "weeps"

'If her heart does ake,
Then let Lyca wake;   25
If my mother sleep,
Lyca shall not weep.

handwritten right: not worried about herself only about parent. [poss- saying if her mother really cannot rest without her, she will wake and return].

handwritten: implication, that this would be a pity

handwritten bottom: t is from sleep that the earth must rise, murder to return to ...d - what is this sleep then - connotations of night = (experience ... also ignorance lack of knowledge)

'Frowning, frowning night,
O'er this desert bright
Let thy moon arise,   30
While I close my eyes.'

Sleeping Lyca lay,
While the beasts of prey
Come from caverns deep,   35
View'd the maid asleep.

The kingly lion stood
And the virgin view'd;
Then he gambol'd round
O'er the hallow'd ground.   40

Leopards, tygers play
Round her as she lay,
While the lion old
Bow'd his mane of gold,

And her bosom lick,   45
And upon her neck
From his eyes of flame
Ruby tears there came;

While the lioness
Loos'd her slender dress,   50
And naked they convey'd
To caves the sleeping maid.

The Little Girl Found

All the night in woe
Lyca's parents go
Over vallies deep,
While the desarts weep.

Handwritten annotations:

Experience is not necessarily bad/nasty.

She is relaxed enough to sleep – But does she not know about experience?

Ambiguity in "sleep"

– disapproving?

no anxiety – (because she is innocent)

traditionally, evil, dangerous

Hell? [for Blake this was not a bad place]

possible to view this as a young girl moving from protection of parents towards experience, of which sexual experience is a part.

very strong and patent in control

innocent, but in particular a holy innocence – sexual.

That's what lions do ⇒ not a threat

virginity possibly seen holy – but this experience from language is perhaps also seen as OK/holy?

Same lion as in "Night" (S I) – both authority figures, quite kindly and good.

experienced

← homage

Passion.

weeping at innocence because she won't be much longer?

Lion represents experience esp. sexual.

Sexual connotation

To worldly experience – anything can happen.

Parents knew of evil potential of experience, worried for Lyca.

Tired and woe-begone,   5
Hoarse with making moan,
Arm in arm seven days
They trac'd the desert ways.

Seven nights they sleep
Among shadows deep,   10
And dream they see their child
Starv'd in desert wild.

Pale thro' pathless ways
The fancied image strays,
Famish'd, weeping, weak,   15
With hollow piteous shriek.

imagine Lyca in terrible state.

Rising from unrest,
The trembling woman prest
With feet of weary woe;
She could no further go.   20

In his arms he bore
Her, arm'd with sorrow sore,
Till before their way
A couching lion lay.

... who represents ... they fear (ie ... perience) becomes ... evolent, when they ... come their terror

Turning back was vain;   25
Soon his heavy mane
Bore them to the ground;
Then he stalk'd around,

seemingly threatening but ...

Smelling to his prey.
But their fears allay   30
When he licks their hands,
And silent by them stands.

... experience ... not all bad —

They look upon his eyes
Fill'd with deep surprise,
And wondering behold
A Spirit arm'd in gold.   35

Before they were worried about experience inhibited & repressed, but now realise "truth"?

This feared experience, turned into spirit (holy?)

On his head a crown,
On his shoulders down
Flow'd his golden hair.
Gone was all their care.   40

'Follow me,' he said;
'Weep not for the maid;
In my palace deep
Lyca lies asleep.'

Then they followed   45
Where the vision led,
And saw their sleeping child
Among tygers wild,

To this day they dwell
In a lonely dell,   50
Nor fear the wolvish howl
Nor the lion's growl.

The Chimney Sweeper

A little black thing among the snow,
Crying ''weep! 'weep!' in notes of woe!
'Where are thy father & mother, say?'
'They are both gone up to the church to pray.

'Because I was happy upon the heath,   5
And smil'd among the winter's snow,
They clothed me in the clothes of death,
And taught me to sing the notes of woe.

'And because I am happy & dance & sing,
They think they have done me no injury;   10
And are gone to praise God & his Priest & King,
Who make up a heaven of our misery.'

Nurse's Song

When the voices of children are heard on the green
And whisp'rings are in the dale,
The days of my youth rise fresh in my mind,
My face turns green and pale.

Then come home my children, the sun is gone down   5
And the dews of night arise;
Your spring & your day are wasted in play,
And your winter and night in disguise.

The Sick Rose

O Rose, thou art sick.
The invisible worm,
That flies in the night
In the howling storm,

Has found out thy bed
Of crimson joy;
And his dark secret love
Does thy life destroy.

The Fly

Little Fly,
Thy summer's play
My thoughtless hand
Has brush'd away.

Am not I   5
A fly like thee?
Or art not thou
A man like me?

For I dance
And drink & sing,
Till some blind hand
Shall brush my wing.

If thought is life
And strength & breath,
And the want
Of thought is death,

Then am I
A happy fly,
If I live
Or if I die.

The Angel

I Dreamt a Dream! what can it mean?
And that I was a maiden Queen,
Guarded by an Angel mild:
Witless woe was ne'er beguil'd!

And I wept both night and day,
And he wip'd my tears away,
And I wept both day and night,
And hid from him my heart's delight.

So he took his wings and fled;
Then the morn blush'd rosy red;
I dried my tears, & arm'd my fears
With ten thousand shields and spears.

Soon my Angel came again;
I was arm'd, he came in vain;
For the time of youth was fled
And grey hairs were on my head.

The Tyger

Tyger, Tyger, burning bright
In the forests of the night, –
What immortal hand or eye
Could frame thy fearful symmetry?

In what distant deeps or skies   5
Burnt the fire of thine eyes?
On what wings dare he aspire?
What the hand dare sieze the fire?

And what shoulder, & what art,
Could twist the sinews of thy heart?   10
And when thy heart began to beat,
What dread hand? & what dread feet?

What the hammer? what the chain?
In what furnace was thy brain?
What the anvil? what dread grasp   15
Dare its deadly terrors clasp?

When the stars threw down their spears
And water'd heaven with their tears,
Did he smile his work to see?
Did he who made the Lamb make thee?   20

Tyger, Tyger, burning bright
In the forests of the night,
What immortal hand or eye
Dare frame thy fearful symmetry?

My Pretty Rose Tree

A flower was offer'd to me,
Such a flower as May never bore;
But I said 'I've a Pretty Rose-tree,'
And I passed the sweet flower o'er.

_Ben seems to say no point in being faithful as, wont benefit ya
Grasp, take what you can._

_Fidelity = Duty [Sooner murder an infant in its cradle, than nurse
unacted desires. – M. of H & H.]_

Then I went to my Pretty Rose-tree,
To tend her by day and by night;
But my Rose turn'd away with jealousy,
And her thorns were my only delight.

to care for, nurture.

how did she know about other.

She gives him cold shoulder, rebuffs him, gives no love.

Ah! Sun-flower

Ah, Sun-flower! weary of time,
Who countest the steps of the Sun,
Seeking after that sweet golden clime
Where the traveller's journey is done;

Where the Youth pined away with desire,
And the pale Virgin shrouded in snow,
Arise from their graves and aspire
Where my Sun-flower wishes to go.

brightly coloured, associated with life and heat

_sunflower, weary and counts the steps – mechanical in Blakian [the hours of folly are measured by the clock.
Is it as frustrated as youth & virgin? in weary time savouring with nothing on earth to look forward to, only after_

– experience? heat passion emotion

– fulfillment, self gratification

unfulfilled, repressed, cold unfilled

(Youth and virgin so out of life and experience they are almost dead.

– reaching up to seeking after the sun

Youth and virgin dead on earth as they do not reach out for what is around them – By-passing to heaven, missing out on earth.

The Lilly

The modest Rose puts forth a thorn,
The humble Sheep a threat'ning horn;
While the Lilly white shall in Love delight,
Nor a thorn nor a threat stain her beauty bright.

natural images, no people, obviously metaphoric

duration in sleep

characteristic not loved by W.

protection, self defence against reproach

openess, delighting in love and experience receptive.

seeming of innocence purity

For BE purity allows it to accept experience as natural – uncorrupting sexuality does not stain wholeness of Lily.

though implication is that Rose and Sheep are stained

The Garden of Love

– "Echoing Green" in experience has become this

I went to the Garden of Love,
And saw what I never had seen:
A Chapel was built in the midst,
Where I used to play on the green.

Eden like place.

what was a playground for child, but becomes different kind of playground for adult.

regularised, religion.

_– E.G._

_World Eden like "Garden of Love" but man corrupts
its, inhibits, regularises._

Chapel - denies its true function by being exclusive

And the gates of this Chapel were shut,   *uncompromising, cold closed, not open or welcoming*
And 'Thou shalt not' writ over the door;
So I turn'd to the Garden of Love
That so many sweet flowers bore,

And I saw it was filled with graves,   *(Death of innocence) on one level perhaps - but overwhelming death of spirit, love, freedom etc, cos of authority*
And tomb-stones where flowers should be;   *death - takes over natural*
And Priests in black gowns were walking their rounds,   *control, rigidity order, regularity conformity*
And binding with briars my joys & desires.

alliteration of b's strong. violent

divergence of 2 opposing sides - church & Alehouse, drinking and abstinence, God & Devil - life vs riches, fuller with both

The Little Vagabond

"without contraries is no progression" T.M.H.H

opposite leaders

Dear Mother, dear Mother, the Church is cold,
But the Ale-house is healthy & pleasant & warm;   *contraries*
Besides I can tell where I am used well,
Such usage in heaven will never do well.

But if at the Church they would give us some Ale,   5
And a pleasant fire our souls to regale,
We'd sing and we'd pray all the live-long day,
Nor ever once wish from the Church to stray.

Then the Parson might preach & drink & sing,   *Church does not correct, make well this - idea that these 102 loyalty would?*
And we'd be as happy as birds in the spring;
And modest dame Lurch, who is always at Church,
Would not have bandy children nor fasting nor birch.

And God, like a father rejoicing to see
His children as pleasant and happy as he,
Would have no more quarrel with the Devil or the Barrel,   15
But kiss him & give him both drink and apparel.

romping rhythm suggestive of alehouse ??

didactic — one side, opinion.

London

I wander thro' each charter'd street
Near where the charter'd Thames does flow,
And mark in every face I meet
Marks of weakness, marks of woe.

In every cry of every Man,
In every Infant's cry of fear,
In every voice, in every ban,
The mind-forg'd manacles I hear:

How the Chimney-sweeper's cry
Every black'ning Church appalls,
And the hapless Soldier's sigh
Runs in blood down Palace walls;

But most thro' midnight streets I hear
How the youthful Harlot's curse
Blasts the new born Infant's tear,
And blights with plagues the Marriage hearse.

The Human Abstract

Pity would be no more
If we did not make somebody Poor;
And Mercy no more could be
If all were as happy as we;

And mutual fear brings peace,
Till the selfish loves increase.
Then Cruelty knits a snare
And spreads his baits with care.

He sits down with holy fears
And waters the ground with tears;
Then Humility takes its root
Underneath his foot.

Soon spreads the dismal shade
Of Mystery over his head,
And the Catterpiller and Fly
Feed on the Mystery;   15

And it bears the fruit of Deceit,
Ruddy and sweet to eat,
And the Raven his nest has made
In its thickest shade.   20

The Gods of the earth and sea
Sought thro' Nature to find this Tree;
But their search was all in vain:
There grows one in the Human Brain.

Infant Sorrow

My mother groan'd, my father wept;
Into the dangerous world I leapt,
Helpless, naked, piping loud,
Like a fiend hid in a cloud.

Struggling in my father's hands,
Striving against my swadling bands,   5
Bound and weary, I thought best
To sulk upon my mother's breast.

A Poison Tree

I was angry with my friend;
I told my wrath, my wrath did end.
I was angry with my foe;
I told it not, my wrath did grow.

And I water'd it in fears,
Night & morning with my tears;
And I sunned it with smiles,
And with soft deceitful wiles.

And it grew both day and night,
Till it bore an apple bright;
And my foe beheld it shine,
And he knew that it was mine,

And into my garden stole
When the night had veil'd the pole;
In the morning glad I see
My foe outstretch'd beneath the tree.

A Little Boy Lost

'Nought loves another as itself,
Nor venerates another so,
Nor is it possible to Thought
A greater than itself to know.

'And Father how can I love you
Or any of my brothers more?
I love you like the little bird
That picks up crumbs around the door.'

The Priest sat by and heard the child;
In trembling zeal he seiz'd his hair;
He led him by his little coat;
And all admir'd the Priestly care.

And standing on the altar high,
'Lo, what a fiend is here!' said he,
'One who sets reason up for judge
Of our most holy Mystery.'

The weeping child could not be heard,
The weeping parents wept in vain;
They strip'd him to his little shirt,
And bound him in an iron chain;   20

And burn'd him in a holy place,
Where many had been burn'd before:
The weeping parents wept in vain.
Are such things done on Albion's shore?

A Little Girl Lost

Children of the future Age
Reading this indignant page,
Know that in a former time
Love! sweet Love! was thought a crime.

In the Age of Gold,
Free from winter's cold,
Youth and maiden bright   5
To the holy light,
Naked in the sunny beams delight.

Once a youthful pair,
Fill'd with softest care,   10
Met in garden bright,
Where the holy light
Had just remov'd the curtains of the night.

There in rising day,
On the grass they play;   15
Parents were afar,
Strangers came not near,
And the maiden soon forgot her fear.

Tired with kisses sweet,   20
They agree to meet
When the silent sleep
Waves o'er heaven's deep,
And the weary tired wanderers weep.

To her father white age or fear.   25
Came the maiden bright;
But his loving look,
Like the holy book,
All her tender limbs with terror shook.

'Ona! pale and weak!   30
To thy father speak.
O the trembling fear!
O the dismal care!
That shakes the blossoms of my hoary hair.'

To Tirzah

Whate'er is Born of Mortal Birth
Must be consumed with the Earth
To rise from Generation free;
Then what have I to do with thee?
The Sexes sprung from Shame & Pride,   5
Blow'd in the morn, in evening died;
But Mercy chang'd Death into Sleep;
The Sexes rose to work & weep.

Thou Mother of my Mortal part
With cruelty didst mould my Heart,   10
And with false self-deceiving tears
Didst bind my Nostrils, Eyes & Ears;

Didst close my Tongue in senseless clay,
And me to Mortal Life betray:
The Death of Jesus set me free: 15
Then what have I to do with thee?

The School Boy

I love to rise in a summer morn,
When the birds sing on every tree;
The distant huntsman winds his horn,
And the sky-lark sings with me.
O! what sweet company.   5

But to go to school in a summer morn,
O! it drives all joy away;
Under a cruel eye outworn
The little ones spend the day
In sighing and dismay.   10

Ah! then at times I drooping sit,
And spend many an anxious hour;
Nor in my book can I take delight,
Nor sit in learning's bower,
Worn thro' with the dreary shower.   15

How can the bird that is born for joy
Sit in a cage and sing?
How can a child when fears annoy
But droop his tender wing,
And forget his youthful spring?   20

O! father & mother, if buds are nip'd
And blossoms blown away,
And if the tender plants are strip'd
Of their joy in the springing day
By sorrow and care's dismay,   25

How shall the summer arise in joy,
Or the summer fruits appear?
Or how shall we gather what griefs destroy,
Or bless the mellowing year
When the blasts of winter appear?   30

The Voice of the Ancient Bard

Youth of delight, come hither,
And see the opening morn,
Image of truth new born.
Doubt is fled, & clouds of reason,
Dark disputes & artful teazing.   5
Folly is an endless maze,
Tangled roots perplex her ways,
How many have fallen there!
They stumble all night over bones of the dead,
And feel they know not what but care,   10
And wish to lead others when they should be led.

A DIVINE IMAGE

Cruelty has a Human Heart,
And Jealousy a Human Face;
Terror the Human Form Divine,
And Secrecy the Human Dress.

The Human Dress is forged Iron,   5
The Human Form a fiery Forge,
The Human Face a Furnace seal'd,
The Human Heart its hungry Gorge.

FROM BLAKE'S NOTEBOOK
(c. 1791–3)

*

I told my love I told my love
I told her all my heart
Trembling cold in ghastly fears
Ah she doth depart

Soon as she was gone from me   5
A traveller came by
Silently invisibly
O was no deny

*

I saw a chapel all of gold
That none did dare to enter in;
And many weeping stood without,
Weeping, mourning, worshipping.

I saw a serpent rise between   5
The white pillars of the door,
And he forc'd & forc'd & forc'd—
Down the golden hinges tore,

And along the pavement sweet,
Set with pearls & rubies bright,   10
All his slimy length he drew,
Till upon the altar white

Vomiting his poison out
On the bread & on the wine.
So I turn'd into a sty   15
And laid me down among the swine.

*

I heard an Angel singing
When the day was springing,
'Mercy, Pity, Peace,
Is the world's release.'

Thus he sung all day   5
Over the new mown hay,
Till the sun went down
And haycocks looked brown.

I heard a Devil curse
Over the heath & the furze,   10
'Mercy could be no more
If there was nobody poor;

'And pity no more could be
If all were as happy as we.'
At his curse the sun went down,   15
And the heavens gave a frown.

Down pour'd the heavy rain
Over the new-reap'd grain;
And Miserie's increase
Is Mercy, Pity, Peace.   20

A Cradle Song

Sleep, Sleep, beauty bright,
Dreaming o'er the joys of night.
Sleep, Sleep; in thy sleep
Little sorrows sit & weep.

Sweet Babe, in thy face   5
Soft desires I can trace,
Secret joys & secret smiles,
Little pretty infant wiles.

As thy softest limbs I feel,
Smiles as of the morning steal   10
O'er thy cheek, & o'er thy breast
Where thy little heart does rest.

O, the cunning wiles that creep
In thy little heart asleep!
When thy little heart does wake   15
Then the dreadful lightnings break

From thy cheek & from thy eye,
O'er the youthful harvests nigh.
Infant wiles & infant smiles
Heaven & Earth of peace beguiles.   20

*

I fear'd the fury of my wind
Would blight all blossoms fair & true,
And my sun it shin'd & shin'd,
And my wind it never blew.

But a blossom fair or true   5
Was not found on any tree;
For all blossoms grew & grew
Fruitless, false, tho' fair to see.

*

Love to faults is always blind,
Always is to joy inclin'd,
Lawless, wing'd & unconfin'd,
And breaks all chains from every mind.

Deceit to secresy confin'd,   5
Lawful, cautious & refin'd,
To every thing but interest blind,
And forges fetters for the mind.

*

Abstinence sows sand all over
The ruddy limbs & flowing hair;
But Desire Gratified
Plants fruits of life & beauty there.

Eternity

He who binds to himself a joy
Does the winged life destroy;
But he who kisses the joy as it flies
Lives in eternity's sun rise.

Riches

The countless gold of a merry heart,
The rubies & pearls of a loving eye,
The indolent never can bring to the mart,
Nor the secret hoard up in his treasury.

Motto to the Songs of Innocence & of Experience

The Good are attracted by Men's perceptions
And think not for themselves,
Till Experience teaches them to catch
And to Cage the Fairies & Elves.

And then the Knave begins to snarl,   5
And the Hypocrite to howl,
And all his good Friends show their private ends,
And the Eagle is known from the Owl.

THE BOOK OF THEL

PLATE 1   I

The daughters of Mne Seraphim led round their sunny flocks,
All but the youngest. She in paleness sought the secret air,
To fade away like morning beauty from her mortal day.
Down by the river of Adona her soft voice is heard,
And thus her gentle lamentation falls like morning dew: 5

'O life of this our spring! why fades the lotus of the water?
Why fade these children of the spring, born but to smile & fall?
Ah! Thel is like a wat'ry bow, and like a parting cloud,
Like a reflection in a glass, like shadows in the water,
Like dreams of infants, like a smile upon an infant's face,   · 10
Like the dove's voice, like transient day, like music in the air.
Ah! gentle may I lay me down and gentle rest my head,
And gentle sleep the sleep of death, and gentle hear the voice
Of him that walketh in the garden in the evening time.'

The Lilly of the Valley, breathing in the humble grass,   15
Answer'd the lovely maid and said: 'I am a wat'ry weed,
And I am very small and love to dwell in lowly vales;
So weak the gilded butterfly scarce perches on my head;
Yet I am visited from heaven, and he that smiles on all
Walks in the valley, and each morn over me spreads his hand   20
Saying, "Rejoice, thou humble grass, thou new-born lilly
      flower,
Thou gentle maid of silent valleys and of modest brooks;
For thou shalt be clothed in light, and fed with morning
      manna,
Till summer's heat melts thee beside the fountains and the
      springs
To flourish in eternal vales". Then why should Thel complain?   25
PLATE 2
Why should the mistress of the vales of Har utter a sigh?'

She ceas'd & smil'd in tears, then sat down in her silver shrine.

Thel answer'd: 'O thou little virgin of the peaceful valley,
Giving to those that cannot crave, the voiceless, the o'erfired;
Thy breath doth nourish the innocent lamb, he smells thy
    milky garments,   5
He crops thy flowers while thou sittest smiling in his face,
Wiping his mild and meekin mouth from all contagious taints.
Thy wine doth purify the golden honey; thy perfume,
Which thou dost scatter on every little blade of grass that
    springs,
Revives the milked cow, & tames the fire-breathing steed.   10
But Thel is like a faint cloud kindled at the rising sun:
I vanish from my pearly throne, and who shall find my place?'

'Queen of the vales,' the Lilly answer'd, 'ask the tender cloud,
And it shall tell thee why it glitters in the morning sky,
And why it scatters its bright beauty thro' the humid air.   15
Descend, O little cloud, & hover before the eyes of Thel.'

The Cloud descended, and the Lilly bow'd her modest head,
And went to mind her numerous charge among the verdant
    grass.

PLATE 3   II

'O little Cloud,' the virgin said, 'I charge thee tell to me
Why thou complainest not when in one hour thou fade away;
Then we shall seek thee, but not find. Ah! Thel is like to thee:
I pass away; yet I complain, and no one hears my voice.'

The Cloud then shew'd his golden head, & his bright form
    emerg'd,   5
Hovering and glittering on the air before the face of Thel:

'O virgin, know'st thou not? Our steeds drink of the golden
    springs

Where Luvah doth renew his horses. Look'st thou on my
    youth,
And fearest thou, because I vanish and am seen no more,
Nothing remains? O maid I tell thee, when I pass away,   10
It is to tenfold life, to love, to peace, and raptures holy.
Unseen descending, weigh my light wings upon balmy
    flowers,
And court the fair eyed dew to take me to her shining tent.
The weeping virgin trembling kneels before the risen sun,
Till we arise link'd in a golden band, and never part,   15
But walk united, bearing food to all our tender flowers.'

'Dost thou, O little Cloud? I fear that I am not like thee;
For I walk thro' the vales of Har, and smell the sweetest
    flowers,
But I feed not the little flowers. I hear the warbling birds,
But I feed not the warbling birds; they fly and seek their food.   20
But Thel delights in these no more, because I fade away;
And all shall say, "Without a use this shining woman liv'd,
Or did she only live to be at death the food of worms?" '

The Cloud reclin'd upon his airy throne and answer'd thus:

'Then if thou art the food of worms, O virgin of the skies,   25
How great thy use, how great thy blessing! Every thing that
    lives
Lives not alone, nor for itself. Fear not, and I will call
The weak worm from its lowly bed, and thou shalt hear its
    voice.
Come forth, worm of the silent valley, to thy pensive queen.'

The helpless worm arose, and sat upon the Lilly's leaf,   30
And the bright Cloud sail'd on, to find his partner in the vale.

PLATE 4   III

Then Thel astonish'd view'd the Worm upon its dewy bed:

'Art thou a Worm? image of weakness, art thou but a Worm?
I see thee like an infant wrapped in the Lilly's leaf.
Ah, weep not, little voice, thou canst not speak, but thou canst
    weep.
Is this a Worm? I see thee lay helpless & naked, weeping,   5
And none to answer, none to cherish thee with mother's
    smiles.'

The Clod of Clay heard the Worm's voice, & rais'd her pitying
    head;
She bow'd over the weeping infant, and her life exhal'd
In milky fondness; then on Thel she fix'd her humble eyes;

'O beauty of the vales of Har, we live not for ourselves.   10
Thou seest me the meanest thing, and so I am indeed:
My bosom of itself is cold, and of itself is dark,
PLATE 5
But he that loves the lowly pours his oil upon my head,
And kisses me, and binds his nuptial bands around my breast,
And says: "Thou mother of my children, I have loved thee,
And I have given thee a crown that none can take away."
But how this is, sweet maid, I know not, and I cannot know;   5
I ponder, and I cannot ponder; yet I live and love.'

The daughter of beauty wip'd her pitying tears with her white
    veil,
And said: 'Alas! I knew not this, and therefore did I weep.
That God would love a Worm I knew, and punish the evil foot
That wilful bruis'd its helpless form; but that he cherish'd it   10
With milk and oil I never knew, and therefore did I weep;
And I complain'd in the mild air, because I fade away,
And lay me down in thy cold bed, and leave my shining lot.'

'Queen of the vales,' the matron Clay answer'd, 'I heard thy
    sighs,
And all thy moans flew o'er my roof, but I have call'd them
    down.   15
Wilt thou, O Queen, enter my house? 'Tis given thee to enter
And to return; fear nothing; enter with thy virgin feet.'

PLATE 6   IV

The eternal gates' terrific porter lifted the northern bar.
Thel enter'd in & saw the secrets of the land unknown.
She saw the couches of the dead, & where the fibrous roots
Of every heart on earth infixes deep its restless twists:
A land of sorrows & of tears where never smile was seen.   5

She wander'd in the land of clouds thro' valleys dark, list'ning
Dolours and lamentations; waiting oft beside a dewy grave
She stood in silence, list'ning to the voices of the ground,
Till to her own grave plot she came, & there she sat down,
And heard this voice of sorrow breathed from the hollow pit: 10

'Why cannot the Ear be closed to its own destruction?
Or the glist'ning Eye to the poison of a smile?
Why are Eyelids stor'd with arrows ready drawn,
Where a thousand fighting men in ambush lie?
Or an Eye of gifts & graces, show'ring fruits & coined gold?   15
Why a Tongue impress'd with honey from every wind?
Why an Ear a whirlpool fierce to draw creations in?
Why a Nostril wide inhaling terror, trembling & affright?
Why a tender curb upon the youthful burning boy?
Why a little curtain of flesh on the bed of our desire?'   20

The Virgin started from her seat, & with a shriek
Fled back unhinder'd till she came into the vales of Har.

Thel's Motto

Does the Eagle know what is in the pit,
Or wilt thou go ask the Mole?
Can Wisdom be put in a silver rod,
Or Love in a golden bowl?

THE MARRIAGE OF HEAVEN AND HELL

PLATE 2

The Argument

Rintrah roars & shakes his fires in the burden'd air;
Hungry clouds swag on the deep.

Once meek, and in a perilous path,
The just man kept his course along
The vale of death.   5
Roses are planted where thorns grow,
And on the barren heath
Sing the honey bees.

Then the perilous path was planted;
And a river and a spring   10
On every cliff and tomb;
And on the bleached bones
Red clay brought forth;

Till the villain left the paths of ease,
To walk in perilous paths, and drive   15
The just man into barren climes.

Now the sneaking serpent walks
In mild humility,
And the just man rages in the wilds
Where lions roam.   20

Rintrah roars & shakes his fires in the burden'd air;
Hungry clouds swag on the deep.

PLATE 3

As a new heaven is begun, and it is now thirty-three years since
its advent, the Eternal Hell revives. And lo! Swedenborg is the

Angel sitting at the tomb; his writings are the linen clothes folded up. Now is the dominion of Edom, & the return of Adam into Paradise; see Isaiah xxxiv & xxxv Chap. ——→ *crucial Blake Ideal*

Without Contraries is no progression. Attraction and Repulsion, Reason and Energy, Love and Hate, are necessary to Human existence.

From these contraries spring what the religious call Good & Evil. Good is the passive that obeys Reason. Evil is the active springing from Energy.

Good is Heaven. Evil is Hell.

PLATE 4   *The Voice of the Devil*

All Bibles or sacred codes have been the causes of the following Errors:

1. That Man has two real existing principles, Viz: a Body & a Soul.

2. That Energy, call'd Evil, is alone from the Body, & that Reason, call'd Good, is alone from the Soul.

3. That God will torment Man in Eternity for following his Energies.

But the following Contraries to these are True:

1. Man has no Body distinct from his Soul; for that call'd Body is a portion of Soul discern'd by the five Senses, the chief inlets of Soul in this age.

2. Energy is the only life and is from the Body, and Reason is the bound or outward circumference of Energy.

3. Energy is Eternal Delight.

PLATES 5–6

Those who restrain desire do so because theirs is weak enough to be restrained; and the restrainer or reason usurps its place & governs the unwilling.

And being restrain'd it by degrees becomes passive, till it is only the shadow of desire.

The history of this is written in Paradise Lost, & the Governor or Reason is call'd Messiah.

And the original Archangel, or possessor of the command of the heavenly host, is call'd the Devil or Satan, and his children are call'd Sin & Death.

But in the Book of Job Milton's Messiah is call'd Satan.

For this history has been adopted by both parties.

It indeed appear'd to Reason as if Desire was cast out; but the Devil's account is that the Messiah fell, & formed a heaven of what he stole from the Abyss.

This is shewn in the Gospel, where he prays to the Father to send the comforter, or Desire, that Reason may have Ideas to build on, the Jehovah of the Bible being no other than he who dwells in flaming fire. Know that after Christ's death, he became Jehovah.

But in Milton, the Father is Destiny, the Son a Ratio of the five senses, & the Holy-ghost Vacuum!

Note. The reason Milton wrote in fetters when he wrote of Angels & God, and at liberty when of Devils & Hell, is because he was a true Poet and of the Devil's party without knowing it.

PLATES 6–7   *A Memorable Fancy*

As I was walking among the fires of hell, delighted with the enjoyments of Genius, which to Angels look like torment and insanity, I collected some of their Proverbs, thinking that as the sayings used in a nation mark its character, so the Proverbs of Hell shew the nature of Infernal wisdom better than any description of buildings or garments.

When I came home, on the abyss of the five senses, where a flat sided steep frowns over the present world, I saw a mighty Devil folded in black clouds hovering on the sides of the rock. With corroding fires he wrote the following sentence now perceived by the minds of men, & read by them on earth:

How do you know but ev'ry Bird that cuts the airy way
Is an immense world of delight, clos'd by your senses five?

PLATE 7   *Proverbs of Hell*

In seed time learn, in harvest teach, in winter enjoy.
Drive your cart and your plow over the bones of the dead.
The road of excess leads to the palace of wisdom.
Prudence is a rich ugly old maid courted by Incapacity.
He who desires but acts not, breeds pestilence.   5
The cut worm forgives the plow.
Dip him in the river who loves water.
A fool sees not the same tree that a wise man sees.
He whose face gives no light, shall never become a star.
Eternity is in love with the productions of time.   10
The busy bee has no time for sorrow.
The hours of folly are measur'd by the clock, but of
wisdom no clock can measure.
All wholesome food is caught without a net or a trap.
Bring out number, weight & measure in a year of dearth.
No bird soars too high if he soars with his own wings.   15
A dead body revenges not injuries.
The most sublime act is to set another before you.
If the fool would persist in his folly he would become wise.
Folly is the cloke of knavery.
Shame is Pride's cloke.   20

PLATE 8
Prisons are built with stones of Law, Brothels with bricks
of Religion.
The pride of the peacock is the glory of God.
The lust of the goat is the bounty of God.
The wrath of the lion is the wisdom of God.
The nakedness of woman is the work of God.   5
Excess of sorrow laughs. Excess of joy weeps.
The roaring of lions, the howling of wolves, the raging of
the stormy sea, and the destructive sword, are portions of
eternity too great for the eye of man.
The fox condemns the trap, not himself.
Joys impregnate. Sorrows bring forth.
Let man wear the fell of the lion, woman the fleece of the
sheep.   10
The bird a nest, the spider a web, man friendship.

The selfish smiling fool & the sullen frowning fool shall be both thought wise, that they may be a rod.

What is now proved was once only imagin'd.

The rat, the mouse, the fox, the rabbet watch the roots; the lion, the tyger, the horse, the elephant watch the fruits.

The cistern contains; the fountain overflows.   15

One thought fills immensity.

Always be ready to speak your mind, and a base man will avoid you.

Every thing possible to be believ'd is an image of truth.

The eagle never lost so much time as when he submitted to learn of the crow.

PLATE 9

The fox provides for himself, but God provides for the lion.

Think in the morning. Act in the noon. Eat in the evening. Sleep in the night.

He who has suffer'd you to impose on him knows you.

As the plow follows words, so God rewards prayers.

The tygers of wrath are wiser than the horses of instruction.   5

Expect poison from the standing water.

You never know what is enough unless you know what is more than enough.

Listen to the fool's reproach! it is a kingly title!

The eyes of fire, the nostrils of air, the mouth of water, the beard of earth.

The weak in courage is strong in cunning.   10

The apple tree never asks the beech how he shall grow, nor the lion the horse how he shall take his prey.

The thankful receiver bears a plentiful harvest.

If others had not been foolish, we should be so.

The soul of sweet delight can never be defil'd.

When thou seest an Eagle, thou seest a portion of Genius; lift up thy head!   15

As the catterpiller chooses the fairest leaves to lay her eggs on, so the priest lays his curse on the fairest joys.

To create a little flower is the labour of ages.

Damn braces. Bless relaxes.

The best wine is the oldest, the best water the newest.

Prayers plow not! Praises reap not! 20

Joys laugh not! Sorrows weep not!

PLATE 10

The head Sublime, the heart Pathos, the genitals Beauty, the hands & feet Proportion.

As the air to a bird or the sea to a fish, so is contempt to the contemptible.

The crow wish'd every thing was black, the owl that every thing was white.

Exuberance is Beauty.

If the lion was advised by the fox, he would be cunning. 5

Improvement makes strait roads, but the crooked roads without Improvement are roads of Genius.

Sooner murder an infant in its cradle than nurse unacted desires.

Where man is not, nature is barren.

Truth can never be told so as to be understood, and not be believ'd.

Enough! or Too much. 10

PLATE 11

The ancient Poets animated all sensible objects with Gods or Geniuses, calling them by the names and adorning them with the properties of woods, rivers, mountains, lakes, cities, nations, and whatever their enlarged & numerous senses could perceive.

And particularly they studied the genius of each city & country, placing it under its mental deity;

Till a system was formed, which some took advantage of & enslav'd the vulgar by attempting to realize or abstract the mental deities from their objects; thus began Priesthood,

Choosing forms of worship from poetic tales.

And at length they pronounc'd that the Gods had order'd such things.

Thus men forgot that All deities reside in the human breast.

PLATES 12–13 *A Memorable Fancy*

The Prophets Isaiah and Ezekiel dined with me, and I asked them how they dared so roundly to assert that God spake to them; and whether they did not think at the time that they would be misunderstood, & so be the cause of imposition.

Isaiah answer'd: 'I saw no God, nor heard any, in a finite organical perception; but my senses discover'd the infinite in every thing, and as I was then perswaded & remain confirm'd, that the voice of honest indignation is the voice of God, I cared not for consequences, but wrote.'

Then I asked: 'Does a firm perswasion that a thing is so, make it so?'

He replied: 'All poets believe that it does, & in ages of imagination this firm perswasion removed mountains; but many are not capable of a firm perswasion of any thing.'

Then Ezekiel said: 'The philosophy of the east taught the first principles of human perception. Some nations held one principle for the origin & some another. We of Israel taught that the Poetic Genius (as you now call it) was the first principle, and all the others merely derivative, which was the cause of our despising the Priests & Philosophers of other countries, and prophecying that all Gods would at last be proved to originate in ours & to be the tributaries of the Poetic Genius. It was this that our great poet, King David, desired so fervently & invokes so patheticly, saying by this he conquers enemies & governs kingdoms. And we so loved our God, that we cursed in his name all the deities of surrounding nations, and asserted that they had rebelled. From these opinions the vulgar came to think that all nations would at last be subject to the Jews.'

'This', said he, 'like all firm perswasions, is come to pass; for all nations believe the Jews' code and worship the Jews' god, and what greater subjection can be?'

I heard this with some wonder, & must confess my own conviction. After dinner I ask'd Isaiah to favour the world with his lost works; he said none of equal value was lost. Ezekiel said the same of his.

I also asked Isaiah what made him go naked and barefoot

three years? He answer'd, 'The same that made our friend Diogenes the Grecian.'

I then asked Ezekiel why he eat dung, & lay so long on his right & left side? He answer'd, 'The desire of raising other men into a perception of the infinite. This the North American tribes practise, & is he honest who resists his genius or conscience only for the sake of present ease or gratification?'

PLATE 14

The ancient tradition that the world will be consumed in fire at the end of six thousand years is true, as I have heard from Hell.

For the cherub with his flaming sword is hereby commanded to leave his guard at tree of life; and when he does, the whole creation will be consumed and appear infinite and holy, whereas it now appears finite & corrupt.

This will come to pass by an improvement of sensual enjoyment.

But first the notion that man has a body distinct from his soul is to be expunged. This I shall do, by printing in the infernal method, by corrosives, which in Hell are salutary and medicinal, melting apparent surfaces away, and displaying the infinite which was hid.

If the doors of perception were cleansed, every thing would appear to man as it is, infinite.

For man has closed himself up, till he sees all things thro' narrow chinks of his cavern.

PLATE 15 *A Memorable Fancy*

I was in a Printing house in Hell & saw the method in which knowledge is transmitted from generation to generation.

In the first chamber was a Dragon-Man, clearing away the rubbish from a cave's mouth; within, a number of Dragons were hollowing the cave.

In the second chamber was a Viper folding round the rock & the cave, and others adorning it with gold, silver and precious stones.

In the third chamber was an Eagle with wings and feathers of air; he caused the inside of the cave to be infinite. Around were numbers of Eagle-like men, who built palaces in the immense cliffs.

In the fourth chamber were Lions of flaming fire, raging around & melting the metals into living fluids.

In the fifth chamber were Unnam'd forms, which cast the metals into the expanse.

There they were receiv'd by Men who occupied the sixth chamber, and took the forms of books & were arranged in libraries.

PLATES 16–17

The Giants who formed this world into its sensual existence and now seem to live in it in chains, are in truth the causes of its life & the sources of all activity; but the chains are the cunning of weak and tame minds which have power to resist energy—according to the proverb, the weak in courage is strong in cunning.

Thus one portion of being is the Prolific, the other the Devouring. To the devourer it seems as if the producer was in his chains, but it is not so; he only takes portions of existence and fancies that the whole.

But the Prolific would cease to be Prolific unless the Devourer as a sea received the excess of his delights.

Some will say, 'Is not God alone the Prolific?' I answer, 'God only Acts and Is in existing beings or Men.'

These two classes of men are always upon earth, & they should be enemies; whoever tries to reconcile them seeks to destroy existence.

Religion is an endeavour to reconcile the two.

Note. Jesus Christ did not wish to unite, but to separate them, as in the Parable of sheep and goats! & he says, 'I came not to send Peace but a Sword.'

Messiah or Satan or Tempter was formerly thought to be one of the Antediluvians who are our Energies.

PLATES 17–20   *A Memorable Fancy*

An Angel came to me and said: 'O pitiable foolish young man! O horrible! O dreadful state! consider the hot burning dungeon thou art preparing for thyself to all eternity, to which thou art going in such career.'

I said: 'Perhaps you will be willing to shew me my eternal lot, & we will contemplate together upon it, and see whether your lot or mine is most desirable.'

So he took me thro' a stable & thro' a church & down into the church vault, at the end of which was a mill. Thro' the mill we went, and came to a cave; down the winding cavern we groped our tedious way till a void boundless as a nether sky appear'd beneath us, & we held by the roots of trees and hung over this immensity. But I said, 'If you please we will commit ourselves to this void, and see whether providence is here also; if you will not, I will.' But he answer'd, 'Do not presume, O young man, but as we here remain, behold thy lot which will soon appear when the darkness passes away.'

So I remain'd with him, sitting in the twisted root of an oak. He was suspended in a fungus, which hung with the head downward into the deep.

By degrees we beheld the infinite Abyss, fiery as the smoke of a burning city; beneath us at an immense distance was the sun, black but shining. Round it were fiery tracks on which revolv'd vast spiders crawling after their prey, which flew or rather swum in the infinite deep, in the most terrific shapes of animals sprung from corruption; & the air was full of them & seem'd composed of them. These are Devils, and are called Powers of the air. I now asked my companion which was my eternal lot; he said, 'Between the black & white spiders.'

But now, from between the black & white spiders, a cloud and fire burst and rolled thro' the deep, blackning all beneath, so that the nether deep grew black as a sea & rolled with a terrible noise. Beneath us was nothing now to be seen but a black tempest, till looking east between the clouds & the waves, we saw a cataract of blood mixed with fire, and not many stone's throw from us appear'd and sunk again the scaly fold of a monstrous serpent. At last, to the east, distant about three degrees, appear'd a fiery crest above the waves; slowly it reared like a ridge of golden rocks till we discover'd two globes of crimson fire, from which the sea fled away in clouds of smoke; and now we saw it was the head of Leviathan. His forehead was divided into streaks of green & purple like those on a tyger's forehead; soon we saw his mouth & red gills hang just above the raging foam, tinging the black deep with beams of blood, advancing toward us with all the fury of a spiritual existence.

My friend the Angel climb'd up from his station into the mill. I remain'd alone, & then this appearance was no more, but I found myself sitting on a pleasant bank beside a river by moonlight, hearing a harper who sung to the harp; & his theme was: 'The man who never alters his opinion is like standing water, & breeds reptiles of the mind.'

But I arose, and sought for the mill, & there I found my Angel, who surprised asked me how I escaped?

I answer'd: 'All that we saw was owing to your metaphysics; for when you ran away, I found myself on a bank by moonlight hearing a harper. But now we have seen my eternal lot, shall I shew you yours?' He laugh'd at my proposal; but I by force suddenly caught him in my arms, & flew westerly thro' the night, till we were elevated above the earth's shadow. Then I flung myself with him directly into the body of the sun. Here I clothed myself in white, & taking in my hand Swedenborg's volumes, sunk from the glorious clime, and passed all the planets till we came to Saturn. Here I staid to rest, & then leap'd into the void between Saturn and the fixed stars.

'Here,' said I, 'is your lot, in this space, if space it may be call'd.' Soon we saw the stable and the church, & I took him to the altar and open'd the Bible, and lo! it was a deep pit, into which I descended driving the Angel before me. Soon we saw seven houses of brick; one we enter'd; in it were a number of monkeys, baboons, & all of that species, chain'd by the middle, grinning and snatching at one another, but withheld by the shortness of their chains. However I saw that they sometimes grew numerous, and then the weak were caught by the strong, and with a grinning aspect, first coupled with & then devour'd, by plucking off first one limb and then another, till the body was left a helpless trunk. This after grinning & kissing it with seeming fondness they devour'd too; and here & there I saw one savourily picking the flesh off of his own tail. As the stench terribly annoy'd us both, we went into the mill, & I in my hand brought the skeleton of a body, which in the mill was Aristotle's Analytics.

So the Angel said: 'Thy phantasy has imposed upon me & thou oughtest to be ashamed.'

I answer'd: 'We impose on one another, & it is but lost time to converse with you whose works are only Analytics.'

PLATES 21–22

I have always found that Angels have the vanity to speak of themselves as the only wise; this they do with a confident insolence sprouting from systematic reasoning.

Thus Swedenborg boasts that what he writes is new, tho' it is only the Contents or Index of already publish'd books.

A man carried a monkey about for a shew, & because he was a little wiser than the monkey, grew vain; and conceiv'd himself as much wiser than seven men. It is so with Swedenborg; he shews the folly of churches & exposes hypocrites, till he imagines that all are religious, & himself the single one on earth that ever broke a net.

Now hear a plain fact: Swedenborg has not written one new truth. Now hear another: he has written all the old falshoods.

And now hear the reason. He conversed with Angels who are all religious, & conversed not with Devils who all hate religion, for he was incapable thro' his conceited notions.

Thus Swedenborg's writings are a recapitulation of all superficial opinions, and an analysis of the more sublime, but no further.

Have now another plain fact: any man of mechanical talents may, from the writings of Paracelsus or Jacob Behmen, produce ten thousand volumes of equal value with Swedenborg's, and from those of Dante or Shakespear an infinite number.

But when he has done this, let him not say that he knows better than his master, for he only holds a candle in sunshine.

PLATES 22–24   *A Memorable Fancy*

Once I saw a Devil in a flame of fire, who arose before an Angel that sat on a cloud, and the Devil utter'd these words:

'The worship of God is: Honouring his gifts in other men, each according to his genius, and loving the greatest men best. Those who envy or calumniate great men hate God, for there is no other God.'

The Angel hearing this became almost blue; but mastering himself he grew yellow, & at last white pink & smiling, and then replied:

'Thou idolater, is not God One? & is not he visible in Jesus Christ? and has not Jesus Christ given his sanction to the law of ten commandments? and are not all other men fools, sinners, & nothings?'

The Devil answer'd: 'Bray a fool in a morter with wheat, yet shall not his folly be beaten out of him. If Jesus Christ is the greatest man, you ought to love him in the greatest degree. Now hear how he has given his sanction to the law of ten commandments: did he not mock at the sabbath, and so mock the sabbath's God? murder those who were murder'd because of him? turn away the law from the woman taken in adultery? steal the labor of others to support him? bear false witness when he omitted making a defence before Pilate? covet when he pray'd for his disciples, and when he bid them shake off the dust of their feet against such as refused to lodge them? I tell you, no virtue can exist without breaking these ten commandments. Jesus was all virtue, and acted from impulse, not from rules.'

When he had so spoken, I beheld the Angel, who stretched out his arms embracing the flame of fire, & he was consumed and arose as Elijah.

Note. This Angel, who is now become a Devil, is my particular friend. We often read the Bible together in its infernal or diabolical sense, which the world shall have if they behave well.

I have also: The Bible of Hell, which the world shall have whether they will or no.

One Law for the Lion & Ox is Oppression.

PLATES 25–27   *A Song of Liberty*

1. The Eternal Female groan'd! it was heard over all the Earth.

2. Albion's coast is sick silent; the American meadows faint!

3. Shadows of Prophecy shiver along by the lakes and the rivers and mutter across the ocean: 'France, rend down thy dungeon!

4. Golden Spain, burst the barriers of old Rome!

5. Cast thy keys, O Rome, into the deep down falling, even to eternity down falling,

6. And weep!'

7. In her trembling hands she took the new born terror howling.

8. On those infinite mountains of light, now barr'd out by the atlantic sea, the new born fire stood before the starry king!

9. Flag'd with grey brow'd snows and thunderous visages, the jealous wings wav'd over the deep.

10. The speary hand burned aloft, unbuckled was the shield; forth went the hand of jealousy among the flaming hair, and hurl'd the new born wonder thro' the starry night.

11. The fire, the fire, is falling!

12. Look up! look up! O citizen of London, enlarge thy countenance; O Jew, leave counting gold! return to thy oil and wine; O African! black African! (go, winged thought, widen his forehead.)

13. The fiery limbs, the flaming hair, shot like the sinking sun into the western sea.

14. Wak'd from his eternal sleep, the hoary element roaring fled away.

15. Down rush'd, beating his wings in vain, the jealous king; his grey brow'd councellors, thunderous warriors, curl'd veterans, among helms, and shields, and chariots, horses, elephants, banners, castles, slings and rocks,

16. Falling, rushing, ruining! buried in the ruins, on Urthona's dens.

17. All night beneath the ruins; then, their sullen flames faded, emerge round the gloomy king.

18. With thunder and fire, leading his starry hosts thro' the waste wilderness, he promulgates his ten commands, glancing his beamy eyelids over the deep in dark dismay,

19. Where the son of fire in his eastern cloud, while the morning plumes her golden breast,

20. Spurning the clouds written with curses, stamps the stony law to dust, loosing the eternal horses from the dens of night, crying,

'Empire is no more! and now the lion & wolf shall cease.'

Chorus

Let the Priests of the Raven of dawn no longer, in deadly black, with hoarse note curse the sons of joy. Nor his accepted brethren, whom, tyrant, he calls free, lay the bound or build the roof. Nor pale religious letchery call that Virginity that wishes but acts not!

For every thing that lives is Holy.

VISIONS OF THE DAUGHTERS OF ALBION

The Eye sees more than the Heart knows.

PLATE iii   *The Argument*

'I loved Theotormon
And I was not ashamed;
I trembled in my virgin fears
And I hid in Leutha's vale.

'I plucked Leutha's flower,   5
And I rose up from the vale;
But the terrible thunders tore
My virgin mantle in twain.'

PLATE 1   *Visions*

Enslav'd, the Daughters of Albion weep: a trembling
      lamentation
Upon their mountains, in their valleys sighs toward America.

For the soft soul of America, Oothoon, wander'd in woe
Along the vales of Leutha, seeking flowers to comfort her;
And thus she spoke to the bright Marygold of Leutha's vale: 5

'Art thou a flower? art thou a nymph? I see thee now a flower,
Now a nymph! I dare not pluck thee from thy dewy bed!'

The Golden nymph replied: 'Pluck thou my flower, Oothoon
      the mild.
Another flower shall spring, because the soul of sweet delight
Can never pass away.' She ceas'd & clos'd her golden shrine.   10

Then Oothoon pluck'd the flower, saying, 'I pluck thee from
      thy bed,
Sweet flower, and put thee here to glow between my breasts,
And thus I turn my face to where my whole soul seeks.'

Over the waves she went in wing'd exulting swift delight,
And over Theotormon's reign took her impetuous course.   15

Bromion rent her with his thunders; on his stormy bed
Lay the faint maid, and soon her woes appall'd his thunders
      hoarse.

Bromion spoke: 'Behold this harlot here on Bromion's bed,
And let the jealous dolphins sport around the lovely maid.
Thy soft American plains are mine, and mine thy north &
    south.   20
Stampt with my signet are the swarthy children of the sun;
They are obedient, they resist not, they obey the scourge;
Their daughters worship terrors and obey the violent.
PLATE 2
Now thou maist marry Bromion's harlot, and protect the child
Of Bromion's rage, that Oothoon shall put forth in nine
    moons' time.'

Then storms rent Theotormon's limbs; he roll'd his waves
    around
And folded his black jealous waters round the adulterate pair.
Bound back to back in Bromion's caves, terror & meekness
    dwell.   5

At entrance Theotormon sits, wearing the threshold hard
With secret tears; beneath him sound like waves on a desart
    shore
The voice of slaves beneath the sun, and children bought with
    money,
That shiver in religious caves beneath the burning fires
Of lust, that belch incessant from the summits of the earth.   10

Oothoon weeps not; she cannot weep! her tears are locked up;
But she can howl incessant, writhing her soft snowy limbs
And calling Theotormon's Eagles to prey upon her flesh:

'I call with holy voice! kings of the sounding air,
Rend away this defiled bosom that I may reflect   15
The image of Theotormon on my pure transparent breast.'

The Eagles at her call descend & rend their bleeding prey.
Theotormon severely smiles; her soul reflects the smile,
As the clear spring mudded with feet of beasts grows pure &
    smiles.

The Daughters of Albion hear her woes, & eccho back her
    sighs.   20

'Why does my Theotormon sit weeping upon the threshold,
And Oothoon hovers by his side, perswading him in vain?
I cry, "Arise, O Theotormon, for the village dog
Barks at the breaking day, the nightingale has done lamenting,
The lark does rustle in the ripe corn, and the Eagle returns   25
From nightly prey and lifts his golden beak to the pure east,
Shaking the dust from his immortal pinions to awake
The sun that sleeps too long. Arise, my Theotormon, I am
    pure,
Because the night is gone that clos'd me in its deadly black."
They told me that the night & day were all that I could see;   30
They told me that I had five senses to inclose me up;
And they inclos'd my infinite brain into a narrow circle,
And sunk my heart into the Abyss, a red round globe, hot
    burning,
Till all from life I was obliterated and erased.
Instead of morn arises a bright shadow, like an eye   35
In the eastern cloud, instead of night a sickly charnel house,
That Theotormon hears me not! To him the night and morn
Are both alike: a night of sighs, a morning of fresh tears;
PLATE 3
And none but Bromion can hear my lamentations.

'With what sense is it that the chicken shuns the ravenous
    hawk?
With what sense does the tame pigeon measure out the
    expanse?
With what sense does the bee form cells? have not the mouse &
    frog
Eyes and ears and sense of touch? yet are their habitations   5
And their pursuits as different as their forms and as their joys.
Ask the wild ass why he refuses burdens, and the meek camel
Why he loves man; is it because of eye, ear, mouth, or skin,
Or breathing nostrils? No, for these the wolf and tyger have.
Ask the blind worm the secrets of the grave, and why her spires 10

Love to curl round the bones of death; and ask the rav'nous
    snake
Where she gets poison, & the wing'd eagle why he loves the
    sun,
And then tell me the thoughts of man that have been hid of old.

'Silent I hover all the night, and all day could be silent,
If Theotormon once would turn his loved eyes upon me.   15
How can I be defil'd when I reflect thy image pure?
Sweetest the fruit that the worm feeds on, & the soul prey'd
    on by woe.
The new wash'd lamb ting'd with the village smoke & the
    bright swan
By the red earth of our immortal river. I bathe my wings,
And I am white and pure to hover round Theotormon's
    breast.'   20

Then Theotormon broke his silence, and he answered:

'Tell me what is the night or day to one o'erflow'd with woe?
Tell me what is a thought? & of what substance is it made?
Tell me what is a joy? & in what gardens do joys grow?
And in what rivers swim the sorrows? and upon what
    mountains   25
PLATE 4
Wave shadows of discontent? and in what houses dwell the
    wretched,
Drunken with woe, forgotten and shut up from cold despair?

'Tell me where dwell the thoughts forgotten till thou call them
    forth?
Tell me where dwell the joys of old? & where the ancient loves?
And when will they renew again & the night of oblivion past?   5
That I might traverse times & spaces far remote and bring
Comforts into a present sorrow and a night of pain.
Where goest thou, O thought? to what remote land is thy
    flight?
If thou returnest to the present moment of affliction

Wilt thou bring comforts on thy wings, and dews and honey
    and balm,   - 10
Or poison from the desart wilds, from the eyes of the envier?'

Then Bromion said, and shook the cavern with his
    lamentation:

'Thou knowest that the ancient trees seen by thine eyes have
    fruit,
But knowest thou that trees and fruits flourish upon the earth
To gratify senses unknown? trees, beasts and birds unknown: 15
Unknown, not unperceiv'd, spread in the infinite microscope,
In places yet unvisited by the voyager, and in worlds
Over another kind of seas, and in atmospheres unknown?
Ah! are there other wars beside the wars of sword and fire?
And are there other sorrows beside the sorrows of poverty?   20
And are there other joys beside the joys of riches and ease?
And is there not one law for both the lion and the ox?
And is there not eternal fire and eternal chains
To bind the phantoms of existence from eternal life?'

Then Oothoon waited silent all the day and all the night;   25
PLATE 5
But when the morn arose, her lamentation renew'd.
The Daughters of Albion hear her woes, & eccho back her
    sighs.

'O Urizen! Creator of men! mistaken Demon of heaven,
Thy joys are tears! thy labour vain to form men to thine image.
How can one joy absorb another? are not different joys   5
Holy, eternal, infinite? and each joy is a Love.

'Does not the great mouth laugh at a gift? & the narrow eyelids
    mock
At the labour that is above payment? and wilt thou take the ape
For thy counsellor? or the dog for a schoolmaster to thy
    children?
Does he who contemns poverty, and he who turns with
    abhorrence   10

From usury, feel the same passion, or are they moved alike?
How can the giver of gifts experience the delights of the
    merchant?
How the industrious citizen the pains of the husbandman?
How different far the fat fed hireling with hollow drum,
Who buys whole corn fields into wastes, and sings upon the
    heath: 15
How different their eye and ear! how different the world to
    them!
With what sense does the parson claim the labour of the
    farmer?
What are his nets & gins & traps, & how does he surround him
With cold floods of abstraction, and with forests of solitude,
To build him castles and high spires, where kings & priests
    may dwell,   20
Till she who burns with youth and knows no fixed lot, is
    bound
In spells of law to one she loaths? and must she drag the chain
Of life in weary lust? must chilling murderous thoughts
    obscure
The clear heaven of her eternal spring? to bear the wintry rage
Of a harsh terror driv'n to madness, bound to hold a rod   25
Over her shrinking shoulders all the day, & all the night
To turn the wheel of false desire, and longings that wake her
    womb
To the abhorred birth of cherubs in the human form,
That live a pestilence & die a meteor & are no more;
Till the child dwell with one he hates, and do the deed he
    loaths,   30
And the impure scourge force his seed into its unripe birth
E'er yet his eyelids can behold the arrows of the day.

'Does the whale worship at thy footsteps as the hungry dog?
Or does he scent the mountain prey, because his nostrils wide
Draw in the ocean? does his eye discern the flying cloud   35
As the raven's eye? or does he measure the expanse like the
    vulture?
Does the still spider view the cliffs where eagles hide their
    young?

Or does the fly rejoice because the harvest is brought in?
Does not the eagle scorn the earth, & despise the treasures
  beneath?
But the mole knoweth what is there, & the worm shall tell it
  thee.   40
Does not the worm erect a pillar in the mouldering church
  yard,
PLATE 6
And a palace of eternity in the jaws of the hungry grave?
Over his porch these words are written: "Take thy bliss, O
  Man!
And sweet shall be thy taste & sweet thy infant joys renew!"

'Infancy, fearless, lustful, happy, nestling for delight
In laps of pleasure! Innocence, honest, open, seeking   5
The vigorous joys of morning light, open to virgin bliss!
Who taught thee modesty, subtil modesty, child of night &
  sleep?
When thou awakest, wilt thou dissemble all thy secret joys,
Or wert thou not awake when all this mystery was disclos'd?
Then com'st thou forth a modest virgin, knowing to
  dissemble,   10
With nets found under thy night pillow, to catch virgin joy
And brand it with the name of whore, & sell it in the night,
In silence, ev'n without a whisper, and in seeming sleep.
Religious dreams and holy vespers light thy smoky fires;
Once were thy fires lighted by the eyes of honest morn. 15
And does my Theotormon seek this hypocrite modesty,
This knowing, artful, secret, fearful, cautious, trembling
  hypocrite?
Then is Oothoon a whore indeed! and all the virgin joys
Of life are harlots, and Theotormon is a sick man's dream,
And Oothoon is the crafty slave of selfish holiness. 20

'But Oothoon is not so, a virgin fill'd with virgin fancies,
Open to joy and to delight where every beauty appears.
If in the morning sun I find it, there my eyes are fix'd
PLATE 7
In happy copulation; if in evening mild, wearied with work,
Sit on a bank and draw the pleasures of this free born joy.

'The moment of desire! the moment of desire! The virgin
That pines for man shall awaken her womb to enormous joys
In the secret shadows of her chamber; the youth shut up from   5
The lustful joy shall forget to generate, & create an amorous
    image
In the shadows of his curtains and in the folds of his silent
    pillow.
Are not these the places of religion? the rewards of continence?
The self enjoyings of self denial? Why dost thou seek religion?
Is it because acts are not lovely that thou seekest solitude,   10
Where the horrible darkness is impressed with reflections of
    desire?

'Father of Jealousy, be thou accursed from the earth!
Why has thou taught my Theotormon this accursed thing?
Till beauty fades from off my shoulders, darken'd and cast out,
A solitary shadow wailing on the margin of non-entity.   15

'I cry, Love! Love! Love! happy, happy Love! free as the
    mountain wind!
Can that be Love, that drinks another as a sponge drinks water?
That clouds with jealousy his nights, with weepings all the
    day,
To spin a web of age around him, grey and hoary! dark!
Till his eyes sicken at the fruit that hangs before his sight?   20
Such is self-love that envies all! a creeping skeleton
With lamplike eyes watching around the frozen marriage bed.

'But silken nets and traps of adamant will Oothoon spread,
And catch for thee girls of mild silver, or of furious gold.
I'll lie beside thee on a bank & view their wanton play   25
In lovely copulation, bliss on bliss with Theotormon.
Red as the rosy morning, lustful as the first born beam,
Oothoon shall view his dear delight, nor e'er with jealous
    cloud
Come in the heaven of generous love, nor selfish blightings
    bring.

'Does the sun walk in glorious raiment on the secret floor   30

PLATE 8

Where the cold miser spreads his gold? or does the bright cloud
    drop
On his stone threshold? does his eye behold the beam that
    brings
Expansion to the eye of pity? or will he bind himself
Beside the ox to thy hard furrow? does not that mild beam blot
The bat, the owl, the glowing tyger, and the king of night?   5
The sea fowl takes the wintry blast for a cov'ring to her limbs,
And the wild snake the pestilence to adorn him with gems &
    gold;
And trees & birds & beasts & men behold their eternal joy.
Arise, you little glancing wings, and sing your infant joy!
Arise and drink your bliss, for every thing that lives is holy!'   10

Thus every morning wails Oothoon, but Theotormon sits
Upon the margin'd ocean conversing with shadows dire.

The Daughters of Albion hear her woes, & eccho back her
    sighs.

AMERICA

A Prophecy

PLATE 1   *Preludium*

The shadowy daughter of Urthona stood before red Orc,
When fourteen suns had faintly journey'd o'er his dark abode.
His food she brought in iron baskets, his drink in cups of iron.
Crown'd with a helmet & dark hair the nameless female stood;
A quiver with its burning stores, a bow like that of night   5

When pestilence is shot from heaven—no other arms she need;
Invulnerable tho' naked, save where clouds roll round her loins
Their awful folds in the dark air. Silent she stood as night;
For never from her iron tongue could voice or sound arise,
But dumb till that dread day when Orc assay'd his fierce
    embrace.   10

'Dark Virgin,' said the hairy Youth, 'thy father stern abhorr'd
Rivets my tenfold chains while still on high my spirit soars.
Sometimes an eagle screaming in the sky, sometimes a lion
Stalking upon the mountains, & sometimes a whale I lash
The raging fathomless abyss; anon a serpent folding   15
Around the pillars of Urthona, and round thy dark limbs,
On the Canadian wilds I fold; feeble my spirit folds,
For chain'd beneath I rend these caverns. When thou bringest
    food
I howl my joy, and my red eyes seek to behold thy face.
In vain! these clouds roll to & fro, & hide thee from my sight.'   20

PLATE 2
Silent as despairing love, and strong as jealousy,
The hairy shoulders rend the links; free are the wrists of fire;
Round the terrific loins he seiz'd the panting struggling womb;
It joy'd. She put aside her clouds & smiled her first-born smile,
As when a black cloud shews its lightnings to the silent deep.

Soon as she saw the terrible boy, then burst the virgin cry:

'I know thee, I have found thee, & I will not let thee go.
Thou art the image of God who dwells in darkness of Africa,
And thou art fall'n to give me life in regions of dark death.
On my American plains I feel the struggling afflictions   10
Endur'd by roots that writhe their arms into the nether deep;
I see a serpent in Canada, who courts me to his love,
In Mexico an Eagle, and a Lion in Peru;
I see a Whale in the South-sea, drinking my soul away.
O what limb rending pains I feel; thy fire & my frost   15
Mingle in howling pains, in furrows by thy lightnings rent.
This is eternal death, and this the torment long foretold.'

PLATE 3   *A Prophecy*

The Guardian Prince of Albion burns in his nightly tent;
Sullen fires across the Atlantic glow to America's shore,
Piercing the souls of warlike men who rise in silent night.
Washington, Franklin, Paine & Warren, Gates, Hancock &
    Green
Meet on the coast glowing with blood from Albion's fiery
    Prince.   5

Washington spoke: 'Friends of America, look over the Atlantic
    sea;
A bended bow is lifted in heaven, & a heavy iron chain
Descends link by link from Albion's cliffs across the sea to bind
Brothers & sons of America, till our faces pale and yellow,
Heads deprest, voices weak, eyes downcast, hands
    work-bruis'd,   10
Feet bleeding on the sultry sands, and the furrows of the whip
Descend to generations that in future times forget.'

The strong voice ceas'd; for a terrible blast swept over the
    heaving sea.
The eastern cloud rent; on his cliffs stood Albion's wrathful
    Prince,
A dragon form clashing his scales at midnight he arose,   15
And flam'd red meteors round the land of Albion beneath.
His voice, his locks, his awful shoulders, and his glowing eyes
PLATE 4
Appear to the Americans upon the cloudy night.

Solemn heave the Atlantic waves between the gloomy nations,
Swelling, belching from its deeps red clouds & raging fires.
Albion is sick, America faints! enrag'd the Zenith grew.
As human blood shooting its veins all round the orbed heaven   5
Red rose the clouds from the Atlantic in vast wheels of blood,
And in the red clouds rose a Wonder o'er the Atlantic sea,
Intense! naked! a Human fire, fierce glowing as the wedge
Of iron heated in the furnace; his terrible limbs were fire,
With myriads of cloudy terrors, banners dark, & towers   10
Surrounded; heat but not light went thro' the murky
    atmosphere.

The King of England looking westward trembles at the vision.

PLATE 5

Albion's Angel stood beside the Stone of night, and saw
The terror like a comet, or more like the planet red
That once inclos'd the terrible wandering comets in its sphere.
Then, Mars, thou wast our center, & the planets three flew
    round
Thy crimson disk; so e'er the Sun was rent from thy red
    sphere.   5
The Spectre glow'd, his horrid length staining the temple long
With beams of blood; & thus a voice came forth, and shook the
    temple:

PLATE 6

'The morning comes, the night decays, the watchmen leave
    their stations;
The grave is burst, the spices shed, the linen wrapped up;
The bones of death, the cov'ring clay, the sinews shrunk &
    dry'd
Reviving shake, inspiring move, breathing! awakening!
Spring like redeemed captives when their bonds & bars are
    burst.   5
Let the slave grinding at the mill run out into the field,
Let him look up into the heavens & laugh in the bright air;
Let the inchained soul, shut up in darkness and in sighing,
Whose face has never seen a smile in thirty weary years,
Rise and look out; his chains are loose, his dungeon doors are
    open;   10
And let his wife and children return from the opressor's
    scourge.
They look behind at every step & believe it is a dream,
Singing: "The Sun has left his blackness, & has found a fresher
    morning,
And the fair Moon rejoices in the clear & cloudless night;
For Empire is no more, and now the Lion & Wolf shall
    cease." '   15

PLATE 7

In thunders ends the voice. Then Albion's Angel wrathful
    burnt
Beside the Stone of Night, and like the Eternal Lion's howl
In famine & war reply'd: 'Art thou not Orc, who
    serpent-form'd
Stands at the gate of Enitharmon to devour her children?
Blasphemous Demon, Antichrist, hater of Dignities,   5
Lover of wild rebellion, and transgressor of God's Law,
Why dost thou come to Angel's eyes in this terrific form?'

PLATE 8

The terror answer'd: 'I am Orc, wreath'd round the accursed
    tree.
The times are ended; shadows pass, the morning 'gins to break;
The fiery joy that Urizen perverted to ten commands,
What night he led the starry hosts thro' the wide wilderness,
That stony law I stamp to dust, and scatter religion abroad   5
To the four winds as a torn book, & none shall gather the
    leaves;
But they shall rot on desart sands, & consume in bottomless
    deeps,
To make the desarts blossom & the deeps shrink to their
    fountains,
And to renew the fiery joy, and burst the stony roof;
That pale religious letchery, seeking Virginity,   10
May find it in a harlot, and in coarse-clad honesty
The undefil'd, tho' ravish'd in her cradle night and morn;
For every thing that lives is holy, life delights in life;
Because the soul of sweet delight can never be defil'd.
Fires inwrap the earthly globe, yet man is not consum'd;   15
Amidst the lustful fires he walks; his feet become like brass,
His knees and thighs like silver, & his breast and head like
    gold.'

PLATE 9

'Sound! sound! my loud war-trumpets & alarm my Thirteen
    Angels!
Loud howls the eternal Wolf! the eternal Lion lashes his tail!

America is dark'ned, and my punishing Demons terrified
Crouch howling before their caverns deep like skins dry'd in
    the wind.
They cannot smite the wheat, nor quench the fatness of the
    earth;   5
They cannot smite with sorrows, nor subdue the plough and
    spade;
They cannot wall the city, nor moat round the castle of princes;
They cannot bring the stubbed oak to overgrow the hills.
For terrible men stand on the shores, & in their robes I see
Children take shelter from the lightnings; there stands
    Washington   10
And Paine and Warren with their foreheads rear'd toward the
    east.
But clouds obscure my aged sight. A vision from afar!
Sound! sound! my loud war-trumpets & alarm my thirteen
    Angels.
Ah vision from afar! Ah rebel form that rent the ancient
Heavens! Eternal Viper self-renew'd, rolling in clouds,   15
I see thee in thick clouds and darkness on America's shore,
Writhing in pangs of abhorred birth. Red flames the crest
    rebellious
And eyes of death. The harlot womb, oft opened in vain,
Heaves in enormous circles. Now the times are return'd upon
    thee,
Devourer of thy parent; now thy unutterable torment renews.   20
Sound! sound! my loud war trumpets & alarm my thirteen
    Angels.
Ah, terrible birth! a young one bursting! where is the weeping
    mouth?
And where the mother's milk? Instead those ever-hissing jaws
And parched lips drop with fresh gore. Now roll thou in the
    clouds!
Thy mother lays her length outstretch'd upon the shore
    beneath.   25
Sound! sound! my loud war-trumpets & alarm my thirteen
    Angels!
Loud howls the eternal Wolf! the eternal Lion lashes his tail!'

PLATE 10

Thus wept the Angel voice, & as he wept the terrible blasts
Of trumpets blew a loud alarm across the Atlantic deep.
No trumpets answer; no reply of clarions or of fifes;
Silent the Colonies remain and refuse the loud alarm.

On those vast shady hills between America & Albion's shore,   5
Now barr'd out by the Atlantic sea, call'd Atlantean hills
Because from their bright summits you may pass to the Golden
   world,
An ancient palace, archetype of mighty Emperies,
Rears its immortal pinnacles, built in the forest of God
By Ariston the king of beauty for his stolen bride.   10

Here on their magic seats the thirteen Angels sat perturb'd,
For clouds from the Atlantic hover o'er the solemn roof.

PLATE 11

Fiery the Angels rose, & as they rose deep thunder roll'd
Around their shores, indignant burning with the fires of Orc;
And Boston's Angel cried aloud as they flew thro' the dark
   night.

He cried: 'Why trembles honesty, and like a murderer
Why seeks he refuge from the frowns of his immortal station?   5
Must the generous tremble & leave his joy to the idle, to the
   pestilence,
That mock him? Who commanded this? what God? what
   Angel?
To keep the gen'rous from experience till the ungenerous
Are unrestrain'd performers of the energies of nature;
Till pity is become a trade, and generosity a science   10
That men get rich by, & the sandy desert is giv'n to the strong.
What God is he writes laws of peace & clothes him in a
   tempest?
What pitying Angel lusts for tears and fans himself with sighs?
What crawling villain preaches abstinence & wraps himself
In fat of lambs? No more I follow, no more obedience pay.'   15

PLATE 12

So cried he, rending off his robe & throwing down his scepter
In sight of Albion's Guardian; and all the thirteen Angels
Rent off their robes to the hungry wind & threw their golden
    scepters
Down on the land of America. Indignant they descended
Headlong from out their heavenly heights, descending swift as
    fires   5
Over the land; naked & flaming are their lineaments seen
In the deep gloom. By Washington & Paine & Warren they
    stood;
And the flame folded, roaring fierce within the pitchy night
Before the Demon red, who burnt towards America
In black smoke, thunders, and loud winds, rejoicing in its
    terror,   10
Breaking in smoky wreaths from the wild deep, & gath'ring
    thick
In flames as of a furnace on the land from North to South.

PLATE 13

What time the thirteen Governors that England sent convene
In Bernard's house, the flames cover'd the land. They rouze,
    they cry,
Shaking their mental chains, they rush in fury to the sea
To quench their anguish; at the feet of Washington down fall'n
They grovel on the sand and writhing lie, while all   5
The British soldiers thro' the thirteen states sent up a howl
Of anguish, threw their swords & muskets to the earth & ran
From their encampments and dark castles, seeking where to
    hide
From the grim flames and from the visions of Orc; in sight
Of Albion's Angel, who enrag'd his secret clouds open'd   10
From north to south, and burnt outstretch'd on wings of
    wrath, cov'ring
The eastern sky, spreading his awful wings across the heavens.
Beneath him roll'd his num'rous hosts, all Albion's Angels
    camp'd
Darken'd the Atlantic mountains, & their trumpets shook the
    valleys,

Arm'd with diseases of the earth to cast upon the Abyss,   15
Their numbers forty millions, must'ring in the eastern sky.

PLATE 14

In the flames stood & view'd the armies drawn out in the sky
Washington, Franklin, Paine & Warren, Allen, Gates & Lee,
And heard the voice of Albion's Angel give the thunderous
    command.
His plagues, obedient to his voice, flew forth out of their
    clouds,
Falling upon America, as a storm to cut them off,   5
As a blight cuts the tender corn when it begins to appear.
Dark is the heaven above, & cold & hard the earth beneath;
And as a plague wind fill'd with insects cuts off man & beast,
And as a sea o'erwhelms a land in the day of an earthquake,
Fury! rage! madness! in a wind swept through America,   10
And the red flames of Orc that folded roaring fierce around
The angry shores, and the fierce rushing of th' inhabitants
    together.
The citizens of New-York close their books & lock their
    chests;
The mariners of Boston drop their anchors and unlade;
The scribe of Pensylvania casts his pen upon the earth;   15
The builder of Virginia throws his hammer down in fear.

Then had America been lost, o'erwhelm'd by the Atlantic,
And Earth had lost another portion of the infinite;
But all rush together in the night in wrath and raging fire.
The red fires rag'd! the plagues recoil'd! then roll'd they back
    with fury   20
PLATE 15
On Albion's Angels. Then the Pestilence began in streaks of
    red
Across the limbs of Albion's Guardian; the spotted plague
    smote Bristol's,
And the Leprosy London's Spirit, sickening all their bands.
The millions sent up a howl of anguish and threw off their
    hammer'd mail,

And cast their swords & spears to earth, & stood a naked
    multitude.   5
Albion's Guardian writhed in torment on the eastern sky,
Pale, quiv'ring toward the brain his glimmering eyes, teeth
    chattering,
Howling & shuddering, his legs quivering, convuls'd each
    muscle & sinew.
Sick'ning lay London's Guardian, and the ancient miter'd
    York,
Their heads on snowy hills, their ensigns sick'ning in the sky.   10

The plagues creep on the burning winds, driven by flames of
    Orc,
And by the fierce Americans rushing together in the night,
Driven o'er the Guardians of Ireland and Scotland and Wales.
They, spotted with plagues, forsook the frontiers, & their
    banners sear'd
With fires of hell deform their ancient heavens with shame &
    woe.   15
Hid in his caves the Bard of Albion felt the enormous plagues,
And a cowl of flesh grew o'er his head, & scales on his back &
    ribs;
And, rough with black scales, all his Angels fright their ancient
    heavens.
The doors of marriage are open, and the Priests in rustling
    scales
Rush into reptile coverts, hiding from the fires of Orc   20
That play around the golden roofs in wreaths of fierce desire,
Leaving the females naked and glowing with the lusts of
    youth.

For the female spirits of the dead, pining in bonds of religion,
Run from their fetters reddening, & in long drawn arches
    sitting
They feel the nerves of youth renew, and desires of ancient
    times   25
Over their pale limbs as a vine when the tender grape appears.

PLATE 16

Over the hills, the vales, the cities, rage the red flames fierce;
The Heavens melted from north to south; and Urizen, who sat
Above all heavens in thunders wrap'd, emerg'd his leprous
    head
From out his holy shrine, his tears in deluge piteous
Falling into the deep sublime. Flag'd with grey-brow'd snows
And thunderous visages, his jealous wings wav'd over the
    deep;
Weeping in dismal howling woe he dark descended, howling
Around the smitten bands, clothed in tears & trembling
    shudd'ring cold.
His stored snows he poured forth, and his icy magazines
He open'd on the deep and on the Atlantic sea white shiv'ring.   10
Leprous his limbs, all over white, and hoary was his visage,
Weeping in dismal howlings before the stern Americans,
Hiding the Demon red with clouds & cold mists from the
    earth;
Till Angels & weak men twelve years should govern o'er the
    strong,
And then their end should come, when France receiv'd the
    Demon's light.   15

Stiff shudderings shook the heav'nly thrones! France, Spain &
    Italy
In terror view'd the bands of Albion and the ancient Guardians
Fainting upon the elements, smitten with their own plagues.
They slow advance to shut the five gates of their law-built
    heaven,
Filled with blasting fancies and with mildews of despair,   20
With fierce disease and lust, unable to stem the fires of Orc;
But the five gates were consum'd, & their bolts and hinges
    melted,
And the fierce flames burnt round the heavens & round the
    abodes of men.

EUROPE

A Prophecy

PLATE iii

'Five windows light the cavern'd Man: thro' one he breathes
    the air;
Thro' one hears music of the spheres; thro' one the eternal vine
Flourishes that he may recieve the grapes; thro' one can look
And see small portions of the eternal world that ever groweth;
Thro' one himself pass out what time he please, but he will not;   5
For stolen joys are sweet, & bread eaten in secret pleasant.'

So sang a Fairy mocking as he sat on a streak'd Tulip,
Thinking none saw him; when he ceas'd I started from the
    trees,
And caught him in my hat as boys knock down a butterfly.
'How know you this,' said I, 'small Sir? where did you learn
    this song?'   10
Seeing himself in my possession, thus he answer'd me:
'My Master, I am yours; command me, for I must obey.'

'Then tell me what is the material world, and is it dead?'
He laughing answer'd: 'I will write a book on leaves of flowers,
If you will feed me on love-thoughts, & give me now and then   15
A cup of sparkling poetic fancies. So, when I am tipsie,
I'll sing to you to this soft lute, and shew you all alive
The world, where every particle of dust breathes forth its joy.'

I took him home in my warm bosom. As we went along
Wild flowers I gather'd, & he shew'd me each eternal flower.   20
He laugh'd aloud to see them whimper because they were
    pluck'd.
They hover'd round me like a cloud of incense. When I came
Into my parlour and sat down, and took my pen to write,
My Fairy sat upon the table, and dictated 'EUROPE.'

PLATE 1   *Preludium*

The nameless shadowy female rose from out the breast of Orc,
Her snaky hair brandishing in the winds of Enitharmon;
And thus her voice arose:

'O mother Enitharmon, wilt thou bring forth other sons,
To cause my name to vanish, that my place may not be found?   5
For I am faint with travel!
Like the dark cloud disburden'd in the day of dismal thunder.

'My roots are brandish'd in the heavens, my fruits in earth
        beneath
Surge, foam and labour into life, first born & first consum'd!
Consumed and consuming!   10
Then why shouldst thou, accursed mother, bring me into life?

'I wrap my turban of thick clouds around my lab'ring head,
And fold the sheety waters as a mantle round my limbs.
Yet the red sun and moon
And all the overflowing stars rain down prolific pains.   15

PLATE 2
'Unwilling I look up to heaven! unwilling count the stars!
Sitting in fathomless abyss of my immortal shrine,
I seize their burning power
And bring forth howling terrors, all devouring fiery kings,

'Devouring & devoured, roaming in dark and desolate
        mountains   5
In forests of eternal death, shrieking in hollow trees.
Ah mother Enitharmon!
Stamp not with solid form this vig'rous progeny of fires.

'I bring forth from my teeming bosom myriads of flames,
And thou dost stamp them with a signet; then they roam
        abroad   10
And leave me void as death.
Ah! I am drown'd in shady woe, and visionary joy.

'And who shall bind the infinite with an eternal band?
To compass it with swaddling bands? and who shall cherish it
With milk and honey?   15
I see it smile & I roll inward & my voice is past.'

She ceast, & roll'd her shady clouds
Into the secret place.

PLATE 3   *A Prophecy*

                    The deep of winter came,
                    What time the secret child
          Descended thro' the orient gates of the eternal day.
          War ceas'd, & all the troops like shadows fled to their abodes.

Then Enitharmon saw her sons & daughters rise around;   5
Like pearly clouds they meet together in the crystal house;
And Los, possessor of the moon, joy'd in the peaceful night,
Thus speaking, while his num'rous sons shook their bright
     fiery wings:

'Again the night is come
That strong Urthona takes his rest,   10
And Urizen unloos'd from chains
Glows like a meteor in the distant north.
Stretch forth your hands and strike the elemental strings!
Awake the thunders of the deep,
PLATE 4
'The shrill winds wake!
Till all the sons of Urizen look out and envy Los.
Seize all the spirits of life and bind
Their warbling joys to our loud strings;
Bind all the nourishing sweets of earth   5
To give us bliss, that we may drink the sparkling wine of Los;
And let us laugh at war,
Despising toil and care,
Because the days and nights of joy in lucky hours renew.'

'Arise, O Orc, from thy deep den,   10
First born of Enitharmon, rise!
And we will crown thy head with garlands of the ruddy vine;
For now thou art bound,
And I may see thee in the hour of bliss, my eldest born.'

The horrent Demon rose, surrounded with red stars of fire,   15
Whirling about in furious circles round the immortal fiend.

Then Enitharmon down descended into his red light,
And thus her voice rose to her children; the distant heavens
    reply.

PLATE 5
'Now comes the night of Enitharmon's joy!
Who shall I call? Who shall I send?
That Woman, lovely Woman! may have dominion?
Arise, O Rintrah, thee I call! & Palamabron, thee!
Go! tell the human race that Woman's love is Sin;   5
That an Eternal life awaits the worms of sixty winters
In an allegorical abode where existence hath never come.
Forbid all Joy, & from her childhood shall the little female
Spread nets in every secret path.

'My weary eyelids draw towards the evening, my bliss is yet
    but new!   10

PLATE 8
'Arise, O Rintrah eldest born, second to none but Orc.
O lion Rintrah, raise thy fury from thy forests black;
Bring Palamabron, horned priest, skipping upon the
    mountains,
And silent Elynittria, the silver bowed queen.
Rintrah, where has thou hid thy bride?   5
Weeps she in desart shades?
Alas, my Rintrah! bring the lovely jealous Ocalythron.

'Arise, my son! bring all thy brethren, O thou king of fire.
Prince of the sun, I see thee with thy innumerable race,
Thick as the summer stars;   10
But each ramping his golden mane shakes,
And thine eyes rejoice because of strength, O Rintrah, furious
    king.'

PLATE 9
Enitharmon slept,
Eighteen hundred years. Man was a Dream!
The night of Nature and their harps unstrung.
She slept in middle of her nightly song,
Eighteen hundred years, a female dream.   5

Shadows of men in fleeting bands upon the winds
Divide the heavens of Europe,
Till Albion's Angel, smitten with his own plagues, fled with
    his bands.
The cloud bears hard on Albion's shore,
Fill'd with immortal demons of futurity.   10
In council gather the smitten Angels of Albion.
The cloud bears hard upon the council house, down rushing
On the heads of Albion's Angels.

One hour they lay buried beneath the ruins of that hall;
But as the stars rise from the salt lake they arise in pain,   15
In troubled mists o'erclouded by the terrors of strugling times.

PLATE 10
In thoughts perturb'd they rose from the bright ruins, silent
    following
The fiery King, who sought his ancient temple serpent-form'd
That stretches out its shady length along the Island white.
Round him roll'd his clouds of war; silent the Angel went,
Along the infinite shores of Thames to golden Verulam.   5
There stand the venerable porches that high-towering rear
Their oak-surrounded pillars, form'd of massy stones, uncut
With tool, stones precious—such eternal in the heavens,

Of colours twelve, few known on earth, give light in the
    opake,
Plac'd in the order of the stars. When the five senses whelm'd   10
In deluge o'er the earth-born man, then turn'd the fluxile eyes
Into two stationary orbs, concentrating all things;
The ever-varying spiral ascents to the heavens of heavens
Were bended downward, and the nostrils' golden gates shut,
Turn'd outward, barr'd and petrify'd against the infinite.   15

Thought chang'd the infinite to a serpent, that which pitieth
To a devouring flame; and man fled from its face and hid
In forests of night. Then all the eternal forests were divided
Into earths rolling in circles of space, that like an ocean rush'd
And overwhelmed all except this finite wall of flesh.   20
Then was the serpent temple form'd, image of infinite
Shut up in finite revolutions, and man became an Angel,
Heaven a mighty circle turning, God a tyrant crown'd.

Now arriv'd the ancient Guardian at the southern porch
That, planted thick with trees of blackest leaf, & in a vale   25
Obscure, inclos'd the Stone of Night. Oblique it stood,
    o'erhung
With purple flowers and berries red, image of that sweet south
Once open to the heavens and elevated on the human neck,
Now overgrown with hair and cover'd with a stony roof.
Downward 'tis sunk beneath th' attractive north, that round
    the feet   30
A raging whirlpool draws the dizzy enquirer to his grave.

PLATE 11
Albion's Angel rose upon the Stone of Night.
He saw Urizen on the Atlantic,
And his brazen Book
That Kings & Priests had copied on Earth
Expanded from North to South.   5

PLATE 12

And the clouds & fires pale roll'd round in the night of
    Enitharmon,
Round Albion's cliffs & London's walls (still Enitharmon
    slept);
Rolling volumes of grey mist involve Churches, Palaces,
    Towers;
For Urizen unclasp'd his Book, feeding his soul with pity.
The youth of England, hid in gloom, curse the pain'd heavens,
    compell'd   5
Into the deadly night to see the form of Albion's Angel.
Their parents brought them forth, & aged ignorance preaches,
    canting,
On a vast rock, perceived by those senses that are clos'd from
    thought—
Bleak, dark, abrupt it stands & overshadows London city.
They saw his boney feet on the rock, the flesh consum'd in
    flames;   10
They saw the Serpent temple lifted above, shadowing the
    Island white;
They heard the voice of Albion's Angel howling in flames of
    Orc,
Seeking the trump of the last doom.

Above the rest the howl was heard from Westminster louder
    and louder.
The Guardian of the secret codes forsook his ancient mansion,   15
Driven out by the flames of Orc; his furr'd robes & false locks
Adhered and grew one with his flesh, and nerves & veins shot
    thro' them.
With dismal torment sick, hanging upon the wind, he fled
Groveling along Great George Street thro' the Park gate. All
    the soldiers
Fled from his sight. He drag'd his torments to the wilderness.   20

Thus was the howl thro' Europe!
For Orc rejoic'd to hear the howling shadows;
But Palamabron shot his lightnings, trenching down his wide
    back,
And Rintrah hung with all his legions in the nether deep.

Enitharmon laugh'd in her sleep to see (O woman's triumph)   25
Every house a den, every man bound; the shadows are fill'd
With spectres, and the windows wove over with curses of iron;
Over the doors 'Thou shalt not,' & over the chimneys 'Fear' is
    written;
With bands of iron round their necks fasten'd into the walls
The citizens; in leaden gyves the inhabitants of suburbs   30
Walk heavy; soft and bent are the bones of villagers.

Between the clouds of Urizen the flames of Orc roll heavy
Around the limbs of Albion's Guardian, his flesh consuming.
Howlings & hissings, shrieks & groans & voices of despair
Arise around him in the cloudy Heavens of Albion. Furious,   35

PLATE 13
The red limb'd Angel seiz'd in horror and torment
The Trump of the last doom; but he could not blow the iron
    tube!
Thrice he assay'd presumptuous to awake the dead to
    Judgment.

A mighty Spirit leap'd from the land of Albion,
Nam'd Newton; he seiz'd the Trump & blow'd the enormous
    blast!   5
Yellow as leaves of Autumn the myriads of Angelic hosts
Fell thro' the wintry skies seeking their graves,
Rattling their hollow bones in howling and lamentation.

Then Enitharmon woke, nor knew that she had slept;
And eighteen hundred years were fled   10
As if they had not been.
She call'd her sons & daughters
To the sports of night,
Within her crystal house;
And thus her song proceeds: 15

'Arise, Ethinthus! tho' the earth-worm call,
Let him call in vain;
Till the night of holy shadows
And human solitude is past!

PLATE 14

'Ethinthus, queen of waters, how thou shinest in the sky!
My daughter, how do I rejoice! for thy children flock around
Like the gay fishes on the wave when the cold moon drinks the
  dew.
Ethinthus! thou art sweet as comforts to my fainting soul,
For now thy waters warble round the feet of Enitharmon.   5

'Manathu–Vorcyon! I behold thee flaming in my halls,
Light of thy mother's soul! I see thy lovely eagles round;
Thy golden wings are my delight, & thy flames of soft
  delusion.

'Where is my lureing bird of Eden? Leutha, silent love!
Leutha, the many colour'd bow delights upon thy wings,   10
Soft soul of flowers, Leutha!
Sweet smiling pestilence! I see thy blushing light;
Thy daughters many changing
Revolve like sweet perfumes ascending, O Leutha, silken
  queen!

'Where is the youthful Antamon, prince of the pearly dew?   15
O Antamon, why wilt thou leave thy mother Enitharmon?
Alone I see thee, crystal form,
Floating upon the bosom'd air
With lineaments of gratified desire.
My Antamon, the seven churches of Leutha seek thy love.   20

'I hear the soft Oothoon in Enitharmon's tents.
Why wilt thou give up woman's secrecy, my melancholy
  child?
Between two moments bliss is ripe.
O Theotormon robb'd of joy, I see thy salt tears flow
Down the steps of my crystal house.   25

'Sotha & Thiralatha, secret dwellers of dreamful caves,
Arise and please the horrent fiend with your melodious songs.
Still all your thunders golden hoof'd, & bind your horses
    black.
Orc! smile upon my children!
Smile, son of my afflictions.   30
Arise, O Orc, and give our mountains joy of thy red light.'

She ceas'd; for All were forth at sport beneath the solemn
    moon,
Waking the stars of Urizen with their immortal songs,
That nature felt thro' all her pores the enormous revelry,
Till morning oped the eastern gate.   35
Then every one fled to his station, & Enitharmon wept.

But terrible Orc, when he beheld the morning in the east,
PLATE 15
Shot from the heights of Enitharmon,
And in the vineyards of red France appear'd the light of his
    fury.

The sun glow'd fiery red!
The furious terrors flew around
On golden chariots raging, with red wheels dropping with
    blood;   5
The Lions lash their wrathful tails;
The Tigers couch upon the prey & suck the ruddy tide;
And Enitharmon groans & cries in anguish and dismay.

Then Los arose; his head he rear'd in snaky thunders clad,
And with a cry that shook all nature to the utmost pole   10
Call'd all his sons to the strife of blood.

THE BOOK OF URIZEN

Preludium

PLATE 2

  Of the primeval Priest's assum'd power,
When Eternals spurn'd back his religion,
And gave him a place in the north,
Obscure, shadowy, void, solitary.

  Eternals, I hear your call gladly.   5
Dictate swift winged words, & fear not
To unfold your dark visions of torment.

PLATE 3   Chap: I

1. Lo, a shadow of horror is risen
In Eternity! Unknown, unprolific,
Self-clos'd, all-repelling: what Demon
Hath form'd this abominable void,
This soul-shudd'ring vacuum? Some said   5
'It is Urizen.' But unknown, abstracted,
Brooding secret, the dark power hid.

2. Times on times he divided, & measur'd
Space by space in his ninefold darkness,
Unseen, unknown; changes appear'd   10
In his desolate mountains, rifted furious
By the black winds of perturbation.

3. For he strove in battles dire,
In unseen conflictions with shapes
Bred from his forsaken wilderness,   15
Of beast, bird, fish, serpent & element,
Combustion, blast, vapour and cloud.

4. Dark revolving in silent activity,
Unseen in tormenting passions,
An activity unknown and horrible,   20
A self-contemplating shadow,
In enormous labours occupied.

5. But Eternals beheld his vast forests.
Age on ages he lay, clos'd, unknown,
Brooding, shut in the deep; all avoid   25
The petrific abominable chaos.

6. His cold horrors silent, dark Urizen
Prepar'd; his ten thousands of thunders
Rang'd in gloom'd array stretch out across
The dread world; & the rolling of wheels,   30
As of swelling seas, sound in his clouds,
In his hills of stor'd snows, in his mountains
Of hail & ice; voices of terror
Are heard, like thunders of autumn
When the cloud blazes over the harvests.

Chap: II

1. Earth was not, nor globes of attraction.
The will of the Immortal expanded
Or contracted his all flexible senses.
Death was not, but eternal life sprung.

2. The sound of a trumpet the heavens   40
Awoke, & vast clouds of blood roll'd
Round the dim rocks of Urizen, so nam'd
That solitary one in Immensity.

3. Shrill the trumpet; & myriads of Eternity
PLATE 4
Muster around the bleak desarts,
Now fill'd with clouds, darkness & waters
That roll'd perplex'd lab'ring, & utter'd
Words articulate, bursting in thunders
That roll'd on the tops of his mountains: 5

4. 'From the depths of dark solitude; from
The eternal abode in my holiness,
Hidden, set apart in my stern counsels
Reserv'd for the days of futurity,
I have sought for a joy without pain,   10
For a solid without fluctuation.
Why will you die, O Eternals?
Why live in unquenchable burnings?

5. 'First I fought with the fire, consum'd
Inwards into a deep world within—   15
A void immense, wild, dark & deep,
Where nothing was, Nature's wide womb.
And self-balanc'd, stretch'd o'er the void,
I alone, even I! the winds merciless
Bound; but condensing, in torrents   20
They fall and fall. Strong I repell'd
The vast waves, & arose on the waters
A wide world of solid obstruction.

6. 'Here alone I, in books form'd of metals,
Have written the secrets of wisdom,   25
The secrets of dark contemplation,
By fightings and conflicts dire
With terrible monsters Sin-bred,
Which the bosoms of all inhabit,
Seven deadly Sins of the soul.   30

7. 'Lo! I unfold my darkness, and on
This rock place with strong hand the Book
Of eternal brass, written in my solitude:

8. 'Laws of peace, of love, of unity,
Of pity, compassion, forgiveness.   35
Let each chuse one habitation,
His ancient infinite mansion,
One command, one joy, one desire,
One curse, one weight, one measure,
One King, one God, one Law.'   40

Chap: III

1. The voice ended. They saw his pale visage
Emerge from the darkness, his hand
On the rock of eternity unclasping
The Book of brass. Rage seiz'd the strong,

2. Rage, fury, intense indignation,   45
In cataracts of fire, blood & gall,
In whirlwinds of sulphurous smoke
And enormous forms of energy;
All the seven deadly sins of the soul
PLATE 5
In living creations appear'd
In the flames of eternal fury.

3. Sund'ring, dark'ning, thund'ring!
Rent away with a terrible crash,
Eternity roll'd wide apart,   5
Wide asunder rolling
Mountainous, all around
Departing, departing, departing,
Leaving ruinous fragments of life,
Hanging, frowning cliffs, & all between   10
An ocean of voidness unfathomable.

4. The roaring fires ran o'er the heav'ns
In whirlwinds & cataracts of blood,
And o'er the dark desarts of Urizen
Fires pour thro' the void on all sides   15
On Urizen's self-begotten armies.

5. But no light from the fires. All was darkness
In the flames of Eternal fury.

6. In fierce anguish & quenchless flames
To the desarts and rocks he ran raging   20
To hide, but he could not; combining
He dug mountains & hills in vast strength;
He piled them in incessant labour,

In howlings & pangs & fierce madness,
Long periods in burning fires labouring,   25
Till hoary, and age-broke, and aged,
In despair and the shadows of death.

7. And a roof, vast petrific around,
On all sides he fram'd; like a womb,
Where thousands of rivers in veins   30
Of blood pour down the mountains to cool
The eternal fires beating without
From Eternals; & like a black globe
View'd by sons of Eternity, standing
On the shore of the infinite ocean,   35
Like a human heart strugling & beating,
The vast world of Urizen appear'd.

8. And Los round the dark globe of Urizen
Kept watch for Eternals to confine
The obscure separation alone;   40
For Eternity stood wide apart,
PLATE 6
As the stars are apart from the earth.

9. Los wept howling around the dark Demon,
And cursing his lot; for in anguish
Urizen was rent from his side,
And a fathomless void for his feet,   5
And intense fires for his dwelling.

10. But Urizen laid in a stony sleep,
Unorganiz'd, rent from Eternity.

11. The Eternals said, 'What is this? Death.
Urizen is a clod of clay.'   10

PLATE 7
12. Los howl'd in a dismal stupor,
Groaning! gnashing! groaning!
Till the wrenching apart was healed.

13. But the wrenching of Urizen heal'd not.
Cold, featureless, flesh or clay,   5
Rifted with direful changes,
He lay in a dreamless night,

14. Till Los rouz'd his fires, affrighted
At the formless unmeasurable death.

PLATE 8   Chap: IV

1. Los, smitten with astonishment,
Frighten'd at the hurtling bones.

2. And at the surging sulphureous
Perturbed Immortal, mad raging

3. In whirlwinds & pitch & nitre   5
Round the furious limbs of Los.

4. And Los formed nets & gins
And threw the nets round about.

5. He watch'd in shudd'ring fear
The dark changes, & bound every change   10
With rivets of iron & brass.

6. And these were the changes of Urizen:

PLATE 10   Chap: IV [a]

1. Ages on ages roll'd over him!
In stony sleep ages roll'd over him!
Like a dark waste stretching, chang'able,
By earthquakes riv'n, belching sullen fires.
On ages roll'd ages in ghastly   5
Sick torment; around him in whirlwinds
Of darkness the eternal Prophet howl'd,
Beating still on his rivets of iron,
Pouring sodor of iron, dividing
The horrible night into watches.   10

2. And Urizen (so his eternal name)
His prolific delight obscur'd more & more
In dark secresy, hiding in surgeing
Sulphureous fluid his phantasies.
The Eternal Prophet heav'd the dark bellows,   15
And turn'd restless the tongs, and the hammer
Incessant beat, forging chains new & new,
Numb'ring with links hours, days & years.

3. The Eternal mind, bounded, began to roll
Eddies of wrath ceaseless round & round,   20
And the sulphureous foam surgeing thick
Settled, a lake, bright & shining clear,
White as the snow on the mountains cold.

4. Forgetfulness, dumbness, necessity!
In chains of the mind locked up   25
Like fetters of ice shrinking together,
Disorganiz'd, rent from Eternity.
Los beat on his fetters of iron,
And heated his furnaces & pour'd
Iron sodor and sodor of brass.   30

5. Restless turn'd the immortal inchain'd,
Heaving dolorous, anguish'd, unbearable,
Till a roof, shaggy, wild, inclos'd
In an orb his fountain of thought.

6. In a horrible dreamful slumber,   35
Like the linked infernal chain,
A vast Spine writh'd in torment
Upon the winds, shooting pain'd
Ribs, like a bending cavern;
And bones of solidness froze   40
Over all his nerves of joy.
And a first Age passed over,
And a state of dismal woe.

PLATE 11

7. From the caverns of his jointed Spine
Down sunk with fright a red
Round globe, hot burning, deep
Deep down into the Abyss,
Panting, Conglobing, Trembling,   5
Shooting out ten thousand branches
Around his solid bones.
And a second Age passed over,
And a state of dismal woe.

8. In harrowing fear rolling round,   10
His nervous brain shot branches
Round the branches of his heart
On high into two little orbs;
And, fixed in two little caves
Hiding carefully from the wind,   15
His Eyes beheld the deep.
And a third Age passed over,
And a state of dismal woe.

9. The pangs of hope began,
In heavy pain, striving, struggling.   20
Two Ears in close volutions
From beneath his orbs of vision
Shot spiring out and petrified
As they grew. And a fourth Age passed,
And a state of dismal woe.   25

10. In ghastly torment sick,
Hanging upon the wind,
PLATE 13
Two Nostrils bent down to the deep.
And a fifth Age passed over,
And a state of dismal woe.

11. In ghastly torment sick,
Within his ribs bloated round,   5
A craving Hungry Cavern.
Thence arose his channel'd Throat,

And like a red flame a Tongue
Of thirst & of hunger appear'd.
And a sixth Age passed over,   10
And a state of dismal woe.

12. Enraged & stifled with torment,
He threw his right Arm to the north,
His left Arm to the south
Shooting out in anguish deep;   15
And his Feet stamp'd the nether Abyss
In trembling & howling & dismay.
And a seventh Age passed over,
And a state of dismal woe.

Chap: V

1. In terrors Los shrunk from his task.   20
His great hammer fell from his hand;
His fires beheld, and sickening
Hid their strong limbs in smoke.
For with noises ruinous loud,
With hurtlings & clashings & groans,   25
The Immortal endur'd his chains,
Tho' bound in a deadly sleep.

2. All the myriads of Eternity,
All the wisdom & joy of life,
Roll like a sea around him,   30
Except what his little orbs
Of sight by degrees unfold.

3. And now his eternal life
Like a dream was obliterated.

4. Shudd'ring, the Eternal Prophet smote   35
With a stroke from his north to south region.
The bellows & hammer are silent now.
A nerveless silence his prophetic voice
Seiz'd; a cold solitude & dark void
The Eternal Prophet & Urizen clos'd.   40

5. Ages on ages roll'd over them,
Cut off from life & light, frozen
Into horrible forms of deformity.
Los suffer'd his fires to decay;
Then he look'd back with anxious desire,   45
But the space, undivided by existence,
Struck horror into his soul.

6. Los wept, obscur'd with mourning;
His bosom earthquak'd with sighs;
He saw Urizen deadly black,   50
In his chains bound, & Pity began,

7. In anguish dividing & dividing,
(For pity divides the soul)
In pangs eternity on eternity.
Life in cataracts pour'd down his cliffs.   55
The void shrunk the lymph into Nerves,
Wand'ring wide on the bosom of night,
And left a round globe of blood
Trembling upon the void.

PLATE 15
Thus the Eternal Prophet was divided
Before the death image of Urizen;
For in changeable clouds and darkness,
In a winterly night beneath,
The Abyss of Los stretch'd immense;   5
And now seen, now obscur'd to the eyes
Of Eternals, the visions remote
Of the dark separation appear'd.
As glasses discover Worlds
In the endless Abyss of space,   10
So the expanding eyes of Immortals
Beheld the dark visions of Los,
And the globe of life blood trembling.

PLATE 18

8. The globe of life blood trembled
Branching out into roots,
Fibrous, writhing upon the winds,
Fibres of blood, milk and tears,
In pangs, eternity on eternity.   5
At length, in tears & cries imbodied,
A female form, trembling and pale,
Waves before his deathy face.

9. All Eternity shudder'd at sight
Of the first female now separate,   10
Pale as a cloud of snow
Waving before the face of Los.

10. Wonder, awe, fear, astonishment
Petrify the eternal myriads
At the first female form now separate.   15
PLATE 19
They call'd her Pity, and fled.

11. 'Spread a Tent with strong curtains around them;
Let cords & stakes bind in the Void,
That Eternals may no more behold them.'

12. They began to weave curtains of darkness;   5
They erected large pillars round the Void,
With golden hooks fasten'd in the pillars;
With infinite labour the Eternals
A woof wove, and called it Science.

Chap: VI

1. But Los saw the Female & pitied.   10
He embrac'd her; she wept, she refus'd
In perverse and cruel delight;
She fled from his arms, yet he follow'd.

2. Eternity shudder'd when they saw
Man begetting his likeness   15
On his own divided image.

3. A time passed over; the Eternals
Began to erect the tent;
When Enitharmon, sick,
Felt a Worm within her womb.   20

4. Yet helpless it lay like a Worm
In the trembling womb
To be moulded into existence.

5. All day the worm lay on her bosom;
All night within her womb   25
The worm lay, till it grew to a serpent
With dolorous hissings & poisons
Round Enitharmon's loins folding.

6. Coil'd within Enitharmon's womb
The serpent grew, casting its scales;   30
With sharp pangs the hissings began
To change to a grating cry.
Many sorrows and dismal throes,
Many forms of fish, bird & beast,
Brought forth an Infant form   35
Where was a worm before.

7. The Eternals their tent finished,
Alarm'd with these gloomy visions,
When Enitharmon groaning
Produc'd a man Child to the light.   40

8. A shriek ran thro' Eternity,
And a paralytic stroke,
At the birth of the Human shadow.

9. Delving earth in his resistless way,
Howling, the Child with fierce flames   45
Issu'd from Enitharmon.

10. The Eternals closed the tent;
They beat down the stakes; the cords
PLATE 20
Stretch'd for a work of eternity.
No more Los beheld Eternity.

11. In his hands he seiz'd the infant;
He bathed him in springs of sorrow;
He gave him to Enitharmon.   5

Chap: VII

1. They named the child Orc; he grew,
Fed with milk of Enitharmon.

2. Los awoke her. O sorrow & pain!
A tight'ning girdle grew
Around his bosom. In sobbings   10
He burst the girdle in twain,
But still another girdle
Oppress'd his bosom. In sobbings
Again he burst it. Again
Another girdle succeeds.   15
The girdle was form'd by day,
By night was burst in twain.

3. These falling down on the rock
Into an iron Chain
In each other link by link lock'd.   20

4. They took Orc to the top of a mountain.
O how Enitharmon wept!
They chain'd his young limbs to the rock
With the Chain of Jealousy
Beneath Urizen's deathful shadow.   25

5. The dead heard the voice of the child,
And began to awake from sleep.
All things heard the voice of the child,
And began to awake to life.

6. And Urizen, craving with hunger,   30
Stung with the odours of Nature,
Explor'd his dens around.

7. He form'd a line & a plummet
To divide the Abyss beneath;
He form'd a dividing rule.   35

8. He formed scales to weigh;
He formed massy weights;
He formed a brazen quadrant;
He formed golden compasses,
And began to explore the Abyss;   40
And he planted a garden of fruits.

9. But Los encircled Enitharmon
With fires of Prophecy
From the sight of Urizen & Orc.

10. And she bore an enormous race.   45

Chap: VIII

1. Urizen explor'd his dens,
Mountain, moor & wilderness,
With a globe of fire lighting his journey,
A fearful journey, annoy'd
By cruel enormities, forms   50
PLATE 23
Of life on his forsaken mountains.

2. And his world teem'd vast enormities,
Fright'ning, faithless, fawning
Portions of life, similitudes
Of a foot, or a hand, or a head,
Or a heart, or an eye; they swam, mischevous   5
Dread terrors, delighting in blood.

3. Most Urizen sicken'd to see
His eternal creations appear,
Sons & daughters of sorrow on mountains,   10
Weeping! wailing! First Thiriel appear'd,
Astonish'd at his own existence,
Like a man from a cloud born; & Utha,

From the waters emerging, laments.
Grodna rent the deep earth, howling,   15
Amaz'd; his heavens immense cracks
Like the ground parch'd with heat. Then Fuzon
Flam'd out, first begotten, last born.
All his eternal sons in like manner;
His daughters from green herbs & cattle,   20
From monsters, & worms of the pit.

4. He, in darkness clos'd, view'd all his race,
And his soul sicken'd! he curs'd
Both sons and daughters; for he saw
That no flesh nor spirit could keep   25
His iron laws one moment.

5. For he saw that life liv'd upon death:
PLATE 25
The Ox in the slaughter house moans,
The Dog at the wintry door.
And he wept & he called it Pity,
And his tears flowed down on the winds.

6. Cold he wander'd on high, over their cities,   5
In weeping & pain & woe;
And where-ever he wander'd in sorrows
Upon the aged heavens,
A cold shadow follow'd behind him
Like a spider's web, moist, cold & dim,   10
Drawing out from his sorrowing soul,
The dungeon-like heaven dividing,
Where ever the footsteps of Urizen
Walk'd over the cities in sorrow;

7. Till a Web, dark & cold, throughout all   15
The tormented element stretch'd
From the sorrows of Urizen's soul.
(And the Web is a Female in embrio.)
None could break the Web, no wings of fire,

8. So twisted the cords & so knotted   20
The meshes, twisted like to the human brain.

9. And all call'd it The Net of Religion.

Chap: IX

1. Then the Inhabitants of those Cities
Felt their Nerves change into Marrow,
And hardening Bones began   25
In swift diseases and torments,
In throbbings & shootings & grindings
Thro' all the coasts; till weaken'd
The Senses inward rush'd, shrinking
Beneath the dark net of infection;   30

2. Till the shrunken eyes, clouded over,
Discern'd not the woven hipocrisy,
But the streaky slime in their heavens,
Brought together by narrowing perceptions,
Appear'd transparent air; for their eyes   35
Grew small like the eyes of a man,
And in reptile forms shrinking together,
Of seven feet stature they remain'd.

3. Six days they shrunk up from existence,
And on the seventh day they rested,   40
And they bless'd the seventh day, in sick hope,
And forgot their eternal life.

4. And their thirty cities divided
In form of a human heart.
No more could they rise at will   45
In the infinite void, but bound down
To earth by their narrowing perceptions
PLATE 28
They lived a period of years,
Then left a noisom body
To the jaws of devouring darkness.

5. And their children wept, & built
Tombs in the desolate places,
And form'd laws of prudence, and call'd them 5
The eternal laws of God.

6. And the thirty cities remain'd,
Surrounded by salt floods, now call'd
Africa: its name was then Egypt. 10

7. The remaining sons of Urizen
Beheld their brethren shrink together
Beneath the Net of Urizen.
Perswasion was in vain;
For the ears of the inhabitants 15
Were wither'd & deafn'd & cold,
And their eyes could not discern
Their brethren of other cities.

8. So Fuzon call'd all together
The remaining children of Urizen,
And they left the pendulous earth: 20
They called it Egypt, & left it.

9. And the salt ocean rolled englob'd.

THE BOOK OF AHANIA

PLATE 2   Chap: Ist

1. Fuzon on a chariot iron-wing'd
On spiked flames rose; his hot visage
Flam'd furious; sparkles his hair & beard
Shot down his wide bosom and shoulders.

On clouds of smoke rages his chariot,   5
And his right hand burns red in its cloud,
Moulding into a vast globe his wrath
As the thunder-stone is moulded,
Son of Urizen's silent burnings.

2. 'Shall we worship this Demon of smoke,'   10
Said Fuzon, 'this abstract non-entity,
This cloudy God seated on waters,
Now seen, now obscur'd, King of Sorrow?'

3. So he spoke, in a fiery flame,
On Urizen frowning indignant,   15
The Globe of wrath shaking on high.
Roaring with fury, he threw
The howling Globe; burning it flew,
Length'ning into a hungry beam. Swiftly

4. Oppos'd to the exulting flam'd beam   20
The broad Disk of Urizen upheav'd
Across the Void many a mile.

5. It was forg'd in mills where the winter
Beats incessant; ten winters the disk
Unremitting endur'd the cold hammer.   25

6. But the strong arm that sent it remember'd
The sounding beam; laughing it tore through
That beaten mass, keeping its direction,
The cold loins of Urizen dividing.

7. Dire shriek'd his invisible Lust.   30
Deep groan'd Urizen! stretching his awful hand,
Ahania (so name his parted soul)
He seiz'd on his mountains of Jealousy.
He groan'd, anguish'd, & called her Sin,
Kissing her and weeping over her;   35
Then hid her in darkness, in silence,
Jealous tho' she was invisible.

8. She fell down, a faint shadow wand'ring
In chaos and circling dark Urizen,
As the moon, anguish'd, circles the earth: 40
Hopeless! abhorr'd! a death-shadow,
Unseen, unbodied, unknown,
The mother of Pestilence.

9. But the fiery beam of Fuzon
Was a pillar of fire to Egypt,   45
Five hundred years wand'ring on earth,
Till Los seiz'd it and beat in a mass
With the body of the sun.

PLATE 3   Chap: IId

1. But the forehead of Urizen gathering,
And his eyes pale with anguish, his lips
Blue & changing, in tears and bitter
Contrition he prepar'd his Bow,

2. Form'd of Ribs, that in his dark solitude,   5
When obscur'd in his forests, fell monsters
Arose. For his dire Contemplations
Rush'd down like floods from his mountains,
In torrents of mud settling thick,
With Eggs of unnatural production   10
Forthwith hatching; some howl'd on his hills,
Some in vales, some aloft flew in air.

3. Of these, an enormous dread Serpent,
Scaled and poisonous horned,
Approach'd Urizen even to his knees   15
As he sat on his dark rooted Oak.

4. With his horns he push'd furious.
Great the conflict & great the jealousy
In cold poisons; but Urizen smote him.

5. First he poison'd the rocks with his blood;   20
Then polish'd his ribs, and his sinews
Dried; laid them apart till winter;
Then a Bow black prepar'd; on this Bow
A poisoned rock plac'd in silence.
He utter'd these words to the Bow: 25

6. 'O Bow of the clouds of secrecy,
O nerve of that lust form'd monster!
Send this rock swift, invisible thro'
The black clouds, on the bosom of Fuzon.'

7. So saying, In torment of his wounds,   30
He bent the enormous ribs slowly:
A circle of darkness! then fixed
The sinew in its rest; then the Rock,
Poisonous source, plac'd with art, lifting difficult
Its weighty bulk; silent the rock lay,   35

8. While Fuzon, his tygers unloosing,
Thought Urizen slain by his wrath.
'I am God,' said he, 'eldest of things!'

9. Sudden sings the rock; swift & invisible
On Fuzon flew; enter'd his bosom.   40
His beautiful visage, his tresses
That gave light to the mornings of heaven,
Were smitten with darkness, deform'd
And outstretch'd on the edge of the forest.

10. But the rock fell upon the Earth,   45
Mount Sinai in Arabia.

Chap: III

1. The Globe shook; and Urizen, seated
On black clouds, his sore wound anointed.
The ointment flow'd down on the void
Mix'd with blood — here the snake gets her poison.   50

2. With difficulty & great pain Urizen
Lifted on high the dead corse;
On his shoulders he bore it to where
A Tree hung over the Immensity.

3. For when Urizen shrunk away   55
From Eternals, he sat on a rock
Barren, a rock which himself
From redounding fancies had petrified.
Many tears fell on the rock,
Many sparks of vegetation.   60
Soon shot the pained root
Of Mystery under his heel.
It grew a thick tree; he wrote
In silence his book of iron;
Till the horrid plant, bending its boughs,   65
Grew to roots when it felt the earth
And again sprung to many a tree.

4. Amaz'd started Urizen! when
He beheld himself compassed round
And high roofed over with trees.   70
He arose, but the stems stood so thick
He with difficulty and great pain
Brought his Books, all but the Book
PLATE 4
Of iron, from the dismal shade.

5. The Tree still grows over the Void,
Enrooting itself all around,
An endless labyrinth of woe!

6. The corse of his first begotten   5
On the accursed Tree of Mystery,
On the topmost stem of this Tree
Urizen nail'd Fuzon's corse.

Chap: IV

1. Forth flew the arrows of pestilence
Round the pale living Corse on the tree;   10

2. For in Urizen's slumbers of abstraction
In the infinite ages of Eternity,
When his Nerves of Joy melted and flow'd
A white Lake on the dark blue air,
In perturb'd pain and dismal torment   15
Now stretching out, now swift conglobing,

3. Effluvia vapor'd above
In noxious clouds; these hover'd thick
Over the disorganiz'd Immortal,
Till petrific pain scurf'd o'er the Lakes   20
As the bones of man, solid & dark.

4. The clouds of disease hover'd wide
Around the Immortal in torment,
Perching around the hurtling bones,
Disease on disease, shape on shape,   25
Winged, screaming in blood & torment.

5. The Eternal Prophet beat on his anvils,
Enrag'd in the desolate darkness;
He forg'd nets of iron around
And Los threw them around the bones.   30

6. The shapes, screaming, flutter'd vain;
Some combin'd into muscles & glands,
Some organs for craving and lust;
Most remain'd on the tormented void,
Urizen's army of horrors.   35

7. Round the pale living Corse on the Tree
Forty years flew the arrows of pestilence.

8. Wailing and terror and woe
Ran thro' all his dismal world;
Forty years all his sons & daughters   40
Felt their skulls harden; then Asia
Arose in the pendulous deep.

9. They reptilize upon the Earth.

10. Fuzon groan'd on the Tree.

Chap: V

1. The lamenting voice of Ahania,   45
Weeping upon the void
And round the Tree of Fuzon:
Distant in solitary night
Her voice was heard, but no form
Had she; but her tears from clouds   50
Eternal fell round the Tree.

2. And the voice cried: 'Ah, Urizen! Love!
Flower of morning! I weep on the verge
Of Non-entity; how wide the Abyss
Between Ahania and thee!   55

3. 'I lie on the verge of the deep,
I see thy dark clouds ascend,
I see thy black forests and floods,
A horrible waste to my eyes!

4. 'Weeping I walk over rocks,   60
Over dens & thro' valleys of death.
Why didst thou despise Ahania,
To cast me from thy bright presence
Into the World of Loneness?

5. 'I cannot touch his hand,   65
Nor weep on his knees, nor hear
His voice & bow, nor see his eyes
And joy, nor hear his footsteps and
My heart leap at the lovely sound!
I cannot kiss the place   70
Whereon his bright feet have trod,
PLATE 5
But I wander on the rocks
With hard necessity.

6. 'Where is my golden palace?
Where my ivory bed?
Where the joy of my morning hour?   5
Where the sons of eternity singing

7. 'To awake bright Urizen, my king,
To arise to the mountain sport,
To the bliss of eternal valleys;

8. 'To awake my king in the morn   10
To embrace Ahania's joy
On the bredth of his open bosom,
From my soft cloud of dew to fall
In showers of life on his harvests?

9. 'When he gave my happy soul   15
To the sons of eternal joy;
When he took the daughters of life
Into my chambers of love;

10. 'When I found babes of bliss on my beds,
And bosoms of milk in my chambers   20
Fill'd with eternal seed,
O! eternal births sung round Ahania
In interchange sweet of their joys.

11. 'Swell'd with ripeness & fat with fatness,
Bursting on winds my odors,   25
My ripe figs and rich pomegranates
In infant joy at thy feet,
O Urizen, sported and sang.

12. 'Then thou with thy lap full of seed,
With thy hand full of generous fire,   30
Walked forth from the clouds of morning,
On the virgins of springing joy,
On the human soul to cast
The seed of eternal science.

13. 'The sweat poured down thy temples;   35
To Ahania return'd in evening
The moisture awoke to birth
My mother's-joys, sleeping in bliss.

14. 'But now, alone, over rocks, mountains,
Cast out from thy lovely bosom.   40
Cruel jealousy, selfish fear,
Self-destroying: how can delight
Renew in these chains of darkness,
Where bones of beasts are strown
On the bleak and snowy mountains,   45
Where bones from the birth are buried
Before they see the light?'

POEMS FROM LETTERS

I

To my Friend Butts I write
My first Vision of Light:
On the yellow sands sitting,
The Sun was Emitting
His Glorious beams   5
From Heaven's high Streams.
Over Sea, over Land
My Eyes did Expand
Into regions of air
Away from all Care,   10
Into regions of fire
Remote from Desire.
The Light of the Morning
Heaven's Mountains adorning,
In particles bright   15
The jewels of Light
Distinct shone & clear.
Amaz'd & in fear
I each particle gazed,

Astonish'd, Amazed;   20
For each was a Man
Human-form'd. Swift I ran,
For they beckon'd to me
Remote by the Sea,
Saying: 'Each grain of Sand,   25
Every stone on the Land,
Each rock & each hill,
Each fountain & rill,
Each herb & each tree,
Mountain, hill, earth & sea,   30
Cloud, Meteor & Star,
Are Men Seen Afar.'
I stood in the Streams
Of Heaven's bright beams
And Saw Felpham sweet   35
Beneath my bright feet
In soft Female charms;
And in her fair arms
My Shadow I knew,
And my wife's shadow too,   40
And My Sister & Friend.
We like Infants descend
In our Shadows on Earth,
Like a weak mortal birth.
My Eyes more & more   45
Like a Sea without Shore
Continue expanding,
The Heavens commanding,
Till the Jewels of Light,
Heavenly Men beaming bright,   50
Appear'd as One Man,
Who Complacent began
My limbs to infold
In his beams of bright gold;
Like dross purg'd away   55
All my mire & my clay.
Soft consum'd in delight
In his bosom Sun bright

I remain'd. Soft he smil'd,
And I heard his voice Mild 60
Saying: 'This is My Fold,
O thou Ram horn'd with gold,
Who awakest from Sleep
On the Sides of the Deep.
On the Mountains around 65
The roarings resound
Of the lion & wolf,
The loud sea & deep gulf.
These are guards of My Fold,
O thou Ram horn'd with gold.' 70
And the voice faded mild.
I remain'd as a Child;
All I ever had known
Before me bright Shone.
I saw you & your wife 75
By the fountains of life.
Such the Vision to me
Appear'd on the Sea.

II

With happiness stretch'd across the hills
In a cloud that dewy sweetness distills,
With a blue sky spread over with wings
And a mild sun that mounts & sings,
With trees & fields full of Fairy elves 5
And little devils who fight for themselves,
Rememb'ring the Verses that Hayley sung
When my heart knock'd against the root of my tongue;
With Angels planted in Hawthorn bowers
And God himself in the passing hours, 10
With Silver Angels across my way
And Golden Demons that none can stay,
With my Father hovering upon the wind
And my Brother Robert just behind,

And my Brother John, the evil one,   15
In a black cloud making his mone—
Tho' dead, they appear upon my path
Notwithstanding my terrible wrath,
They beg, they intreat, they drop their tears,
Fill'd full of hopes, fill'd full of fears—   20
With a thousand Angels upon the Wind
Pouring disconsolate from behind
To drive them off—& before my way
A frowning Thistle implores my stay.
What to others a trifle appears   25
Fills me full of smiles or tears;
For double the vision my Eyes do see,
And a double vision is always with me.
With my inward Eye, 'tis an old Man grey,
With my outward, a Thistle across my way.   30
'If thou goest back,' the thistle said,
'Thou art to endless woe betray'd;
For here does Theotormon lower,
And here is Enitharmon's bower,
And Los the terrible thus hath sworn,   35
Because thou backward dost return,
Poverty, Envy, old age & fear
Shall bring thy Wife upon a bier,
And Butts shall give what Fuseli gave,
A dark black Rock & a gloomy Cave.'   40

I struck the Thistle with my foot,
And broke him up from his delving root:
'Must the duties of life each other cross?
Must every joy be dung & dross?
Must my dear Butts feel cold neglect   45
Because I give Hayley his due respect?
Must Flaxman look upon me as wild
And all my friends be with doubts beguil'd?
Must my Wife live in my Sister's bane,
Or my Sister survive on my Love's pain?   50
The curses of Los, the terrible shade,
And his dismal terrors make me afraid.'

So I spoke, & struck in my wrath
The old man weltering upon my path.
Then Los appear'd in all his power;   55
In the Sun he appear'd, descending before
My face in fierce flames. In my double sight
'Twas outward a Sun, inward Los in his might.

'My hands are labour'd day & night,
And Ease comes never in my sight.   60
My Wife has no indulgence given
Except what comes to her from heaven.
We eat little, we drink less;
This Earth breeds not our happiness.
Another Sun feeds our life's streams;   65
We are not warmed with thy beams.
Thou measurest not the Time to me,
Nor yet the Space that I do see;
My Mind is not with thy light array'd;
Thy Terrors shall not make me afraid.'   70
When I had my Defiance given,
The Sun stood trembling in heaven;
The Moon, that glow'd remote below,
Became leprous & white as snow;
And every soul of men on the Earth   75
Felt affliction & sorrow & sickness & dearth.
Los flam'd in my path, & the Sun was hot
With the bows of my Mind & the arrows of Thought.
My bowstring fierce with ardour breathes,
My arrows glow in their golden sheaves;   80
My brothers & father march before;
The heavens drop with human gore.

Now I a fourfold vision see,
And a fourfold vision is given to me;
'Tis fourfold in my supreme delight   85
And threefold in soft Beulah's night,
And twofold Always. May God us keep
From single vision & Newton's sleep.

FROM BLAKE'S NOTEBOOK
(c. 1802–4)

My Spectre around me night & day
Like a Wild beast guards my way;
My Emanation far within
Weeps incessantly for my Sin.

A Fathomless & boundless Deep,   5
There we wander, there we weep.
On the hungry craving wind
My Spectre follows thee behind.

He scents thy footsteps in the snow
Wheresoever thou dost go,   10
Thro' the wintry hail & rain:
'When wilt thou return again?

'Dost thou not in Pride & scorn
Fill with tempests all my morn?
And with jealousies & fears   15
Fill my pleasant nights with tears?

'Seven of my sweet loves thy knife
Has bereaved of their life;
Their marble tombs I built with tears,
And with cold & shuddering fears.   20

'Seven more loves weep night & day
Round the tombs where my loves lay,
And seven more loves attend each night
Around my couch with torches bright.

'And Seven more Loves in my bed   25
Crown with wine my mournful head,
Pitying & forgiving all
Thy transgressions great & small.

'When wilt thou return & view
My loves, & them to life renew?   30
When wilt thou return & live?
When wilt thou pity, as I forgive?'

'Never, Never I return:
Still for Victory I burn!
Living, thee alone I'll have,   35
And when dead I'll be thy Grave.

'Thro' the Heav'n & Earth & Hell
Thou shalt never, never quell;
I will fly & thou pursue,
Night & Morn the flight renew.'   40

'Till I turn from Female Love
And root up the Infernal Grove,
I shall never worthy be
To Step into Eternity.

'And to end thy cruel mocks   45
Annihilate thee on the rocks,
And another form create
To be subservient to my Fate.

'Let us agree to give up Love
And root up the infernal grove;   50
Then we shall return & see
The worlds of happy Eternity.

'& Throughout all Eternity
I forgive you, you forgive me;
As our dear Redeemer said,   55
"This the Wine & this the Bread." '

*

Mock on, Mock on, Voltaire, Rousseau!
Mock on, Mock on—'tis all in vain!
You throw the sand against the wind,
And the wind blows it back again.

And every sand becomes a Gem 5
Reflected in the beams divine;
Blown back they blind the mocking Eye,
But still in Israel's paths they shine.

The Atoms of Democritus
And Newton's Particles of Light 10
Are sands upon the Red sea shore,
Where Israel's tents do shine so bright.

Morning

To find the Western path,
Right thro' the Gates of Wrath
I urge my way.
Sweet Mercy leads me on
With soft repentant moan; 5
I see the break of day.

The war of swords & spears
Melted by dewy tears
Exhales on high;
The Sun is freed from fears 10
And with soft grateful tears
Ascends the sky.

FROM THE PICKERING MS

The Mental Traveller

I travel'd thro' a Land of Men,
A Land of Men & Women too,
And heard & saw such dreadful things
As cold Earth wanderers never knew.

For there the Babe is born in joy   5
That was begotten in dire woe,
Just as we Reap in joy the fruit
Which we in bitter tears did sow.

And if the Babe is born a Boy
He's given to a Woman Old,   10
Who nails him down upon a rock,
Catches his shrieks in cups of gold.

She binds iron thorns around his head,
She pierces both his hands & feet,
She cuts his heart out at his side   15
To make it feel both cold & heat.

Her fingers number every Nerve,
Just as a Miser counts his gold;
She lives upon his shrieks & cries,
And she grows young as he grows old,   20

Till he becomes a bleeding youth
And she becomes a Virgin bright;
Then he rends up his Manacles
And binds her down for his delight.

He plants himself in all her Nerves,   25
Just as a Husbandman his mould;
And she becomes his dwelling place
And Garden, fruitful seventy fold.

An Aged Shadow soon he fades,
Wand'ring round an Earthly Cot,   30
Full filled all with gems & gold
Which he by industry had got.

And these are the gems of the Human Soul:
The rubies & pearls of a lovesick eye,
The countless gold of the akeing heart,   35
The martyr's groan & the lover's sigh.

They are his meat, they are his drink;
He feeds the Beggar & the Poor
And the wayfaring Traveller;
For ever open is his door.   40

His grief is their eternal joy;
They make the roofs & walls to ring;
Till from the fire on the hearth
A little Female Babe does spring.

And she is all of solid fire   45
And gems & gold, that none his hand
Dares stretch to touch her Baby form,
Or wrap her in his swaddling-band.

But She comes to the Man she loves,
If young or old, or rich or poor;   50
They soon drive out the aged Host,
A Beggar at another's door.

He wanders weeping far away
Untill some other take him in;
Oft blind & age-bent, sore distrest,   55
Untill he can a Maiden win.

And to allay his freezing Age
The Poor Man takes her in his arms;
The Cottage fades before his sight,
The Garden & its lovely Charms;   60

The Guests are scatter'd thro' the land,
For the Eye altering alters all;
The Senses roll themselves in fear,
And the flat Earth becomes a Ball;

The Stars, Sun, Moon, all shrink away—   65
A desart vast without a bound,
And nothing left to eat or drink,
And a dark desart all around.

The honey of her Infant lips,
The bread & wine of her sweet smile, 70
The wild game of her roving eye,
Does him to Infancy beguile.

For as he eats & drinks he grows
Younger & younger every day;
And on the desart wild they both 75
Wander in terror & dismay.

Like the wild Stag she flees away,
Her fear plants many a thicket wild;
While he pursues her night & day,
By various arts of Love beguil'd; 80

By various arts of Love & Hate,
Till the wide desart planted o'er
With Labyrinths of wayward Love,
Where roams the Lion, Wolf & Boar,

Till he becomes a wayward Babe, 85
And she a weeping Woman Old.
Then many a Lover wanders here,
The Sun & Stars are nearer roll'd,

The trees bring forth sweet Extacy
To all who in the desart roam, 90
Till many a City there is Built
And many a pleasant Shepherd's home.

But when they find the frowning Babe,
Terror strikes thro' the region wide;
They cry, 'the Babe! the Babe is Born!' 95
And flee away on every side.

For who dare touch the frowning form
His arm is wither'd to its root;
Lions, Boars, Wolves, all howling flee,
And every Tree does shed its fruit. 100

And none can touch that frowning form,
Except it be a Woman Old;
She nails him down upon the Rock,
And all is done as I have told.

The Crystal Cabinet

The Maiden caught me in the Wild,
Where I was dancing merrily;
She put me into her Cabinet,
And Lock'd me up with a golden Key.

This Cabinet is form'd of Gold   5
And Pearl & Crystal shining bright,
And within it opens into a World
And a little lovely Moony Night.

Another England there I saw,
Another London with its Tower,   10
Another Thames & other Hills,
And another pleasant Surrey Bower,

Another Maiden like herself,
Translucent, lovely, shining clear,
Threefold each in the other clos'd—   15
O, what a pleasant trembling fear!

O, what a smile! a threefold Smile
Fill'd me, that like a flame I burn'd.
I bent to Kiss the lovely Maid,
And found a Threefold Kiss return'd.   20

I strove to seize the inmost Form
With ardor fierce & hands of flame,
But burst the Crystal Cabinet
And like a Weeping Babe became,

A weeping Babe upon the wild,   25
And weeping Woman, pale, reclin'd;
And in the outward air again
I fill'd with woes the passing Wind.

Auguries of Innocence

To see a World in a Grain of Sand
And a Heaven in a Wild Flower,
Hold Infinity in the palm of your hand
And Eternity in an hour.

A Robin Red breast in a Cage   5
Puts all Heaven in a Rage.
A dove house fill'd with doves & Pigeons
Shudders Hell thro' all its regions.
A Dog starv'd at his Master's Gate
Predicts the ruin of the State.   10
A Horse misus'd upon the Road
Calls to Heaven for Human blood.
Each outcry of the hunted Hare
A fibre from the Brain does tear.
A Skylark wounded in the wing,   15
A Cherubim does cease to sing.
The Game Cock clip'd & arm'd for fight
Does the Rising Sun affright.
Every Wolf's & Lion's howl
Raises from Hell a Human Soul.   20
The wild deer wand'ring here & there
Keeps the Human Soul from Care.
The Lamb misus'd breeds Public strife,
And yet forgives the Butcher's Knife.
The Bat that flits at close of Eve   25
Has left the Brain that won't Believe.
The Owl that calls upon the Night
Speaks the Unbeliever's fright.
He who shall hurt the little Wren

Shall never be belov'd by Men.   30
He who the Ox to wrath has mov'd
Shall never be by Woman lov'd.
The wanton Boy that kills the Fly
Shall feel the Spider's enmity.
He who torments the Chafer's sprite   35
Weaves a Bower in endless Night.
The Catterpiller on the Leaf
Repeats to thee thy Mother's grief.
Kill not the Moth nor Butterfly,
For the Last Judgment draweth nigh.   40
He who shall train the Horse to war
Shall never pass the Polar Bar.
The Beggar's Dog & Widow's Cat,
Feed them & thou wilt grow fat.
The Gnat that sings his Summer's song   45
Poison gets from Slander's tongue.
The poison of the Snake & Newt
Is the sweat of Envy's Foot.
The Poison of the Honey Bee
Is the Artist's Jealousy.   50
The Prince's Robes & Beggar's Rags
Are Toadstools on the Miser's Bags.
A truth that's told with bad intent
Beats all the Lies you can invent.
It is right it should be so;   55
Man was made for Joy & Woe,
And when this we rightly know,
Thro' the World we safely go.
Joy & Woe are woven fine,
A Clothing for the Soul divine;   60
Under every grief & pine
Runs a joy with silken twine.
The Babe is more than swadling Bands;
Throughout all these Human Lands
Tools were made, & Born were hands—   65
Every Farmer Understands.
Every Tear from Every Eye
Becomes a Babe in Eternity;

This is caught by Females bright
And return'd to its own delight.   70
The Bleat, the Bark, Bellow & Roar
Are Waves that Beat on Heaven's Shore.
The Babe that weeps the Rod beneath
Writes Revenge in realms of death.
The Beggar's Rags fluttering in Air   75
Does to Rags the Heavens tear.
The Soldier arm'd with Sword & Gun
Palsied strikes the Summer's Sun.
The poor Man's Farthing is worth more
Than all the Gold on Afric's Shore.   80
One Mite wrung from the Lab'rer's hands
Shall buy & sell the Miser's Lands;
Or if protected from on high
Does that whole Nation sell & buy.
He who mocks the Infant's Faith   85
Shall be mock'd in Age & Death.
He who shall teach the Child to Doubt
The rotting Grave shall ne'er get out.
He who respects the Infant's faith
Triumphs over Hell & Death.   90
The Child's Toys & the Old Man's Reasons
Are the Fruits of the Two seasons.
The Questioner who sits so sly
Shall never know how to Reply.
He who replies to words of Doubt   95
Doth put the Light of Knowledge out.
The Strongest Poison ever known
Came from Cæsar's Laurel Crown.
Nought can deform the Human Race
Like to the Armour's iron brace.   100
When Gold & Gems adorn the Plow
To peaceful Arts shall Envy Bow.
A Riddle, or the Cricket's Cry,
Is to Doubt a fit Reply.
The Emmet's Inch & Eagle's Mile   105
Make Lame Philosophy to smile.
He who Doubts from what he sees

Will ne'er Believe, do what you Please.
If the Sun & Moon should doubt,
They'd immediately Go out.   110
To be in a Passion you Good may do,
But no Good if a Passion is in you.
The Whore & Gambler, by the State
Licenc'd, build that Nation's Fate.
The Harlot's cry from Street to Street   115
Shall weave Old England's winding Sheet.
The Winner's Shout, the Loser's Curse,
Dance before dead England's Hearse.
Every Night & every Morn
Some to Misery are Born.   120
Every Morn & every Night
Some are Born to sweet delight.
Some are Born to sweet delight,
Some are Born to Endless Night.
We are led to Believe a Lie   125
When we see not Thro' the Eye,
Which was Born in a Night to perish in a Night,
When the Soul Slept in Beams of Light.
God Appears & God is Light
To those poor Souls who dwell in Night,   130
But does a Human Form Display
To those who Dwell in Realms of Day.

FROM *THE FOUR ZOAS*

Night I
Four Mighty Ones are in every Man. A Perfect Unity
Cannot Exist but from the Universal Brotherhood of Eden,   10
The Universal Man, to Whom be Glory Evermore, Amen.

What are the Natures of those Living Creatures the Heavenly
    Father only
Knoweth; no Individual Knoweth nor Can know in all
    Eternity.

Los was the fourth immortal starry one, & in the Earth
Of a bright Universe Empery attended day & night,   15
Days & nights of revolving joy. Urthona was his name
In Eden. In the Auricular Nerves of Human life,
Which is the Earth of Eden, he his Emanations propagated,
Fairies of Albion, afterwards Gods of the Heathen. Daughter
    of Beulah, Sing
His fall into Division & his Resurrection to Unity.   20

*   *   *

Night I
'Hear! I will sing a Song of Death; it is a Song of Vala!   260
The Fallen Man takes his repose; Urizen sleeps in the porch.
Luvah and Vala woke, and flew up from the Human Heart
Into the Brain; from thence upon the pillow Vala slumber'd.
And Luvah seiz'd the Horses of Light, & rose into the Chariot
    of Day.

*   *   *

Night II
'What is the price of Experience? do men buy it for a song,
Or wisdom for a dance in the street? No, it is bought with the
    price
Of all that a man hath—his house, his wife, his children.
Wisdom is sold in the desolate market where none come to
    buy,   400
And in the wither'd field where the farmer plows for bread in
    vain.

It is an easy thing to triumph in the summer's sun
And in the vintage, & to sing on the waggon loaded with corn;
It is an easy thing to talk of patience to the afflicted,

To speak the laws of prudence to the houseless wanderer,   405
To listen to the hungry ravens' cry in wintry season,
When the red blood is fill'd with wine & with the marrow of
    lambs;
It is an easy thing to laugh at wrathful elements,
To hear the dog howl at the wintry door, the ox in the
    slaughter house moan,
To see a god on every wind, & a blessing on every blast,   410
To hear sounds of love in the thunderstorm that destroys our
    enemy's house,
To rejoice in the blight that covers his field, & the sickness that
    cuts off his children,
While our olive & vine sing & laugh round our door & our
    children bring fruit & flowers.

Then the groan & the dolor are quite forgotten, & the slave
    grinding at the mill,
And the captive in chains, & the poor in the prison, & the
    soldier in the field   415
When the shatter'd bone hath laid him groaning among the
    happier dead.

It is an easy thing to rejoice in the tents of prosperity;
Thus could I sing & thus rejoice, but it is not so with me!'

      *   *   *

Night III
'Then, O my dear lord, listen to Ahania, listen to the vision,
The vision of Ahania in the slumbers of Urizen,
When Urizen slept in the porch and the Ancient Man was
    smitten.

The Darkning Man walk'd on the steps of fire before his halls,
And Vala walk'd with him in dreams of soft deluding slumber.   45
He looked up & saw thee, Prince of Light, thy splendor faded,
But saw not Los nor Enitharmon, for Luvah hid them in
    shadow,
In a soft cloud Outstretch'd across; and Luvah dwelt in the
    cloud.

Then Man ascended mourning into the splendors of his
    palace;
Above him rose a Shadow from his wearied intellect   50
Of living gold, pure, perfect, holy; in white linen pure he
    hover'd,
A sweet, entrancing self delusion, a watry vision of Man,
Soft exulting in existence, all the Man absorbing.

Man fell upon his face prostrate before the watry shadow,
Saying, 'O Lord, whence is this change? Thou knowest I am
    nothing'.   55
And Vala trembled & coverd her face, & her locks were spread
    on the pavement.

I heard, astonishd at the Vision, & my heart trembled within
    me;
I heard the voice of the Slumberous Man, and thus he spoke
Idolatrous to his own Shadow, words of Eternity uttering:
"O, I am nothing when I enter into judgment with thee.   60
If thou withdraw thy breath, I die & vanish into Hades;
If thou dost lay thine hand upon me, behold I am silent;
If thou withold thine hand, I perish like a fallen leaf.
O, I am nothing, & to nothing must return again;
If thou withdraw thy breath, behold I am oblivion." '   65

*   *   *

Night VI
For Urizen beheld the terrors of the Abyss, wand'ring among
The ruin'd spirits, once his children & the children of Luvah.
Scar'd at the sound of their own sigh that seems to shake the
    immense
They wander Moping, in their heart a Sun, a Dreary moon,   90
A Universe of fiery constellations in their brain,
An Earth of wintry woe beneath their feet, & round their loins
Waters or winds or clouds or brooding lightnings & pestilential
    plagues.
Beyond the bounds of their own self their senses cannot
    penetrate.

As the tree knows not what is outside of its leaves & bark   95
And yet it drinks the summer joy & fears the winter sorrow,
So in the regions of the grave none knows his dark compeer,
Tho' he partakes of his dire woes & mutual returns the pang,
The throb, the dolor, the convulsion in soul-sickening woes
. . .

Then came he among fiery cities & castles built of burning
      steel.   115
Then he beheld the forms of tygers & of Lions, dishumaniz'd
      men.
Many in serpents & in worms, stretch'd out enormous length
Over the sullen mould & slimy tracks, obstruct his way,
Drawn out from deep to deep, woven by ribb'd
And scaled monsters, or arm'd in iron shell or shell of brass 120
Or gold, a glittering torment shining & hissing in eternal pain;
Some, columns of fire or of water, sometimes stretch'd out in
      height,
Sometimes in length, sometimes englobing, wandering in
      vain, seeking for ease.
His voice to them was but an inarticulate thunder, for their
      Ears
Were heavy & dull, & their eyes & nostrils closed up.   125
Oft he stood by a howling victim, Questioning in words
Soothing or Furious; no one answer'd; every one wrap'd up
In his own sorrow howl'd regardless of his words, nor voice
Of sweet response could he obtain, tho' oft assay'd with tears.
He knew they were his Children ruin'd in his ruin'd world. 130

Oft would he stand & question a fierce scorpion glowing with
      gold;
In vain: the terror heard not; then a lion he would Seize
By the fierce mane, staying his howling course; in vain the
      voice
Of Urizen, in vain the Eloquent tongue. A Rock, a Cloud, a
      Mountain,
Were now not Vocal as in Climes of happy Eternity   135
Where the lamb replies to the infant voice & the lion to the man
      of years,

Giving them sweet instructions; Where the Cloud, the River &
    the Field
Talk with the husbandman & shepherd. But these attack'd him
    sore,
Seizing upon his feet & rending the Sinews, that in Caves
He hid to recure his obstructed powers with rest & oblivion.   140

Here he had time enough to repent of his rashly threaten'd
    curse.
He saw them curs'd beyond his Curse; his soul melted with
    fear.
He could not take their fetters off, for they grew from the soul,
Nor could he quench the fires, for they flam'd out from the
    heart,
Nor could he calm the Elements, because himself was Subject.   145
So he threw his flight in terror & pain, & in repentant tears.

*   *   *

Night VII
And Urizen read in his book of brass in sounding tones:

'Listen, O Daughters, to my voice, Listen to the Words of
    Wisdom.   110
So shall you govern over all. Let Moral Duty tune your
    tongue,
But be your hearts harder than the nether millstone.
To bring the shadow of Enitharmon beneath our wondrous
    tree
That Los may Evaporate like smoke & be no more,
Draw down Enitharmon to the Spectre of Urthona   115
And let him have dominion over Los the terrible shade.
Compell the poor to live upon a Crust of bread by soft mild
    arts.
Smile when they frown, frown when they smile; & when a
    man looks pale
With labour & abstinence, say he looks healthy & happy;
And when his children sicken, let them die—there are enough   120
Born, even too many, & our Earth will be overrun

Without these arts. If you would make the poor live with
    temper,
With pomp give every crust of bread you give; with gracious
    cunning
Magnify small gifts; reduce a man to want a gift & then give
    with pomp.
Say he smiles if you hear him sigh. If pale, say he is ruddy. 125
Preach temperance: say he is overgorg'd & drowns his wit
In strong drink, tho' you know that bread & water are all
He can afford. Flatter his wife, pity his children, till we can
Reduce all to our will, as spaniels are taught with art.
Lo, how the heart & brain are formed in the breeding womb 130
Of Enitharmon! how it buds with life & forms the bones,
The little heart, the liver & the red blood in its labyrinths!
By gratified desire, by strong devouring appetite, she fills
Los with ambitious fury that his race shall all devour.'

Then Orc cried: 'Curse thy Cold hypocrisy! Already round thy
    tree 135
In scales that shine with gold & rubies thou beginnest to
    weaken
My divided Spirit. Like a worm I rise in peace, unbound
From wrath. Now when I rage, my fetters bind me more.
O torment! O torment! A Worm compelled! Am I a worm?
Is it in strong deceit that man is born? In strong deceit 140
Thou dost restrain my fury, that the worm may fold the tree.
Avaunt, Cold hypocrite! I am chain'd or thou couldst not use
    me thus.
The Man shall rage, bound with this Chain; the worm in
    silence creep.
Thou wilt not cease from rage. Grey Demon, silence all thy
    storms;
Give me example of thy mildness, King of furious hail-storms. 145
Art thou the cold attractive power that holds me in this chain?
I well remember how I stole thy light & it became fire
Consuming. Thou Know'st me now, O Urizen, Prince of
    Light;
And I know thee. Is this the triumph, this the Godlike State
That lies beyond the bounds of Science in the Grey obscure?' 150

Terrified Urizen heard Orc, now certain that he was Luvah;
And Orc began to Organize a Serpent body,
Despising Urizen's light & turning it into flaming fire,
Receiving as a poison'd Cup Receives the heavenly wine,
And turning affection into fury & thought into abstraction,   155
A Self-consuming dark devourer rising into the heavens.

Urizen, envious, brooding, sat, & saw the secret terror
Flame high in pride & laugh to scorn the source of his deceit,
Nor knew the source of his own, but thought himself the Sole
    author
Of all his wandering Experiments in the horrible Abyss.   160
He knew that weakness stretches out in breadth & length; he
    knew
That wisdom reaches high & deep; and therefore he made Orc,
In Serpent form compell'd, stretch out & up the mysterious
    tree.
He suffer'd him to Climb that he might draw all human forms
Into submission to his will; nor knew the dread result.   165

*   *   *

Night IX
Urizen wept in the dark deep, anxious his Scaly form
To reassume the human; & he wept in the dark deep
Saying: 'O that I had never drank the wine nor eat the bread
Of dark mortality, nor cast my view into futurity, nor turn'd   165
My back dark'ning the present, clouding with a cloud,
And building arches high, & cities, turrets & towers and domes
Whose smoke destroy'd the pleasant garden & whose running
    Kennels
Chok'd the bright rivers, burd'ning with my Ships the angry
    deep;
Thro' Chaos seeking for delight, & in spaces remote   170
Seeking the Eternal which is always present to the wise;
Seeking for pleasure which unsought falls round the infant's
    path
And on the fleeces of mild flocks who neither care nor labour.
But I, the labourer of ages, whose unwearied hands

Are thus deform'd with hardness, with the sword & with the
 spear 175
And with the Chisel & the mallet, I, whose labours vast
Order the nations, separating family by family,
Alone enjoy not. I alone, in misery supreme,
Ungratified give all my joy unto this Luvah & Vala.
Then Go, O dark futurity! I will cast thee forth from these 180
Heavens of my brain, nor will I look upon that void
Which I have made; for lo, futurity is in this moment!
Let Orc consume, let Tharmas rage, let dark Urthona give
All strength to Los & Enitharmon, & let Los self-curs'd 185
Rend down this fabric, as a wall ruin'd & family extinct.
Rage, Orc! Rage, Tharmas! Urizen no longer curbs your rage.'

So Urizen spoke. He shook his snows from off his Shoulders &
 arose
As on a Pyramid of mist, his white robes scattering
The fleecy white; renew'd, he shook his aged mantles off 190
Into the fires. Then glorious, bright, Exulting in his joy,
He sounding rose into the heavens in naked majesty,
In radiant Youth.

* * *

FROM *MILTON*

PLATE 1   *Preface*

. . .

And did those feet in ancient time
Walk upon England's mountains green?
And was the holy Lamb of God
On England's pleasant pastures seen?

And did the Countenance Divine   5
Shine forth upon our clouded hills?
And was Jerusalem builded here
Among these dark Satanic Mills?

Bring me my Bow of burning gold;
Bring me my Arrows of desire;   10
Bring me my Spear; O clouds unfold!
Bring me my Chariot of fire!

I will not cease from Mental Fight,
Nor shall my Sword sleep in my hand,
Till we have built Jerusalem   15
In England's green & pleasant Land.

Would to God that all the Lord's people were Prophets.
                                        Numbers XI. 29

PLATE 2   *Book the First*

Daughters of Beulah! Muses who inspire the Poet's Song,
Record the journey of immortal Milton thro' your Realms
Of terror & mild moony lustre, in soft sexual delusions
Of varied beauty, to delight the wanderer and repose
His burning thirst & freezing hunger! Come into my hand   5
By your mild power, descending down the Nerves of my right
    arm
From out the Portals of my Brain, where by your ministry
The Eternal Great Humanity Divine planted his Paradise,
And in it caus'd the Spectres of the Dead to take sweet forms
In likeness of himself. Tell also of the False Tongue! vegetated 10
Beneath your land of shadows, of its sacrifices and
Its offerings, even till Jesus, the image of the Invisible God,
Became its prey, a curse, an offering and an atonement
For Death Eternal in the heavens of Albion, & before the Gates
Of Jerusalem his Emanation, in the heavens beneath Beulah.   15

Say first! what mov'd Milton, who walk'd about in Eternity
One hundred years, pond'ring the intricate mazes of
    Providence,
Unhappy tho' in heav'n—he obey'd, he murmur'd not, he was
    silent
Viewing his Sixfold Emanation scatter'd thro' the deep
In torment—To go into the deep, her to redeem & himself
    perish?   20
What cause at length mov'd Milton to this unexampled deed?
A Bard's prophetic Song! for sitting at eternal tables,
Terrific among the Sons of Albion in chorus solemn & loud,
A Bard broke forth! all sat attentive to the awful man.

*   *   *

PLATE 14
Then Milton rose up from the heavens of Albion ardorous.   10
The whole Assembly wept prophetic, seeing in Milton's face
And in his lineaments divine the shades of Death & Ulro.
He took off the robe of the promise, & ungirded himself from
    the oath of God.

And Milton said: 'I go to Eternal Death! The Nations still
Follow after the detestable Gods of Priam, in pomp   15
Of warlike selfhood contradicting and blaspheming.
When will the Resurrection come to deliver the sleeping body
From corruptibility? O when, Lord Jesus, wilt thou come?
Tarry no longer, for my soul lies at the gates of death.
I will arise and look forth for the morning of the grave;   20
I will go down to the sepulcher to see if morning breaks;
I will go down to self annihilation and eternal death,
Lest the Last Judgment come & find me unannihilate,
And I be seiz'd & giv'n into the hands of my own Selfhood.
The Lamb of God is seen thro' mists & shadows, hov'ring   25
Over the sepulchers in clouds of Jehovah & winds of Elohim,
A disk of blood, distant; & heav'ns & earths roll dark between.
What do I here before the Judgment? without my Emanation?
With the daughters of memory & not with the daughters of
    inspiration?

I in my Selfhood am that Satan; I am that Evil One!   30
He is my Spectre! In my obedience to loose him from my
    Hells,
To claim the Hells, my Furnaces, I go to Eternal Death.'

*   *   *

PLATE 21
But Milton entering my Foot, I saw in the nether
Regions of the Imagination—also all men on Earth   5
And all in Heaven saw in the nether regions of the Imagination
In Ulro beneath Beulah—the vast breach of Milton's descent.
But I knew not that it was Milton, for man cannot know
What passes in his members till periods of Space & Time
Reveal the secrets of Eternity; for more extensive   10
Than any other earthly things are Man's earthly lineaments.

And all this Vegetable World appear'd on my left Foot,
As a bright sandal form'd immortal of precious stones & gold:
I stooped down & bound it on to walk forward thro' Eternity.

*   *   *

PLATE 22
                         . . . what time I bound my sandals
On to walk forward thro' Eternity, Los descended to me;   5
And Los behind me stood, a terrible flaming Sun, just close
Behind my back. I turned round in terror, and behold!
Los stood in that fierce glowing fire, & he also stoop'd down
And bound my sandals on in Udan-Adan. Trembling I stood
Exceedingly with fear & terror, standing in the Vale   10
Of Lambeth; but he kissed me, and wish'd me health,
And I became One Man with him arising in my strength.
'Twas too late now to recede. Los had enter'd into my soul;
His terrors now posses'd me whole! I arose in fury & strength.

'I am that Shadowy Prophet who Six Thousand Years ago   15
Fell from my station in the Eternal bosom. Six Thousand
    Years

Are finish'd. I return! both Time & Space obey my will.
I in Six Thousand Years walk up and down; for not one
 Moment
Of Time is lost, nor one Event of Space unpermanent,
But all remain; every fabric of Six Thousand Years   20
Remains permanent. Tho' on the Earth where Satan
Fell and was cut off all things vanish & are seen no more,
They vanish not from me & mine, we guard them first & last.
The generations of men run on in the tide of Time,
But leave their destin'd lineaments permanent for ever & ever.' 25

   * * *

PLATE 24
Los is by mortals nam'd Time; Enitharmon is nam'd Space.
But they depict him bald & aged who is in eternal youth,
All powerful, and his locks flourish like the brows of morning. 70
He is the Spirit of Prophecy, the ever apparent Elias.
Time is the mercy of Eternity; without Time's swiftness,
Which is the swiftest of all things, all were eternal torment.
All the Gods of the Kingdoms of Earth labour in Los's Halls:
Every one is a fallen Son of the Spirit of Prophecy.   75
He is the Fourth Zoa, that stood around the Throne Divine.

   * * *

PLATE 25
Thou seest the Constellations in the deep & wondrous Night;
They rise in order and continue their immortal courses
Upon the mountains & in vales, with harp & heavenly song,
With flute & clarion, with cups & measures fill'd with foaming
 wine.
Glitt'ring the streams reflect the Vision of beatitude,   70
And the calm Ocean joys beneath & smooths his awful waves.
PLATE 26
These are the Sons of Los, & these the Labourers of the
 Vintage.

Thou seest the gorgeous clothed Flies that dance & sport in
    summer
Upon the sunny brooks & meadows; every one the dance
Knows in its intricate mazes of delight artful to weave,
Each one to sound his instruments of music in the dance,   5
To touch each other & recede, to cross & change & return.
These are the Children of Los. Thou seest the Trees on
    mountains;
The wind blows heavy, loud they thunder thro' the darksom
    sky,
Uttering prophecies & speaking instructive words to the sons
Of men. These are the Sons of Los, these the Visions of
    Eternity;   10
But we see only as it were the hem of their garments
When with our vegetable eyes we view these wondrous
    Visions.

. . .

And every Generated Body in its inward form
Is a garden of delight & a building of magnificence,
Built by the Sons of Los in Bowlahoola & Allamanda;
And the herbs & flowers & furniture & beds & chambers
Continually woven in the Looms of Enitharmon's Daughters,   35
In bright Cathedron's golden Dome with care & love & tears.
For the various Classes of Men are all mark'd out determinate
In Bowlahoola, & as the Spectres choose their affinities
So they are born on Earth, & every Class is determinate;
But not by Natural, but by Spiritual power alone, Because   40
The Natural power continually seeks & tends to Destruction,
Ending in Death, which would of itself be Eternal Death.
And all are Class'd by Spiritual & not by Natural power.

And every Natural Effect has a Spiritual Cause, and Not
A Natural; for a Natural Cause only seems: it is a Delusion   45
Of Ulro, & a ratio of the perishing Vegetable Memory.

*   *   *

PLATE 28

But others of the Sons of Los build Moments & Minutes &
    Hours
And Days & Months & Years & Ages & Periods, wondrous
    buildings;
And every Moment has a Couch of gold for soft repose,   45
(A Moment equals a pulsation of the artery),
And between every two Moments stands a Daughter of Beulah
To feed the Sleepers on their Couches with maternal care.
And Every Minute has an azure Tent with silken Veils;   50
And Every Hour has a bright golden Gate carved with skill;
And every Day & Night has Walls of brass & Gates of adamant,
Shining like precious stones & ornamented with appropriate
    signs;
And every Month a silver paved Terrace builded high;
And every Year invulnerable Barriers with high Towers;   55
And every Age is Moated deep with Bridges of silver & gold;
And every Seven Ages is Incircled with a Flaming Fire.
Now Seven Ages is amounting to Two Hundred Years:
Each has its Guard, each Moment, Minute, Hour, Day, Month
    & Year.
All are the work of Fairy hands of the Four Elements.   60
The Guard are Angels of Providence on duty evermore.
Every Time less than a pulsation of the artery
Is equal in its period & value to Six Thousand Years;
PLATE 29
For in this Period the Poet's Work is Done, and all the Great
Events of Time start forth & are conciev'd in such a Period,
Within a Moment, a Pulsation of the Artery.

The Sky is an immortal Tent built by the Sons of Los;
And every Space that a Man views around his dwelling-place,   5
Standing on his own roof or in his garden on a mount
Of twenty-five cubits in height, such space is his Universe;
And on its verge the Sun rises & sets, the Clouds bow
To meet the flat Earth & the Sea in such an order'd Space.
The Starry heavens reach no further, but here bend and set   10
On all sides, & the two Poles turn on their valves of gold;
And if he move his dwelling-place, his heavens also move

Where'er he goes, & all his neighbourhood bewail his loss.
Such are the Spaces called Earth, & such its dimension.
As to that false appearance which appears to the reasoner,   15
As of a Globe rolling thro' Voidness, it is a delusion of Ulro.
The Microscope knows not of this, nor the Telescope; they alter
The ratio of the Spectator's Organs, but leave Objects
      untouch'd.
For every Space larger than a red globule of Man's blood
Is visionary, and is created by the Hammer of Los;   20
And every Space smaller than a Globule of Man's blood opens
Into Eternity, of which this vegetable Earth is but a shadow.
The red Globule is the unwearied Sun by Los created
To measure Time and Space to mortal Men every morning.
Bowlahoola & Allamanda are placed on each side   25
Of that Pulsation & that Globule, terrible their power.

*   *   *

Book the Second

. . .

PLATE 31
Thou hearest the Nightingale begin the Song of Spring.
The Lark sitting upon his earthly bed, just as the morn
Appears, listens silent; then springing from the waving
      Corn-field loud   30
He leads the Choir of Day! trill, trill, trill, trill,
Mounting upon the wings of light into the Great Expanse,
Reecchoing against the lovely blue & shining heavenly Shell,
His little throat labours with inspiration; every feather
On throat & breast & wings vibrates with the effluence Divine.   35
All Nature listens silent to him, & the awful Sun
Stands still upon the Mountain looking on this little Bird
With eyes of soft humility & wonder, love & awe.
Then loud from their green covert all the Birds begin their
      Song:

The Thrush, the Linnet & the Goldfinch, Robin & the Wren   40
Awake the Sun from his sweet reverie upon the Mountain;
The Nightingale again assays his song, & thro' the day
And thro' the night warbles luxuriant, every Bird of Song
Attending his loud harmony with admiration & love.
This is a Vision of the lamentation of Beulah over Ololon.   45

Thou perceivest the Flowers put forth their precious Odours,
And none can tell how from so small a center comes such
    sweets,
Forgetting that within that Center Eternity expands
Its ever during doors that Og & Anak fiercely guard.
First, e'er the morning breaks, joy opens in the flowery
    bosoms,   50
Joy even to tears, which the Sun rising dries; first the Wild
    Thyme
And Meadow-sweet, downy & soft, waving among the reeds,
Light springing on the air, lead the sweet Dance: they wake
The Honeysuckle sleeping on the Oak; the flaunting beauty
Revels along upon the wind; the White-thorn, lovely May,   55
Opens her many lovely eyes; listening the Rose still sleeps—
None dare to wake her; soon she bursts her crimson curtain'd
    bed
And comes forth in the majesty of beauty; every Flower,
The Pink, the Jessamine, the Wall-flower, the Carnation,
The Jonquil, the mild Lilly opes her heavens; every Tree   60
And Flower & Herb soon fill the air with an innumerable
    Dance,
Yet all in order sweet & lovely. Men are sick with Love.
Such is a Vision of the lamentation of Beulah over Ololon.

PLATE 32
And Milton oft sat upon the Couch of Death, & oft conversed
In vision & dream beatific with the Seven Angels of the
    Presence.

'I have turned my back upon these Heavens builded on cruelty.
My Spectre still wandering thro' them follows my Emanation;
He hunts her footsteps thro' the snow & the wintry hail & rain.   5

The idiot Reasoner laughs at the Man of Imagination,
And from laughter proceeds to murder by undervaluing
    calumny.'

Then Hillel, who is Lucifer, replied over the Couch of Death,
And thus the Seven Angels instructed him, & thus they
    converse:

'We are not Individuals but States, Combinations of
    Individuals.   10
We were Angels of the Divine Presence, & were Druids in
    Annandale,
Compell'd to combine into Form by Satan, the Spectre of
    Albion,
Who made himself a God & destroyed the Human Form
    Divine.
But the Divine Humanity & Mercy gave us a Human Form
Because we were combin'd in Freedom & holy Brotherhood;   15
While those combin'd by Satan's Tyranny, first in the blood of
    War
And Sacrifice & next in Chains of imprisonment, are Shapeless
    Rocks
Retaining only Satan's Mathematic Holiness, Length, Bredth
    & Highth,
Calling the Human Imagination, which is the Divine Vision &
    Fruition
In which Man liveth eternally, madness & blasphemy,
    against   20
Its own Qualities, which are Servants of Humanity, not Gods
    or Lords.
Distinguish therefore States from Individuals in those States.
States change, but Individual Identities never change nor cease.
You cannot go to Eternal Death in that which can never Die.
Satan & Adam are States Created into Twenty-seven
    Churches,   25
And thou, O Milton, art a State, about to be Created
Called Eternal Annihilation, that none but the Living shall
Dare to enter; & they shall enter triumphant over Death
And Hell & the Grave: States that are not, but ah! Seem to be.

'Judge then of thy Own Self: thy Eternal Lineaments explore,   30
What is Eternal & what Changeable, & what Annihilable?
The Imagination is not a State: it is the Human Existence itself.
Affection or Love becomes a State when divided from
    Imagination.
The Memory is a State always, & the Reason is a State
Created to be Annihilated & a new Ratio Created.   35
Whatever can be Created can be Annihilated. Forms cannot.
The Oak is cut down by the Ax, the Lamb falls by the Knife,
But their Forms Eternal Exist For-ever. Amen. Hallelujah!'

Thus they converse with the Dead, watching round the Couch
    of Death.
For God himself enters Death's Door always with those that
    enter,   40
And lays down in the Grave with them, in Visions of Eternity,
Till they awake & see Jesus, & the Linen Clothes lying
That the Females had Woven for them, & the Gates of their
    Father's House.

*   *   *

PLATE 35
There is a Moment in each Day that Satan cannot find,
Nor can his Watch Fiends find it; but the Industrious find
This Moment & it multiply; & when it once is found
It renovates every Moment of the Day if rightly placed.   45
In this Moment Ololon descended to Los & Enitharmon
Unseen beyond the Mundane Shell, Southward in Milton's
    track.

Just in this Moment when the morning odours rise abroad
And first from the Wild Thyme, stands a Fountain in a rock
Of crystal flowing into two Streams: one flows thro'
    Golgonooza
And thro' Beulah to Eden beneath Los's western wall;   50
The other flows thro' the Aerial Void & all the Churches,
Meeting again in Golgonooza beyond Satan's Seat.

The Wild Thyme is Los's Messenger to Eden, a mighty
    Demon,
Terrible, deadly & poisonous his presence in Ulro dark;   55
Therefore he appears only a small Root creeping in grass,
Covering over the Rock of Odours his bright purple mantle
Beside the Fount, above the Lark's Nest in Golgonooza.
Luvah slept here in death, & here is Luvah's empty Tomb.
Ololon sat beside this Fountain on the Rock of Odours.   60

Just at the place to where the Lark mounts is a Crystal Gate:
It is the enterance of the First Heaven, named Luther; for
The Lark is Los's Messenger thro' the Twenty-seven
    Churches,
That the Seven Eyes of God, who walk even to Satan's Seat
Thro' all the Twenty-seven Heavens, may not slumber nor
    sleep.   65
But the Lark's Nest is at the Gate of Los, at the eastern
Gate of wide Golgonooza, & the Lark is Los's Messenger.

PLATE 36

When on the highest lift of his light pinions he arrives
At that bright Gate, another Lark meets him, & back to back
They touch their pinions, tip tip, and each descend
To their respective Earths, & there all night consult with
    Angels
Of Providence & with the eyes of God all night in slumbers   5
Inspired, & at the dawn of day send out another Lark
Into another Heaven to carry news upon his wings.
Thus are the Messengers dispatch'd till they reach the Earth
    again
In the East Gate of Golgonooza; & the Twenty-eighth bright
Lark met the Female Ololon descending into my Garden.   10
Thus it appears to Mortal eyes & those of the Ulro Heavens,
But not thus to Immortals; the Lark is a mighty Angel.

For Ololon step'd into the Polypus within the Mundane
    Shell—
They could not step into Vegetable Worlds without becoming
The enemies of Humanity, except in a Female Form—   15

And as One Female, Ololon and all its mighty Hosts
Appear'd, a Virgin of twelve years. Nor time nor space was
To the perception of the Virgin Ololon, but as the
Flash of lightning, but more quick, the Virgin in my Garden
Before my Cottage stood; for the Satanic Space is delusion.   20

For when Los join'd with me he took me in his fi'ry whirlwind.
My Vegetated portion was hurried from Lambeth's shades;
He set me down in Felpham's Vale & prepar'd a beautiful
Cottage for me, that in three years I might write all these
    Visions
To display Nature's cruel holiness, the deceits of Natural
    Religion.   25
Walking in my Cottage Garden, sudden I beheld
The Virgin Ololon & address'd her as a Daughter of Beulah:

'Virgin of Providence, fear not to enter into my Cottage.
What is thy message to thy friend? What am I now to do?
Is it again to plunge into deeper affliction? Behold me   30
Ready to obey, but pity thou my Shadow of Delight.
Enter my Cottage, comfort her, for she is sick with fatigue.'

PLATE 37

The Virgin answer'd: 'Knowest thou of Milton who
    descended
Driven from Eternity? Him I seek! terrified at my Act
In Great Eternity which thou knowest, I come him to seek.'

So Ololon utter'd in words distinct the anxious thought:
Mild was the voice, but more distinct than any earthly.   5
That Milton's Shadow heard; & condensing all his Fibres
Into a strength impregnable of majesty & beauty infinite,
I saw he was the Covering Cherub & within him Satan
And Rahab, in an outside which is fallacious, within
Beyond the outline of Identity, in the Selfhood deadly.   10
And he appear'd the Wicker Man of Scandinavia, in whom
Jerusalem's children consume in flames among the Stars.

Descending down into my Garden, a Human Wonder of God
Reaching from heaven to earth, a Cloud & Human Form,
I beheld Milton with astonishment, & in him beheld   1
The Monstrous Churches of Beulah, the Gods of Ulro dark,
Twelve monstrous dishumaniz'd terrors, Synagogues of
     Satan,
A Double Twelve & Thrice Nine: such their divisions.

*   *   *

PLATE 38
And Milton, collecting all his fibres into impregnable strength,   5
Descended down a Paved work of all kinds of precious stones
Out from the eastern sky; descending down into my Cottage
Garden, clothed in black, severe & silent he descended.

The Spectre of Satan stood upon the roaring sea & beheld
Milton within his sleeping Humanity; trembling & shudd'ring   10
He stood upon the waves, a Twenty-seven-fold mighty
     Demon,
Gorgeous & beautiful; loud roll his thunders against Milton.
Loud Satan thunder'd, loud & dark upon mild Felpham shore;
Not daring to touch one fibre he howl'd round upon the Sea.

I also stood in Satan's bosom & beheld its desolations: 15
A ruin'd Man, a ruin'd building of God not made with hands;
Its plains of burning sand, its mountains of marble terrible;
Its pits & declivities flowing with molten ore & fountains
Of pitch & nitre; its ruin'd palaces & cities & mighty works;
Its furnaces of affliction, in which his Angels & Emanations   20
Labour with blacken'd visages among its stupendous ruins,
Arches & pyramids & porches, colonades & domes,
In which dwells Mystery, Babylon; here is her secret place;
From hence she comes forth on the Churches in delight;
Here is her Cup fill'd with its poisons, in these horrid vales,   25
And here her scarlet Veil woven in pestilence & war;
Here is Jerusalem bound in chains, in the Dens of Babylon.

In the Eastern porch of Satan's Universe Milton stood & said:

'Satan! my Spectre! I know my power thee to annihilate
And be a greater in thy place, & be thy Tabernacle,   30
A covering for thee to do thy will, till one greater comes
And smites me as I smote thee & becomes my covering.
Such are the Laws of thy false Heav'ns; but Laws of Eternity
Are not such. Know thou, I come to Self Annihilation.
Such are the Laws of Eternity, that each shall mutually   35
Annihilate himself for other's good, as I for thee.
Thy purpose & the purpose of thy Priests & of thy Churches
Is to impress on men the fear of death, to teach
Trembling & fear, terror, constriction, abject selfishness.
Mine is to teach Men to despise death & to go on   40
In fearless majesty annihilating Self, laughing to scorn
Thy Laws & terrors, shaking down thy Synagogues as webs.
I come to discover before Heav'n & Hell the Self righteousness
In all its Hypocritic turpitude, opening to every eye
These wonders of Satan's holiness, shewing to the Earth   45
The Idol Virtues of the Natural Heart, & Satan's Seat
Explore in all its Selfish Natural Virtue, & put off
In Self annihilation all that is not of God alone,
To put off Self & all I have, ever & ever. Amen.'

Satan heard, Coming in a cloud with trumpets & flaming
    fire,   50
Saying: 'I am God the judge of all, the living & the dead.
Fall therefore down & worship me; submit thy supreme
Dictate to my eternal Will, & to my dictate bow.
I hold the Balances of Right & Just, & mine the Sword.
Seven Angels bear my Name & in those Seven I appear;   55
But I alone am God, & I alone in Heav'n & Earth
Of all that live dare utter this; others tremble & bow,
PLATE 39
Till All Things become One Great Satan, in Holiness
Oppos'd to Mercy, and the Divine Delusion, Jesus, be no
    more.'

Suddenly around Milton on my Path the Starry Seven
Burn'd terrible! My Path became a solid fire, as bright
As the clear Sun, & Milton silent came down on my Path.   5

And there went forth from the Starry limbs of the Seven,
Forms
Human, with Trumpets innumerable, sounding articulate
As the Seven spake; and they stood in a mighty Column of Fire
Surrounding Felpham's Vale, reaching to the Mundane Shell,
Saying:

'Awake, Albion awake! reclaim thy Reasoning Spectre,
Subdue   10
Him to the Divine Mercy. Cast him down into the Lake
Of Los that ever burneth with fire, ever & ever, Amen!
Let the Four Zoas awake from Slumbers of Six Thousand
Years.'

Then loud the Furnaces of Los were heard, & seen as Seven
Heavens
Stretching from south to north over the mountains of Albion.   15
Satan heard; trembling round his Body, he incircled it;
He trembled with exceeding great trembling & astonishment,
Howling in his Spectre round his Body, hung'ring to devour
But fearing for the pain; for if he touches a Vital
His torment is unendurable. Therefore he cannot devour,   20
But howls round it as a lion round his prey continually.
Loud Satan thunder'd, loud & dark upon mild Felpham's
Shore,
Coming in a Cloud with Trumpets & with Fiery Flame,
An awful Form eastward, from midst of a bright Paved-work
Of precious stones by Cherubim surrounded, so permitted   25
(Lest he should fall apart in his Eternal Death) to imitate
The Eternal Great Humanity Divine surrounded by
His Cherubim & Seraphim in ever happy Eternity.
Beneath sat Chaos: Sin on his right hand, Death on his left;
And Ancient Night spread over all the heav'n his Mantle of
Laws.   30
He trembled with exceeding great trembling & astonishment.

Then Albion rose up in the Night of Beulah on his Couch
Of dread repose seen by the visionary eye; his face is toward

The east, toward Jerusalem's Gates; groaning he sat above
His rocks. London & Bath & Legions & Edinburgh   35
Are the four pillars of his Throne; his left foot near London
Covers the shades of Tyburn; his instep from Windsor
To Primrose Hill stretching to Highgate & Holloway;
London is between his knees, its basements fourfold;
His right foot stretches to the sea on Dover cliffs, his heel   40
On Canterbury's ruins; his right hand covers lofty Wales,
His left Scotland; his bosom girt with gold involves
York, Edinburgh, Durham & Carlisle, & on the front
Bath, Oxford, Cambridge, Norwich; his right elbow
Leans on the Rocks of Erin's Land, Ireland, ancient nation;   45
His head bends over London. He sees his embodied Spectre
Trembling before him with exceeding great trembling & fear.
He views Jerusalem & Babylon, his tears flow down.
He mov'd his right foot to Cornwall, his left to the rocks of
    Bognor;
He strove to rise to walk into the Deep, but strength failing   50
Forbad; & down with dreadful groans he sunk upon his Couch
In moony Beulah. Los, his strong Guard, walks round beneath
    the Moon.

Urizen faints in terror, striving among the Brooks of Arnon
With Milton's Spirit. As the Plowman or Artificer or Shepherd
While in the labours of his Calling sends his Thought abroad   55
To labour in the ocean or in the starry heaven, So Milton
Labour'd in Chasms of the Mundane Shell, tho' here before
My Cottage midst the Starry Seven, where the Virgin Ololon
Stood trembling in the Porch. Loud Satan thunder'd on the
    stormy Sea,
Circling Albion's Cliffs in which the Four-fold World resides,   60
Tho' seen in fallacy outside, a fallacy of Satan's Churches.

PLATE 40
Before Ololon Milton stood & perceiv'd the Eternal Form
Of that mild Vision; wondrous were their acts, by me
    unknown
Except remotely; and I heard Ololon say to Milton:

'I see thee strive upon the Brooks of Arnon. There a dread
And awful Man I see, o'ercover'd with the mantle of years.   5
I behold Los & Urizen, I behold Orc & Tharmas,
The Four Zoas of Albion, & thy Spirit with them striving,
In Self annihilation giving thy life to thy enemies.
Are those who contemn Religion & seek to annihilate it
Become in their Feminine portions the causes & promoters   10
Of these Religions? How is this thing, this Newtonian
      Phantasm,
This Voltaire & Rousseau, this Hume & Gibbon &
      Bolingbroke,
This Natural Religion, this impossible absurdity?
Is Ololon the cause of this? O where shall I hide my face?
These tears fall for the little ones, the Children of Jerusalem,   15
Lest they be annihilated in thy annihilation.'

No sooner she had spoke but Rahab Babylon appear'd
Eastward upon the Paved work across Europe & Asia,
Glorious as the midday Sun, in Satan's bosom glowing,
A Female hidden in a Male, Religion hidden in War,   20
Nam'd Moral Virtue, cruel two-fold Monster shining bright,
A Dragon red & hidden Harlot which John in Patmos saw.

And all beneath the Nations innumerable of Ulro
Appear'd, the Seven Kingdoms of Canaan & Five Baalim
Of Philistea into Twelve divided, call'd after the Names   25
Of Israel, as they are in Eden—Mountain, River & Plain,
City & sandy Desert intermingled beyond mortal ken.

But turning toward Ololon in terrible majesty, Milton
Replied: 'Obey thou the Words of the Inspired Man.
All that can be annihilated must be annihilated   30
That the Children of Jerusalem may be saved from slavery.
There is a Negation, & there is a Contrary;
The Negation must be destroy'd to redeem the Contraries.
The Negation is the Spectre, the Reasoning Power in Man.
This is a false Body, an Incrustation over my Immortal   35
Spirit, a Selfhood which must be put off & annihilated alway.

To cleanse the Face of my Spirit by Self-examination,
PLATE 41
To bathe in the Waters of Life, to wash off the Not Human,
I come in Self-annihilation & the grandeur of Inspiration;
To cast off Rational Demonstration by Faith in the Saviour,
To cast off the rotten rags of Memory by Inspiration,
To cast off Bacon, Locke & Newton from Albion's covering,   5
To take off his filthy garments, & clothe him with Imagination;
To cast aside from Poetry all that is not Inspiration,
That it no longer shall dare to mock with the aspersion of
      Madness
Cast on the Inspired by the tame high finisher of paltry Blots
Indefinite, or paltry Rhymes, or paltry Harmonies,   10
Who creeps into State Government like a caterpiller to destroy;
To cast off the idiot Questioner who is always questioning
But never capable of answering, who sits with a sly grin
Silent plotting when to question, like a thief in a cave,
Who publishes doubt & calls it knowledge, whose Science is
      Despair,   15
Whose pretence to knowledge is Envy, whose whole Science is
To destroy the wisdom of ages to gratify ravenous Envy,
That rages round him like a Wolf day & night without rest.
He smiles with condescension, he talks of Benevolence &
      Virtue,
And those who act with Benevolence & Virtue they murder
      time on time.   20
These are the destroyers of Jerusalem, these are the murderers
Of Jesus, who deny the Faith & mock at Eternal Life,
Who pretend to Poetry that they may destroy Imagination
By imitation of Nature's Images drawn from Remembrance.
These are the Sexual Garments, the Abomination of
      Desolation,   25
Hiding the Human Lineaments as with an Ark & Curtains,
Which Jesus rent & now shall wholly purge away with Fire
Till Generation is swallow'd up in Regeneration.'

Then trembled the Virgin Ololon & reply'd in clouds of
      despair:

'Is this our Feminine Portion, the Six-fold Miltonic Female? 30
Terribly this Portion trembles before thee, O awful Man!
Altho' our Human Power can sustain the severe contentions
Of Friendship, our Sexual cannot, but flies into the Ulro.
Hence arose all our terrors in Eternity; & now remembrance
Returns upon us. Are we Contraries, O Milton, Thou & I? 35
O Immortal! how were we led to War the Wars of Death?
Is this the Void Outside of Existence, which if enter'd into
PLATE 42
Becomes a Womb? & is this the Death Couch of Albion?
Thou goest to Eternal Death, & all must go with thee.'

So saying, the Virgin divided Six-fold, & with a shriek
Dolorous that ran thro' all Creation, a Double- Six-fold
    Wonder,
Away from Ololon she divided & fled into the depths 5
Of Milton's Shadow, as a Dove upon the stormy Sea.

Then as a Moony Ark Ololon descended to Felpham's Vale
In clouds of blood, in streams of gore, with dreadful
    thunderings
Into the Fires of Intellect that rejoic'd in Felpham's Vale
Around the Starry Eight. With one accord the Starry Eight
    became 10
One Man, Jesus the Saviour, wonderful! Round his limbs
The Clouds of Ololon folded as a Garment dipped in blood,
Written within & without in woven letters; & the Writing
Is the Divine Revelation in the Litteral expression,
A Garment of War. I heard it nam'd the Woof of Six Thousand
    Years. 15

And I beheld the Twenty-four Cities of Albion
Arise upon their Thrones to Judge the Nations of the Earth;
And the Immortal Four in whom the Twenty-four appear
    Four-fold
Arose around Albion's body. Jesus wept & walked forth
From Felpham's Vale clothed in Clouds of blood, to enter into
Albion's Bosom, the bosom of death, & the Four surrounded
    him

In the Column of Fire in Felpham's Vale. Then to their mouths
    the Four
Applied their Four Trumpets & them sounded to the Four
    winds.

Terror struck in the Vale. I stood at that immortal sound;
My bones trembled. I fell outstretch'd upon the path   25
A moment, & my Soul return'd into its mortal state,
To Resurrection & Judgment in the Vegetable Body;
And my sweet Shadow of Delight stood trembling by my side.

Immediately the Lark mounted with a loud trill from
    Felpham's Vale,
And the Wild Thyme from Wimbleton's green & impurpled
    Hills;   30
And Los & Enitharmon rose over the Hills of Surrey.
Their clouds roll over London with a south wind. Soft
    Oothoon
Pants in the Vales of Lambeth, weeping o'er her Human
    Harvest.
Los listens to the Cry of the Poor Man, his Cloud
Over London in volume terrific, low bended in anger.   35

Rintrah & Palamabron view the Human Harvest beneath.
Their Wine-presses & Barns stand open; the Ovens are
    prepar'd,
The Waggons ready; terrific Lions & Tygers sport & play.
All Animals upon the Earth are prepar'd in all their strength
PLATE 43
To go forth to the Great Harvest & Vintage of the Nations.

Finis

FROM JERUSALEM

PLATE 4
Of the Sleep of Ulro! and of the passage through
Eternal Death! and of the awaking to Eternal Life.

This theme calls me in sleep night after night, & ev'ry morn
Awakes me at sun-rise; then I see the Saviour over me
 Spreading his beams of love & dictating the words of this mild
      song.   5

'Awake! awake, O sleeper of the land of shadows, wake!
    expand!
I am in you and you in me, mutual in love divine:
Fibres of love from man to man thro' Albion's pleasant land.
In all the dark Atlantic vale down from the hills of Surrey
A black water accumulates. Return, Albion, return!   10
Thy brethren call thee; and thy fathers and thy sons,
Thy nurses and thy mothers, thy sisters and thy daughters
Weep at thy soul's disease, and the Divine Vision is darken'd.
Thy Emanation that was wont to play before thy face,
Beaming forth with her daughters into the Divine bosom—   15
Where hast thou hidden thy Emanation, lovely Jerusalem,
From the vision and fruition of the Holy-one?
I am not a God afar off, I am a brother and friend;
Within your bosoms I reside, and you reside in me.
Lo! we are One, forgiving all Evil, Not seeking recompense.   20
Ye are my members, O ye sleepers of Beulah, land of shades!'

But the perturbed Man away turns down the valleys dark:

'Phantom of the over heated brain! shadow of immortality!
Seeking to keep my soul a victim to thy Love! which binds
Man, the enemy of man, into deceitful friendships.   25
Jerusalem is not; her daughters are indefinite.
By demonstration man alone can live, and not by faith.
My mountains are my own, and I will keep them to myself:

The Malvern and the Cheviot, the Wolds, Plinlimmon &
    Snowdon   30
Are mine. Here will I build my Laws of Moral Virtue.
Humanity shall be no more, but war & princedom & victory!'

So spoke Albion in jealous fears, hiding his Emanation
Upon the Thames and Medway, rivers of Beulah, dissembling
His jealousy before the throne divine, darkening, cold!

. . .

PLATE 5
Trembling I sit day and night, my friends are astonish'd at me,
Yet they forgive my wanderings. I rest not from my great task!
To open the Eternal Worlds, to open the immortal Eyes
Of Man inwards into the Worlds of Thought, into Eternity
Ever expanding in the Bosom of God, the Human
    Imagination.   20
O Saviour pour upon me thy Spirit of meekness & love;
Annihilate the Selfhood in me, be thou all my life!
Guide thou my hand, which trembles exceedingly upon the
    rock of ages,
While I write of the building of Golgonooza, & of the terrors of
    Entuthon;
Of Hand & Hyle & Coban, of Kwantok, Peachey, Brereton,
    Slayd & Hutton;   25
Of the terrible sons & daughters of Albion and their
    Generations.

                *   *   *

PLATE 15
I see the Four-fold Man, The Humanity in deadly sleep
And its fallen Emanation, The Spectre & its cruel Shadow.
I see the Past, Present & Future existing all at once
Before me. O Divine Spirit, sustain me on thy wings,
That I may awake Albion from his long & cold repose!   10
For Bacon & Newton, sheath'd in dismal steel, their terrors
    hang

Like iron scourges over Albion. Reasonings like vast Serpents
Infold around my limbs, bruising my minute articulations.

I turn my eyes to the Schools & Universities of Europe
And there behold the Loom of Locke, whose Woof rages dire,   15
Wash'd by the Water-wheels of Newton. Black the cloth
In heavy wreathes folds over every Nation. Cruel Works
Of many Wheels I view, wheel without wheel, with cogs
    tyrannic
Moving by compulsion each other, not as those in Eden,
    which
Wheel within Wheel in freedom revolve in harmony & peace.   20

        *   *   *

PLATE 27
    The fields from Islington to Marybone,
To Primrose Hill and Saint John's Wood,
    Were builded over with pillars of gold,
And there Jerusalem's pillars stood.

    Her Little-ones ran on the fields,   5
The Lamb of God among them seen,
    And fair Jerusalem, his Bride,
Among the little meadows green.

    Pancrass & Kentish-town repose
Among her golden pillars high,   10
    Among her golden arches which
Shine upon the starry sky.

    The Jew's-harp-house & the Green Man,
The Ponds where Boys to bathe delight,
    The fields of Cows by Willan's farm,   15
Shine in Jerusalem's pleasant sight.

    She walks upon our meadows green,
The Lamb of God walks by her side,
    And every English Child is seen
Children of Jesus & his Bride,   20

Forgiving trespasses and sins
Lest Babylon with cruel Og
   With Moral & Self-righteous Law
Should crucify in Satan's Synagogue!

   What are those golden Builders doing   25
Near mournful ever-weeping Paddington,
   Standing above that mighty Ruin
Where Satan the first victory won,

   Where Albion slept beneath the Fatal Tree,
And the Druids' golden Knife   30
   Rioted in human gore,
In Offerings of Human Life?

   They groan'd aloud on London Stone,
They groan'd aloud on Tyburn's Brook;
   Albion gave his deadly groan,   35
And all the Atlantic Mountains shook.

   Albion's Spectre from his Loins
Tore forth in all the pomp of War,
   Satan his name; in flames of fire
He stretch'd his Druid Pillars far.   40

   Jerusalem fell from Lambeth's Vale
Down thro' Poplar & Old Bow,
   Thro' Malden & acros the Sea,
In War & howling, death & woe.

   The Rhine was red with human blood,   45
The Danube roll'd a purple tide,
   On the Euphrates Satan stood,
And over Asia stretch'd his pride.

   He wither'd up sweet Zion's Hill
From every Nation of the Earth;   50
   He wither'd up Jerusalem's Gates,
And in a dark Land gave her birth.

He wither'd up the Human Form
By laws of sacrifice for sin,
    Till it became a Mortal Worm,   55
But O! translucent all within.

The Divine Vision still was seen,
Still was the Human Form Divine
    Weeping in weak & mortal clay,
O Jesus, still the Form was thine.   60

And thine the Human Face, & thine
The Human Hands & Feet & Breath,
    Entering thro' the Gates of Birth
And passing thro' the Gates of Death.

And O thou Lamb of God, whom I   65
Slew in my dark self-righteous pride,
    Art thou return'd to Albion's Land,
And is Jerusalem thy Bride?

Come to my arms & never more
Depart, but dwell for ever here;   70
    Create my Spirit to thy Love;
Subdue my Spectre to thy Fear.

Spectre of Albion! warlike Fiend!
In clouds of blood & ruin roll'd,
    I here reclaim thee as my own,   75
My Selfhood! Satan! arm'd in gold.

Is this thy soft Family-Love,
Thy cruel Patriarchal pride,
    Planting thy Family alone,
Destroying all the World beside?   80

A man's worst enemies are those
Of his own house & family;
    And he who makes his law a curse,
By his own law shall surely die.

   In my Exchanges every Land   85
  Shall walk, & mine in every Land
   Mutual shall build Jerusalem,
  Both heart in heart & hand in hand.

    *   *   *

PLATE 31

Fearing that Albion should turn his back against the Divine
  Vision,
Los took his globe of fire to search the interiors of Albion's
Bosom, in all the terrors of friendship entering the caves
Of despair & death to search the tempters out, walking among 5
Albion's rocks & precipices, caves of solitude & dark despair;
And saw every Minute Particular of Albion degraded &
  murder'd,
But saw not by whom; they were hidden within in the minute
  particulars
Of which they had possess'd themselves; and there they take
  up
The articulations of a man's soul and laughing throw it down 10
Into the frame, then knock it out upon the plank, & souls are
  bak'd
In bricks to build the pyramids of Heber & Terah. But Los
Search'd in vain; clos'd from the minutia he walk'd difficult.
He came down from Highgate thro' Hackney & Holloway
  towards London
Till he came to old Stratford, & thence to Stepney & the Isle 15
Of Leutha's Dogs, thence thro' the narrows of the River's side,
And saw every minute particular, the jewels of Albion,
  running down
The kennels of the streets & lanes as if they were abhorr'd.
Every Universal Form was become barren mountains of
  Moral
Virtue, and every Minute Particular harden'd into grains of
  sand,   20
And all the tendernesses of the soul cast forth as filth & mire,
Among the winding places of deep contemplation intricate,

To where the Tower of London frown'd dreadful over
      Jerusalem,
A building of Luvah, builded in Jerusalem's eastern gate, to be
His secluded Court. Thence to Bethlehem, where was builded   25
Dens of despair in the house of bread; enquiring in vain
Of stones and rocks he took his way, for human form was
      none;
And thus he spoke, looking on Albion's City with many tears:

'What shall I do? what could I do, if I could find these
      Criminals?
I could not dare to take vengeance, for all things are so
      constructed   30
And built by the Divine hand that the sinner shall always
      escape,
And he who takes vengeance alone is the criminal of
      Providence.
If I should dare to lay my finger on a grain of sand
In way of vengeance, I punish the already punish'd. O whom
Should I pity if I pity not the sinner who is gone astray?   35
O Albion, if thou takest vengeance, if thou revengest thy
      wrongs,
Thou art for ever lost! What can I do to hinder the Sons
Of Albion from taking vengeance? or how shall I them
      perswade?'

So spoke Los, travelling thro' darkness & horrid solitude.
And he beheld Jerusalem in Westminster & Marybone   40
Among the ruins of the Temple, and Vala who is her Shadow,
Jerusalem's Shadow bent northward over the Island white.

*   *   *

PLATE 38
Turning from Universal Love, petrific as he went,
His cold against the warmth of Eden rag'd with loud
Thunders of deadly war (the fever of the human soul),
Fires and clouds of rolling smoke. But mild the Saviour
      follow'd him,   10

Displaying the Eternal Vision, the Divine Similitude,
In loves and tears of brothers, sisters, sons, fathers and friends,
Which if Man ceases to behold, he ceases to exist,

Saying, 'Albion! Our wars are wars of life, & wounds of love
With intellectual spears & long winged arrows of thought.   15
Mutual in one another's love and wrath all renewing
We live as One Man; for contracting our infinite senses
We behold multitude; or expanding, we behold as one,
As One Man all the Universal Family; and that One Man
We call Jesus the Christ; and he in us, and we in him   20
Live in perfect harmony in Eden, the land of life,
Giving, receiving, and forgiving each other's trespasses.
He is the Good shepherd, he is the Lord and master,
He is the Shepherd of Albion, he is all in all
In Eden, in the garden of God, and in heavenly Jerusalem.   25
If we have offended, forgive us; take not vengeance against us.'

*   *   *

PLATE 52
       I saw a Monk of Charlemaine
Arise before my sight;
       I talk'd with the Grey Monk as we stood
In beams of infernal light.

       Gibbon arose with a lash of steel   5
And Voltaire with a wracking wheel;
       The Schools, in clouds of learning roll'd,
Arose with War in iron & gold.

       'Thou lazy Monk,' they sound afar,
'In vain condemning glorious War!   10
       And in your Cell you shall ever dwell:
Rise, War, & bind him in his Cell!'

       The blood red ran from the Grey Monk's side;
His hands & feet were wounded wide,
       His body bent, his arms & knees   15
Like to the roots of ancient trees.

When Satan first the black bow bent
And the Moral Law from the Gospel rent,
    He forg'd the Law into a Sword
And spill'd the blood of mercy's Lord.   20

    Titus! Constantine! Charlemaine!
O Voltaire! Rousseau! Gibbon! Vain
    Your Grecian Mocks and Roman Sword
Against this image of his Lord!

    For a Tear is an Intellectual thing,   25
And a Sigh is the Sword of an Angel King,
    And the bitter groan of a Martyr's woe
Is an Arrow from the Almightie's Bow.

                *   *   *

PLATE 60
But the Divine Lamb stood beside Jerusalem; oft she saw   50
The lineaments Divine & oft the Voice heard, & oft she said:

'O Lord & Saviour, have the Gods of the Heathen pierced thee?
Or hast thou been pierced in the House of thy Friends?
Art thou alive, & livest thou for evermore? Or art thou
Not but a delusive shadow, a thought that liveth not?   55
Babel mocks, saying there is no God nor Son of God,
That thou, O Human Imagination, O Divine Body, art all
A delusion; but I know thee, O Lord, when thou arisest upon
My weary eyes, even in this dungeon & this iron mill.
The Stars of Albion cruel rise; thou bindest to sweet influences, 60
For thou also sufferest with me, altho' I behold thee not;
And altho' I sin & blaspheme thy holy name, thou pitiest me,
Because thou knowest I am deluded by the turning mills
And by these visions of pity & love because of Albion's death.'

Thus spake Jerusalem, & thus the Divine Voice replied: 65
'Mild Shade of Man, pitiest thou these Visions of terror & woe?
Give forth thy pity & love; fear not! lo, I am with thee always.
Only believe in me that I have power to raise from death

Thy Brother who Sleepeth in Albion; fear not, trembling
    Shade.

PLATE 61

Behold in the Visions of Elohim Jehovah, behold Joseph &
    Mary

And be comforted, O Jerusalem, in the Visions of Jehovah
    Elohim.'

She looked & saw Joseph the Carpenter in Nazareth, & Mary
His espoused Wife. And Mary said, 'If thou put me away from
    thee,
Dost thou not murder me?' Joseph spoke in anger & fury,
    'Should I   5
Marry a Harlot & an Adulteress?' Mary answer'd, 'Art thou
    more pure
Than thy Maker who forgiveth Sins & calls again Her that is
    Lost?
Tho' She hates, he calls her again in love. I love my dear
    Joseph,
But he driveth me away from his presence; yet I hear the voice
    of God
In the voice of my Husband; tho' he is angry for a moment, he
    will not   10
Utterly cast me away. If I were pure, never could I taste the
    sweets
Of the Forgiveness of Sins; if I were holy, I never could
    behold the tears
Of love of him who loves me in the midst of his anger in
    furnace of fire.'

'Ah my Mary!' said Joseph, weeping over & embracing her
    closely in
His arms, 'Doth he forgive Jerusalem, & not exact Purity from
    her who is   15
Polluted? I heard his voice in my sleep & his Angel in my
    dream,
Saying, "Doth Jehovah Forgive a Debt only on condition that
    it shall

Be Payed? Doth he Forgive Pollution only on conditions of
    Purity?
That Debt is not Forgiven! That Pollution is not Forgiven!
Such is the Forgiveness of the Gods, the Moral Virtues of the   20
Heathen, whose tender Mercies are Cruelty. But Jehovah's
    Salvation
Is without Money & without Price, in the Continual
    Forgiveness of Sins,
In the Perpetual Mutual Sacrifice in Great Eternity. For
    behold,
There is none that liveth & Sinneth not! And this is the
    Covenant
Of Jehovah: If you Forgive one-another, so shall Jehovah
    Forgive You,   25
That He Himself may Dwell among You. Fear not then to take
To thee Mary thy Wife, for she is with Child by the Holy
    Ghost." '

Then Mary burst forth into a Song; she flowed like a River of
Many Streams in the arms of Joseph & gave forth her tears of
    joy
Like many waters, and Emanating into gardens & palaces upon   30
Euphrates, & to forests & floods & animals wild & tame from
Gihon to Hiddekel, & to corn fields & villages & inhabitants
Upon Pison & Arnon & Jordan. And I heard the voice among
The Reapers, Saying, 'Am I Jerusalem the lost Adulteress? or
    am I
Babylon come up to Jerusalem?' And another voice answer'd
    Saying: 35

'Does the voice of my Lord call me again? Am I pure thro' his
    Mercy
And Pity? Am I become lovely as a Virgin in his sight, who am
Indeed a Harlot drunken with the Sacrifice of Idols? Does he
Call her pure as he did in the days of her Infancy when She
Was cast out to the loathing of her person? The Chaldean took   40
Me from my Cradle. The Amalekite stole me away upon his
    Camels

Before I had ever beheld with love the Face of Jehovah, or
    known
That there was a God of Mercy. O Mercy, O Divine
    Humanity!
O Forgiveness & Pity & Compassion! If I were Pure I should
    never
Have known Thee; If I were Unpolluted I should never have   45
Glorified thy Holiness, or rejoiced in thy great Salvation.'

Mary leaned her side against Jerusalem. Jerusalem received
The Infant into her hands in the Visions of Jehovah. Times
    passed on.
Jerusalem fainted over the Cross & Sepulcher. She heard the
    voice:
'Wilt thou make Rome thy Patriarch Druid, & the Kings of
    Europe his   50
Horsemen? Man in the Resurrection changes his Sexual
    Garments at Will.
Every Harlot was once a Virgin, every Criminal an Infant
    Love.

PLATE 62

Repose on me till the morning of the Grave. I am thy life.'

Jerusalem replied: 'I am an outcast; Albion is dead.
I am left to the trampling foot & the spurning heel;
A Harlot I am call'd; I am sold from street to street;
I am defaced with blows & with the dirt of the Prison.
And wilt thou become my Husband, O my Lord & Saviour?   5
Shall Vala bring thee forth? Shall the Chaste be ashamed also?
I see the Maternal Line, I behold the Seed of the Woman:
Cainah & Ada & Zillah, & Naamah, Wife of Noah,
Shuah's daughter & Tamar & Rahab the Canaanites,   10
Ruth the Moabite, & Bathsheba of the daughters of Heth,
Naamah the Ammonite, Zibeah the Philistine, & Mary.
These are the Daughters of Vala, Mother of the Body of death.
But I, thy Magdalen, behold thy Spiritual Risen Body.
Shall Albion arise? I know he shall arise at the Last Day.   15
I know that in my flesh I shall see God; but Emanations
Are weak, they know not whence they are, nor whither tend.'

Jesus replied, 'I am the Resurrection & the Life.
I Die & pass the limits of possibility, as it appears
To individual perception. Luvah must be Created   20
And Vala; for I cannot leave them in the gnawing Grave,
But will prepare a way for my banished-ones to return.
Come now with me into the villages, walk thro' all the cities.
Tho' thou art taken to prison & judgment, starved in the
    streets,
I will command the cloud to give thee food, & the hard rock   25
To flow with milk & wine; tho' thou seest me not a season,
Even a long season & a hard journey & a howling wilderness,
Tho' Vala's cloud hide thee & Luvah's fires follow thee,
Only believe & trust in me. Lo, I am always with thee.'

So spoke the Lamb of God while Luvah's Cloud reddening
    above   30
Burst forth in streams of blood upon the heavens, & dark night
Involv'd Jerusalem; & the Wheels of Albion's Sons turn'd
    hoarse
Over the Mountains, & the fires blaz'd on Druid Altars,
And the Sun set in Tyburn's Brook where Victims howl & cry.

But Los beheld the Divine Vision among the flames of the
    Furnaces.   35
Therefore he lived & breathed in hope; but his tears fell
    incessant
Because his Children were clos'd from him apart, &
    Enitharmon
Dividing in fierce pain. Also the Vision of God was clos'd in
    clouds
Of Albion's Spectres, that Los in despair oft sat & often
    ponder'd
On Death Eternal, in fierce shudders upon the mountains of
    Albion   40
Walking, & in the vales in howlings fierce. Then to his Anvils
Turning, anew began his labours, tho' in terrible pains.

*   *   *

PLATE 65

Then left the Sons of Urizen the plow & harrow, the loom,
The hammer & the chisel & the rule & compasses; from
     London fleeing,
They forg'd the sword on Cheviot, the chariot of war & the
     battle-ax,
The trumpet fitted to mortal battle, & the flute of summer in
     Annandale.   15
And all the Arts of Life they chang'd into the Arts of Death in
     Albion:
The hour-glass contemn'd because its simple workmanship
Was like the workmanship of the plowman, & the water wheel
That raises water into cisterns broken & burn'd with fire
Because its workmanship was like the workmanship of the
     shepherd.   20
And in their stead, intricate wheels invented, wheel without
     wheel,
To perplex youth in their outgoings & to bind to labours in
     Albion
Of day & night the myriads of eternity; that they may grind
And polish brass & iron hour after hour, laborious task,
Kept ignorant of its use; that they might spend the days of
     wisdom   25
In sorrowful drudgery to obtain a scanty pittance of bread;
In ignorance to view a small portion & think that All,
And call it Demonstration, blind to all the simple rules of life.

       *   *   *

PLATE 90

But still the thunder of Los peals loud, & thus the thunders cry:
'These beautiful Witchcrafts of Albion are gratifyd by Cruelty.
PLATE 91
It is easier to forgive an Enemy than to forgive a Friend.
The man who permits you to injure him deserves your
     vengeance;
He also will receive it. Go Spectre! obey my most secret desire,
Which thou knowest without my speaking. Go to these Fiends
     of Righteousness.

Tell them to obey their Humanities & not pretend Holiness   5
When they are murderers, as far as my Hammer & Anvil
   permit.
Go, tell them that the worship of God is honouring his gifts
In other men & loving the greatest men best, each according
To his Genius, which is the Holy Ghost in Man. There is no
   other
God than that God who is the intellectual fountain of
   Humanity.   10
He who envies or calumniates, which is murder & cruelty,
Murders the Holy-one. Go, tell them this, & overthrow their
   cup,
Their bread, their altar-table, their incense & their oath,
Their marriage & their baptism, their burial & consecration.
I have tried to make friends by corporeal gifts but have only   15
Made enemies. I never made friends but by spiritual gifts,
By severe contentions of friendship & the burning fire of
   thought.
He who would see the Divinity must see him in his Children,
One first, in friendship & love, then a Divine Family, & in the
   midst
Jesus will appear; so he who wishes to see a Vision, a perfect
   Whole,   20
Must see it in its Minute Particulars, Organized, & not as thou,
O Fiend of Righteousness, pretendest; thine is a Disorganized
And snowy cloud, brooder of tempests & destructive War.
You smile with pomp & rigor, you talk of benevolence &
   virtue;
I act with benevolence & Virtue & get murder'd time after
   time.   25
You accumulate Particulars & murder by analyzing, that you
May take the aggregate, & you call the aggregate Moral Law,
And you call that swell'd & bloated Form a Minute Particular.
But General Forms have their vitality in Particulars, & every
Particular is a Man, a Divine Member of the Divine Jesus.'   30

So Los cried at his Anvil, in the horrible darkness weeping.

The Spectre builded stupendous Works, taking the Starry
    Heavens
Like to a curtain & folding them according to his will,
Repeating the Smaragdine Table of Hermes to draw Los down
Into the Indefinite, refusing to believe without demonstration.   35
Los reads the Stars of Albion; the Spectre reads the Voids
Between the Stars, among the arches of Albion's Tomb
    sublime,
Rolling the Sea in rocky paths, forming Leviathan
And Behemoth, the War by Sea enormous & the War
By Land astounding, erecting pillars in the deepest Hell   40
To reach the heavenly arches. Los beheld undaunted; furious
His heav'd Hammer; he swung it round & at one blow
In unpitying ruin driving down the pyramids of pride,
Smiting the Spectre on his Anvil, & the integuments of his Eye
And Ear unbinding in dire pain, with many blows   45
Of strict severity self-subduing, & with many tears labouring.

Then he sent forth the Spectre; all his pyramids were grains
Of sand, & his pillars dust on the fly's wing, & his starry
Heavens a moth of gold & silver mocking his anxious grasp.
Thus Los alter'd his Spectre, & every Ratio of his Reason   50
He alter'd time after time, with dire pain & many tears,
Till he had completely divided him into a separate space.

Terrified Los sat to behold, trembling & weeping & howling:
'I care not whether a Man is Good or Evil; all that I care
Is whether he is a Wise Man or a Fool. Go, put off Holiness   55
And put on Intellect, or my thund'rous Hammer shall drive
    thee
To wrath which thou condemnest, till thou obey my voice.'

So Los terrified cries, trembling & weeping & howling:
    'Beholding,
PLATE 92
What do I see? The Briton, Saxon, Roman, Norman
    amalgamating
In my Furnaces into One Nation, the English, & taking refuge

In the Loins of Albion; the Canaanite united with the fugitive
Hebrew, whom she divided into Twelve & sold into Egypt,
Then scatter'd the Egyptian & Hebrew to the four Winds.   5
This sinful Nation Created in our Furnaces & Looms is
    Albion.'

So Los spoke. Enitharmon answer'd in great terror in
    Lambeth's Vale:

'The Poet's Song draws to its period, & Enitharmon is no
    more.
For if he be that Albion I can never weave him in my Looms;
But when he touches the first fibrous thread, like filmy dew   10
My Looms will be no more & I annihilate vanish for ever.
Then thou wilt Create another Female according to thy Will.'

Los answer'd swift as the shuttle of gold: 'Sexes must vanish &
    cease
To be when Albion arises from his dread repose, O lovely
    Enitharmon:
When all their Crimes, their Punishments, their Accusations of
    Sin,   15
All their Jealousies, Revenges, Murders, hidings of Cruelty in
    Deceit
Appear only in the Outward Spheres of Visionary Space and
    Time,
In the shadows of Possibility, by Mutual Forgiveness for
    evermore,
And in the Vision & in the Prophecy, that we may Foresee &
    Avoid
The terrors of Creation & Redemption & Judgment.   20

        *   *   *

PLATE 94
Albion cold lays on his Rock; storms & snows beat round him,
Beneath the Furnaces & the starry Wheels & the Immortal
    Tomb;

Howling winds cover him; roaring seas dash furious against
  him;
In the deep darkness broad lightnings glare, long thunders roll.

The weeds of Death inwrap his hands & feet, blown incessant   5
And wash'd incessant by the for-ever restless sea-waves
  foaming abroad
Upon the white Rock. England, a Female Shadow, as deadly
  damps
Of the Mines of Cornwall & Derbyshire, lays upon his bosom
  heavy,
Moved by the wind in volumes of thick cloud, returning,
  folding round
His loins & bosom, unremovable by swelling storms & loud
  rending   10
Of enraged thunders. Around them the Starry Wheels of their
  Giant Sons
Revolve, & over them the Furnaces of Los, & the Immortal
  Tomb around,
Erin sitting in the Tomb to watch them unceasing night and
  day.
And the Body of Albion was closed apart from all Nations.

Over them the famish'd Eagle screams on boney Wings, and
  around   15
Them howls the Wolf of famine; deep heaves the Ocean black,
  thundering
Around the wormy Garments of Albion, then pausing in
  deathlike silence.

Time was Finished! The Breath Divine Breathed over Albion
Beneath the Furnaces & starry Wheels and in the Immortal
  Tomb;
And England, who is Brittannia, awoke from Death on
  Albion's bosom.   20
She awoke pale & cold; she fainted seven times on the Body of
  Albion.

'O pitious Sleep, O pitious Dream! O God, O God, awake!
    I have slain
In Dreams of Chastity & Moral Law, I have Murdered Albion!
    Ah!
In Stone-henge & on London Stone & in the Oak Groves of
    Malden
I have Slain him in my Sleep with the Knife of the Druid.
    O England,   25
O all ye Nations of the Earth, behold ye the Jealous Wife!
The Eagle & the Wolf & Monkey & Owl & the King & Priest
    were there.'

PLATE 95

Her voice pierc'd Albion's clay cold ear; he moved upon the
    Rock.
The Breath Divine went forth upon the morning hills; Albion
    mov'd
Upon the Rock; he open'd his eyelids in pain, in pain he mov'd
His stony members; he saw England. Ah! shall the Dead live
    again?

The Breath Divine went forth over the morning hills. Albion
    rose   5
In anger, the wrath of God breaking bright flaming on all sides
    around
His awful limbs. Into the Heavens he walked, clothed in
    flames,
Loud thund'ring, with broad flashes of flaming lightning &
    pillars
Of fire, speaking the Words of Eternity in Human Forms, in
    direful
Revolutions of Action & Passion, thro' the Four Elements on
    all sides   10
Surrounding his awful Members. Thou seest the Sun in heavy
    clouds
Struggling to rise above the Mountains. In his burning hand
He takes his Bow, then chooses out his arrows of flaming gold.
Murmuring the Bowstring breathes with ardor! clouds roll
    round the

Horns of the wide Bow, loud sounding winds sport on the
    mountain brows, 15
Compelling Urizen to his Furrow & Tharmas to his Sheepfold
And Luvah to his Loom. Urthona he beheld, mighty labouring
    at
His Anvil, in the Great Spectre Los, unwearied labouring &
    weeping.
Therefore the Sons of Eden praise Urthona's Spectre in songs,
Because he kept the Divine Vision in time of trouble. 20

As the Sun & Moon lead forward the Visions of Heaven &
    Earth,
England, who is Brittannia, enter'd Albion's bosom rejoicing,
Rejoicing in his indignation, adoring his wrathful rebuke.
She who adores not your frowns will only loathe your smiles.

PLATE 96

As the Sun & Moon lead forward the Visions of Heaven &
    Earth,
England, who is Brittannia, entered Albion's bosom rejoicing.

Then Jesus appeared, standing by Albion as the Good
    Shepherd
By the lost Sheep that he hath found, & Albion knew that it
Was the Lord, the Universal Humanity; & Albion saw his Form 5
A Man, & they conversed as Man with Man in Ages of
    Eternity.
And the Divine Appearance was the likeness & similitude of
    Los.

Albion said: 'O Lord, what can I do? my Selfhood cruel
Marches against thee, deceitful, from Sinai & from Edom
Into the Wilderness of Judah, to meet thee in his pride. 10
I behold the Visions of my deadly Sleep of Six Thousand Years
Dazling around thy skirts like a Serpent of precious stones &
    gold.
I know it is my Self, O my Divine Creator & Redeemer.'

Jesus replied: 'Fear not Albion; unless I die thou canst not live,
But if I die I shall arise again & thou with me.   15
This is Friendship & Brotherhood; without it Man Is Not.'

So Jesus spoke. The Covering Cherub coming on in darkness
Overshadow'd them, & Jesus said: 'Thus do Men in Eternity
One for another, to put off, by forgiveness, every sin.'

Albion reply'd: 'Cannot Man exist without Mysterious   20
Offering of Self for Another? is this Friendship &
        Brotherhood?
I see thee in the likeness & similitude of Los my Friend.'

Jesus said: 'Wouldest thou love one who never died
For thee, or ever die for one who had not died for thee?
And if God dieth not for Man & giveth not himself   25
Eternally for Man, Man could not exist; for Man is Love,
As God is Love. Every kindness to another is a little Death
In the Divine Image, nor can Man exist but by Brotherhood.'

So saying, the Cloud overshadowing divided them asunder.
Albion stood in terror, not for himself but for his Friend   30
Divine, & Self was lost in the contemplation of faith
And wonder at the Divine Mercy & at Los's sublime honour.

'Do I sleep amidst danger to Friends? O my Cities & Counties,
Do you sleep? Rouze up, rouze up! Eternal Death is abroad!'

So Albion spoke, & threw himself into the Furnaces of
        affliction.   35
All was a Vision, all a Dream! The Furnaces became
Fountains of Living Waters flowing from the Humanity
        Divine.
And all the Cities of Albion rose from their Slumbers, and All
The Sons & Daughters of Albion on soft clouds, Waking from
        Sleep.
Soon all around remote the Heavens burnt with flaming fires,   40
And Urizen & Luvah & Tharmas & Urthona arose into
Albion's Bosom. Then Albion stood before Jesus in the Clouds
Of Heaven, Fourfold among the Visions of God in Eternity.

PLATE 97

'Awake, Awake, Jerusalem! O lovely Emanation of Albion,
Awake and overspread all Nations as in Ancient Time;
For lo! the Night of Death is past and the Eternal Day
Appears upon our Hills! Awake, Jerusalem, and come away!'

So spake the Vision of Albion, & in him so spake in my hearing   5
The Universal Father. Then Albion stretch'd his hand into
    Infinitude,
And took his Bow. Fourfold the Vision: for bright beaming
    Urizen
Lay'd his hand on the South & took a breathing Bow of carved
    Gold;
Luvah his hand stretch'd to the East & bore a Silver Bow,
    bright shining;
Tharmas Westward a Bow of Brass, pure flaming, richly
    wrought;   10
Urthona Northward in thick storms a Bow of Iron, terrible
    thundering.

And the Bow is a Male & Female, & the Quiver of the Arrows
    of Love
Are the Children of this Bow, a Bow of Mercy &
    Loving-kindness, laying
Open the hidden Heart in Wars of mutual Benevolence, Wars
    of Love.
And the Hand of Man grasps firm between the Male & Female
    Loves.   15
And he Clothed himself in Bow & Arrows, in awful state,
    Fourfold,
In the midst of his Twenty-eight Cities, each with his Bow
    breathing.

PLATE 98

Then each an Arrow flaming from his Quiver fitted carefully;
They drew fourfold the unreprovable String, bending thro' the
    wide Heavens
The horned Bow Fourfold; loud sounding flew the flaming
    Arrow fourfold.

Murmuring the Bowstring breathes with ardor. Clouds roll
    round the horns
Of the wide Bow; loud sounding Winds sport on the
    Mountains' brows.   5
The Druid Spectre was Annihilate, loud thund'ring, rejoicing,
    terrific, vanishing,
Fourfold Annihilation; & at the clangor of the Arrows of
    Intellect
The innumerable Chariots of the Almighty appear'd in
    Heaven,
And Bacon & Newton & Locke, & Milton & Shakespear &
    Chaucer,
A Sun of blood red wrath surrounding heaven on all sides
    around,   10
Glorious, incomprehensible by Mortal Man, & each Chariot
    was Sexual Threefold.

And every Man stood Fourfold. Each Four Faces had: One to
    the West,
One toward the East, One to the South, One to the North; the
    Horses Fourfold.
And the dim Chaos brighten'd beneath, above, around! Eyed
    as the Peacock,
According to the Human Nerves of Sensation, the Four
    Rivers of the Water of Life.   15

South stood the Nerves of the Eye; East, in Rivers of bliss, the
    Nerves of the
Expansive Nostrils; West flow'd the Parent Sense, the Tongue;
    North stood
The labyrinthine Ear. Circumscribing & Circumcising the
    excrementitious
Husk & Covering, into Vacuum evaporating, revealing the
    lineaments of Man,
Driving outward the Body of Death in an Eternal Death &
    Resurrection,   20
Awaking it to Life among the Flowers of Beulah, rejoicing in
    Unity

In the Four Senses, in the Outline, the Circumference & Form,
 for ever
In Forgiveness of Sins which is Self Annihilation; it is the
 Covenant of Jehovah.

The Four Living Creatures, Chariots of Humanity Divine
 Incomprehensible,
In beautiful Paradises expand. These are the Four Rivers of
 Paradise   25
And the Four Faces of Humanity, fronting the Four Cardinal
 Points
Of Heaven, going forward, forward irresistible from Eternity
 to Eternity.

And they conversed together in Visionary forms dramatic,
 which bright
Redounded from their Tongues in thunderous majesty, in
 Visions,
In new Expanses, creating exemplars of Memory and of
 Intellect,   30
Creating Space, Creating Time, according to the wonders
 Divine
Of Human Imagination, throughout all the Three Regions
 immense
Of Childhood, Manhood & Old Age; & the all tremendous
 unfathomable Non Ens
Of Death was seen in regenerations terrific or complacent,
 varying
According to the subject of discourse; & every Word & every
 Character   35
Was Human according to the Expansion or Contraction, the
 Translucence or
Opakeness of Nervous fibres. Such was the variation of Time
 & Space,
Which vary according as the Organs of Perception vary; &
 they walked
To & fro in Eternity as One Man, reflecting each in each &
 clearly seen

And seeing, according to fitness & order. And I heard Jehovah
    speak   40
Terrific from his Holy Place, & saw the Words of the Mutual
    Covenant Divine
On Chariots of gold & jewels, with Living Creatures starry &
    flaming
With every Colour. Lion, Tyger, Horse, Elephant, Eagle,
    Dove, Fly, Worm
And the all wondrous Serpent clothed in gems & rich array
    Humanize
In the Forgiveness of Sins according to thy Covenant, Jehovah.
    They Cry: 45

'Where is the Covenant of Priam, the Moral Virtues of the.
    Heathen?
Where is the Tree of Good & Evil that rooted beneath the cruel
    heel
Of Albion's Spectre, the Patriarch Druid? Where are all his
    Human Sacrifices
For Sin in War, & in the Druid Temples of the Accuser of Sin,
    beneath
The Oak Groves of Albion that cover'd the whole Earth
    beneath his Spectre?   50
Where are the Kingdoms of the World & all their glory that
    grew on Desolation,
The Fruit of Albion's Poverty Tree, when the Triple Headed
    Gog-Magog Giant
Of Albion Taxed the Nations into Desolation, & then gave the
    Spectrous Oath?'

Such is the Cry from all the Earth, from the Living Creatures
    of the Earth
And from the great City of Golgonooza in the Shadowy
    Generation,   55
And from the Thirty-two Nations of the Earth among the
    Living Creatures.

PLATE 99

All Human Forms identified, even Tree, Metal, Earth & Stone;
    all
Human Forms identified, living, going forth & returning
    wearied
Into the Planetary lives of Years, Months, Days & Hours;
    reposing,
And then Awaking into his Bosom in the Life of Immortality.

And I heard the Name of their Emanations: they are named
    Jerusalem.   5

The End of the Song
of Jerusalem

FROM *FOR THE SEXES*
THE GATES OF PARADISE

The Gates of Paradise

Mutual Forgiveness of each Vice,
Such are the Gates of Paradise.
Against the Accuser's chief desire
Who walkd among the Stones of Fire
Jehovah's Finger Wrote the Law,   5
Then Wept, then rose in Zeal & Awe
And the Dead Corpse from Sinai's heat
Buried beneath his Mercy Seat.
O Christians, Christians, tell me Why
You rear it on your Altars high.   10

*   *   *

To the Accuser Who Is the God of This World

Truly, My Satan, thou art but a Dunce,
And dost not know the Garment from the Man.
Every Harlot was a Virgin once,
Nor canst thou ever change Kate into Nan.

Tho' thou art Worship'd by the Names Divine   5
Of Jesus & Jehovah, thou art still
The Son of Morn in weary Night's decline,
The lost Traveller's Dream under the Hill.

FROM *THE EVERLASTING GOSPEL*

(j)

There is not one Moral Virtue that Jesus Inculcated but Plato & Cicero did Inculcate before him. What then did Christ Inculcate? Forgiveness of Sins. This alone is the Gospel, & this is the Life & Immortality brought to light by Jesus, Even the Covenant of Jehovah, which is This: If you forgive one another your Trespasses so shall Jehovah forgive you, That he himself may dwell among you; but if you Avenge, you Murder the Divine Image & he cannot dwell among you because you Murder him; he arises Again & you deny that he is Arisen & are blind to Spirit.

(d)

Was Jesus Humble? or did he
Give any Proofs of Humility?
Boast of high Things with Humble tone,
And give with Charity a Stone?

When but a Child he ran away, 5
And left his Parents in dismay.
When they had wander'd three days long
These were the words upon his tongue:
'No Earthly Parents I confess;
I am doing my Father's business.' 10
When the rich learned Pharisee
Came to consult him secretly,
Upon his heart with Iron pen
He wrote, 'Ye must be born again.'
He was too proud to take a bribe; 15
He spoke with authority, not like a Scribe.
He says, with most consummate Art,
'Follow me, I am meek & lowly of heart,'
As that is the only way to escape
The Miser's net & the Glutton's trap. 20
What can be done with such desperate Fools
Who follow after the Heathen Schools?
I was standing by when Jesus died;
What I call'd Humility they call'd Pride.
He who loves his Enemies betrays his Friends; 25
This surely is not what Jesus intends,
But the sneaking Pride of Heroic Schools,
And the Scribes' & Pharisees' Virtuous Rules.
For he acts with honest, triumphant Pride;
And this is the cause that Jesus died. 30
He did not die with Christian Ease,
Asking pardon of his Enemies.
If he had, Caiaphas would forgive;
Sneaking submission can always live.
He had only to say that God was the devil, 35
And the devil was God, like a Christian Civil,
Mild Christian regrets to the devil confess
For affronting him thrice in the Wilderness;
He had soon been bloody Caesar's Elf,
And at last he would have been Caesar himself, 40
Like Dr. Priestly & Bacon & Newton.
Poor Spiritual Knowledge is not worth a button,
For thus the Gospel Sir Isaac confutes:

'God can only be known by his Attributes,
And as to the Indwelling of the Holy Ghost   45
Or of Christ & his Father, it's all a boast
And Pride & Vanity of the imagination,
That disdains to follow this World's Fashion.'
To teach Doubt & Experiment
Certainly was not what Christ meant.   50
What was he doing all that time,
From twelve years old to manly prime?
Was he then Idle, or the Less
About his Father's business?
Or was his wisdom held in scorn   55
Before his wrath began to burn
In Miracles throughout the Land,
That quite unnerv'd Caiaphas' hand?
If he had been Antichrist, Creeping Jesus,
He'd have done any thing to please us;   60
Gone sneaking into Synagogues,
And not us'd the Elders & Priests like dogs,
But Humble as a Lamb or Ass
Obey'd himself to Caiaphas.
God wants not Man to Humble himself: 65
This is the trick of the ancient Elf.
This is the Race that Jesus ran:
Humble to God, Haughty to Man,
Cursing the Rulers before the People
Even to the temple's highest Steeple;   70
And when he Humbled himself to God
Then descended the Cruel Rod:
'If thou humblest thyself, thou humblest me;
Thou also dwell'st in Eternity.
Thou art a Man, God is no more;   75
Thy own humanity learn to adore,
For that is my Spirit of Life.
Awake! arise to Spiritual Strife,
And thy Revenge abroad display
In terrors at the Last Judgment day.   80
God's Mercy & Long Suffering
Is but the Sinner to Judgment to bring.

Thou on the Cross for them shalt pray,
And take Revenge at the Last Day.'
Jesus replied, & thunders hurl'd: 85
'I never will Pray for the World.
Once I did so when I pray'd in the Garden;
I wish'd to take with me a Bodily Pardon.'
Can that which was of woman born,
In the absence of the Morn,   90
When the Soul fell into Sleep,
And Archangels round it weep,
Shooting out against the Light
Fibres of a deadly night,
Reasoning upon its own dark Fiction,   95
In Doubt which is Self Contradiction?
Humility is only doubt,
And does the Sun & Moon blot out,
Rooting over with thorns & stems
The buried Soul & all its gems.   100
This Life's dim Windows of the Soul
Distorts the Heavens from Pole to Pole,
And leads you to Believe a Lie
When you see with, not thro', the Eye,
That was born in a night to perish in a night,   105
When the Soul slept in the beams of Light.

Notes

Abbreviations

A. = America;   Ahania = Book of Ahania;   B. = Blake;
E. = Europe;   F.Z. = The Four Zoas;   J. = Jerusalem;
M. = Milton;   M.H.H. = Marriage of Heaven and Hell;
P.S. = Poetical Sketches;   S.E. = Songs of Experience;
S.I. = Songs of Innocence; S.I.E. = Songs of Innocence and of Experience;
Thel = Book of Thel;   U. = Book of Urizen;
V.D.A. = Visions of the Daughters of Albion.

The editions of Blake listed in the bibliography are referred to by the names of the editors. Quotations from the editions of Erdman and Keynes are labelled E. and K.

Poetical Sketches (p. 1). Printed for B. by friends in 1783 for private distribution. B. wrote MS emendations in a few copies and gave them to friends and patrons, but does not seem to have taken much interest in the volume. The Advertisement states, how reliably one cannot be sure, that the poems were written between B.'s twelfth and his twentieth year.

To Spring (p. 1). The first of four unrhymed poems on the seasons; 'To Winter' is the fourth. B. combines traditional personifications of the dawn and of spring into a fresh picture of a godlike figure coming, it is hoped, to bring love and fertility to the land. Compare and contrast Orc in *A.* Preludium.
     12 *mourns*: primarily, longs for; but perhaps recalls also the mourning for Adonis and other fertility gods, who die in winter and return in spring.

To Winter (p. 1).
     7–12. This more than usually vigorous personification proceeds from the same imagination as will create Urizen, also associated with the north, rocks, the freezing up of life (mental as well as physical), opposed to the animating Orc. B. is already concerned with psychological states, not just describing scenery.

16 *Hecla*: probably the mountain in Iceland rather than that in the Hebrides.

Song: 'How sweet I roam'd' (p. 2). Stated by an acquaintance of B., B.H. Malkin in his *A Father's Memories of His Child* (1806), to have been written 'before the age of fourteen'.

10. *Phoebus*: or Apollo, god of the sun and of poetry. There is a transition from the prince of love (Eros or Cupid) to the god of poetry, but presumably the two are associated, not contrasted—the experience of the 'golden pleasures' of love and of being inspired to write poetry may both paradoxically lead to confinement. The speaker roam'd freely (1–2) till he saw the prince—there is already a hint of danger. The speaker is lured from the open fields into the enclosed garden, and then into the golden cage.

Song: 'My silks and fine array' (p. 3). Reminiscent of some Elizabethan songs (e.g. Shakespeare's 'Come away, come away, death' in *Twelfth Night*, dirge in *Cymbeline*), but a fresh creation rather than a mere imitation. This kind of poem is usually by a male lover to a cruel mistress.

Song: 'I love the jocund dance' (p. 4). An early song of innocence (cf. 'The Ecchoing Green'), but containing more poetic diction than the poems in *S.I.* In spite of the elements of conventional pastoralism it seems, though it may not be, an expression of personal experience; so one wonders whether 'Kitty' (18) is Catherine Boucher, whom Blake married in 1782. If so the Advertisement's dating of *P.S.* must be extended.

Mad Song (p. 6). Mad songs, characterized by lack of logical sequence and frantic emotion, were a poetic fashion; six appeared in Percy's *Reliques of Ancient Poetry* (1765). But, especially in the last stanza, this is more than an exercise in a fashionable mode.

13–16. The feeling is mirrored in the disorder of rhyme and rhythm.

17–24. The speaker recognizes the 'comforts' that come with the light, but experiences the light as 'frantic pain' and turns away from it to a cloud, darkness, night. He is 'like a fiend' (he condemns himself, though he acts with eagerness), and moves 'with howling woe' (woe because of the light? or because of turning away? or both?). The combination of contrary feelings is more extreme and more dramatically expressed than in 'How sweet I roam'd', but both poems show the young poet's awareness of strange contradictions in experience. The poem suggests not just the experience of a madman, but that of the artist fearing his own inspiration, of anyone fearing the light and its claims. Cf. Earth's turning away from the Bard's call in 'Earth's Answer' in *S.E.*

To the Muses (p. 6). Directed against the conventionality and lack of inspiration of much contemporary verse, this poem is itself fairly conventional in diction and imagery—deliberately exemplifying the languid movement it deplores?

1–4. There is a Mount Ida in Crete, associated with Zeus, and one near Troy, where the judgment of Paris took place, leading to the Trojan war, celebrated by Homer. The Muses were daughters of Zeus, and associated with Apollo. Poetry, of old divinely inspired and dealing with great subjects, has become tame.

All Religions Are One and **There Is No Natural Religion** (pp. 7–8). Because of the simple and hesitant technique these are assumed to be B.'s earliest works in relief etching, and are conjecturally dated 1788. Each proposition was engraved on a separate, small plate, from which impressions were taken on separate sheets of paper. Probably B. never arranged a complete copy and left only a stack of loose sheets at his death, which were later arranged into various incomplete sets. The correct arrangement of most of the plates is self-evident, but not of the Conclusion, Application and 'Therefore' plates in *There Is No Natural Religion*. In editions until recently the Conclusion was placed at the end of (a), but a copy of (b) found in 1953 suggests that it belongs in (b). See Keynes's note in his Trianon Press edition (1971). Keynes arranges: Application, Conclusion, 'Therefore'. I follow Grant and Johnson in their Norton edition (1979) in putting the Application after the Conclusion.

In *All Religions Are One* B. challenges contemporary assumptions. Most thinkers then (and now?) said that our knowledge is derived from sensations arranged into categories and reasoned upon; and that, if anything beyond what can be deduced in this way is known, it must come by revelation from God. B. challenges both empirical philosophy and orthodox religion. The 'true faculty of knowing' is the poetic genius or imagination, which is present in all of us and is the indwelling divinity and the source of all religions and philosophies.

In *There Is No Natural Religion* (a) B. states what the consequences of believing that man's perceptions are bounded by his bodily sensations would be. It would not be possible to erect any religion on such a foundation. He is here refuting eighteenth-century deism. In (b) he states his own view, developing the line of argument in *All Religions Are One*. In the Application he reverses what many would regard as common sense—that reason is the faculty that enables us to see objectively, to see things as they are, whereas imagination is subjective and fanciful. On the contrary, he says, the 'Ratio', a system organized by the reason on the basis of the known facts discovered by the senses, is man-made; seeing it we see only ourselves. Seeing imaginatively we see the infinite in all things, we see God.

Therefore: Cf. St Athanasius, *De Incarnatione*, ch.54: 'For He became a man that we might become divine.'

Songs of Innocence (p. 10). An early version of 'Laughing Song' was written into a copy of *P.S.*, and early versions of 'Holy Thursday', 'Nurse's Song' and 'The Little Boy Lost' are included in *An Island in the Moon*, written *c.* 1784–5. In the latter B. humorously satirizes some of his acquaintances and London personalities of the day, including himself (he appears as Mr Quid the Cynic). The surrounding satire provides a strong contrast and an ironic undertone to the songs. The young B. was Mr Quid and the writer of the pessimistic *Tiriel* (1788) as well as the visionary of innocence; but that does not mean that the vision is, or that he came to think it, an illusion. He continued to issue copies of *S.I.* after *S.E.* was added to form a joint volume in 1794. The vision of innocence is complemented, not cancelled, by the 'experienced' vision of the later poems.

S.I. may be compared and contrasted with other volumes of hymns and songs for children, sometimes with designs, popular at that time, e.g. Isaac Watts's *Divine and Moral Songs for the Use of Children* (1715), Charles Wesley's *Hymns for Children* (1763), Mrs Barbauld's *Hymns in Prose for Children* (1787). B. uses, transforms, undermines these. His songs are more radiant, more visionary, less moralistic. See J. Holloway's *Blake: The Lyric Poetry* (1968).

The order of the poems in *S.I.* varies from copy to copy, and 'The Little Girl Lost', 'The Little Girl Found', 'The Schoolboy' and 'The Voice of the Ancient Bard', originally in *S.I.*, were in late copies transferred to *S.E.* The order used here is that of copy Z and of some other late copies of *S.I.E.* Copy Z was reproduced in facsimile by the Trianon Press (1955) and less expensively by O.U.P. (1967).

Introduction (p. 10).

5. *pipe*: The piper accepts the command of the child. He, and we in reading *S.I.*, are led into acceptance of childlike vision. The child is a laughing, happy child, yet has strange power (he rides on a cloud). The familiar and the divine are combined, as in the lamb.

8. *he wept*: 'He wept with joy' (12). 'Excess of sorrow laughs. Excess of joy weeps' (*M.H.H.* 8). This is the primary meaning, but underneath is awareness of the lamb (both animal and Jesus) as victim as well as embodiment of innocence.

The Shepherd (p. 11). Like 'Introduction' combines simple, pastoral imagery with suggestions of an underlying Christian meaning, of the shepherd as the Good Shepherd (John 10:1–16). But whereas in John the shepherd leads the sheep, here he follows them.

The Little Black Boy (p. 13). Subverts the pious missionary hymn by showing that it is the black boy, because of his ability to love, who will bring the white boy to God, not the other way round.

9–20. The mother innocently comforts her son for the rejection he will suffer in this life by pointing to another one. That she thus postpones hope to another world is an implied criticism of the situation in which she is placed, but not of her.

23. Both black and white bodies are 'clouds', which we have to wear for a time until we can bear the beams of God's love. Some stress that this is the boy's view, not necessarily B.'s—which is true; but to say that there is an implied criticism of the boy's dualistic notion of soul and body is to bring in knowledge of later poems, not to read this one.

The Blossom (p. 14). It is possible to impose symbolic, especially sexual, interpretations, but better to read as a beautiful evocation of a state of innocence which includes the speaker (a young girl?), blossom (also alive, is happy, sees) and birds. Birth, burgeoning—in leaves, blossom and the girl's bosom—merriment, appetite ('swift as arrow') and sorrow ('sobbing' brings in the thought of sorrow, even if it does not always imply sadness in *S.I.*) exist together as parts of an accepted natural order.

The Chimney Sweeper (p. 14). Boys, sometimes as young as four, were sold to sweeps for about £5 (the younger the more valuable), and made to go up often very narrow, sometimes lighted, chimneys; constantly grimy they were treated as outcasts; they usually died young. Agitation in the 1780s led to a law being passed that boys should not be used as sweeps under the age of eight, should be thoroughly washed once a week and should not be made to go up lighted chimneys, but this law was not enforced. The poem makes a similar, more extreme, effect to that of 'The Little Black Boy'. In both an elder (the speaker here is presumably a more experienced sweep than Tom Dacre) comforts a boy, leading to the boy having a vision of a state of being opposite to that in which he exists. Both elders and both boys are innocent, are not blamed for not being able to envisage any escape from the 'Coffin' of their actual lives except in a future life or in dreams. But the effect is not at all to suggest that slavery, racialism or the exploitation of children is to be condoned because innocence can survive in the most appalling conditions; quite the reverse.

    24. The conventional moral is the boy's, not the poet's. What the poem has shown is that Tom can be happy because he still has the capacity for vision, not because he does his duty in the sense the elder boy may intend.

The Little Boy Lost (p. 15). A slightly amended version of a poem in *An Island in the Moon*, where it is sung by Quid the Cynic—a satirical self-portrait of B. By itself a poem of experience, a so far unanswered cry for love.

    8. *the vapour*: the will-o'-the-wisp, marsh lights.

Laughing Song (p. 16).

    7. The early version, written into a copy of *P.S.*, had 'Edessa, and Lyca, and Emilie', more 'poetical' names.

A Cradle Song (p. 16). Cf. 'A Cradle Hymn' by Isaac Watts, and see 'Blake, Watts, and Mrs Barbauld' by V. de S. Pinto in *The Divine Vision*. The main difference, apart from B's much subtler rhythm, is that Watts's mother contrasts her child with Jesus rather than seeing the 'holy image' in him.

    12. The repeated word 'beguiles' (12, 16, 32) has a slightly ambivalent effect. Here the meaning is 'charms away'; the terrors of the night are charmed away, heaven and earth are charmed into peace. But one is aware of the other possible meaning—'tricks,

deceives'—which will be the meaning in the Notebook 'A Cradle Song'. For the time being the sleep of the child is successfully protected, but one is conscious of the surrounding dangers.

20. The weeping of the mother and of the child Jesus (24–5) cannot this time be explained away as a weeping for joy. Cf. 'Introduction' and note. The child will have to suffer; the mother suffers for him, and Jesus for both.

The Divine Image (p. 17). Asserts in abstract language what is more concretely and movingly suggested in the preceding poem.

Holy Thursday (p. 18). A slightly amended version of a draft in *An Island in the Moon*, where it was sung by the complacent Obtuse Angle. It was well known in the 1780s, when the annual services of thanksgiving began to be held in St Paul's in order to accommodate the increased number of children in the Charity Schools, that the children were not always treated kindly by their guardians. There were complaints of constant flogging and of semi-starvation, the masters and mistresses making money by stinting the rations. Nevertheless this is a song of innocence, even though knowledge of the actual conditions and of the original context underlines the questions that the poem itself suggests. Why are the children walking in regimented ranks to give thanks for charity? The speaker rightly sees the 'radiance' of the children, but we question his acceptance of the conditions in which they are shown.

Night (p. 18). The first three stanzas beautifully evoke a sense of unity between different forms of life, and of protection, as in 'Cradle Song' in *S.I.* Then, realistically, it is acknowledged that, in this life, the protective powers cannot prevent the wolves and tigers from rushing dreadful. They remove the 'mild spirits' to new worlds, where the lion is so transformed as to eat grass (44). Cf. Isaiah 11:6: 'The wolf also shall dwell with the lamb, and the leopard shall lie down with the kid; and the calf and the young lion and the fatling together; and a little child shall lead them.'

37. *his*: Jesus's.

Nurse's Song (p. 21). Little altered from the draft in *An Island in the Moon*, sung by Mrs Nannicantipot, a slightly mocking portrait of Mrs Barbauld, writer of pious hymns for children; but removed from the ironic context. The elder, her own heart 'at rest', allows the children's play to continue. Adult anxiety is brought in by her fear of the dews of night, but is soon dismissed. Cf. 'The Ecchoing Green' and 'Nurse's Song' in *S.E.*

Infant Joy (p. 22). An imaginary dialogue between a mother and her two-day-old baby. Cf. 'Cradle Song' in *S.I.* and 'Infant Sorrow' in *S.E.*

A Dream (p. 22). Spoken presumably by a child, whose bed is guarded by an angel, as the mother ant in his dream is protected by glow-worm and beetle. Cf. 'The Little Boy Lost' and 'Found', and 'Night'.

On Another's Sorrow (p. 23).
   9–12. Cf. Cowper in 'Hark my soul! It is the Lord':

> Can a woman's tender care
> Cease towards the child she bare?
> Yes, she may forgetful be,
> Yet will I remember thee.

Cowper uses the uncertainty of human compassion to show by contrast the certainty of the divine; B. makes the fact of human compassion point to the divine.

26–7. Notice the present tenses.

Songs of Experience (p. 24). 'Songs of Experience, in Illuminated Printing . . . price 5s' was advertised for sale by B. in October 1793. Most of the poems had been drafted in his brother Robert's sketchbook since the latter's death in 1787, probably in 1791–3. See *The Notebook of William Blake*, ed. Erdman and Moore (1973). In 1794 B. brought the two sets of songs together, and added a new title page for the joint volume. 'To Tirzah' was added later, and B. continued until late in life to reorder the plates. The poems are given slightly different nuances of meaning by being placed in different contexts and by variations in colouring. Each copy is unique.

Introduction (p. 24). Not in the Notebook. This does not provide evidence for the suggestion that it was written later than 'Earth's Answer', which in that case was not originally an answer to it. On the contrary it may well have been written early, not long after the in some ways similar 'Voice of the Ancient Bard', originally in *S.I.* It has been understood in two (at least) opposed ways. (1) The Bard is an inspired prophet, who speaks for the Holy Word, which, weeping compassionately over the fallen soul, unlike the God of Genesis 3 who rebukes and punishes, could restore the soul if it would listen. The coming dawn could be the occasion and emblem of a return to the light; but Earth perversely turns away. (2) The Bard, an authoritarian figure contrasted to the Piper in 'Introduction' to *S.I.*, has listened too much to the supposedly 'Holy' Word, which is a tyrannous father-figure. This Holy Word weeps over sin (rather than forgiving and restoring), and calls upon the fallen soul to obey and to accept the restrictions of the present, while hoping for some hypothetical heaven in the future. Perhaps the poem is a deliberately enigmatic entry into the state of experience. See 'Voice of the Ancient Bard', which suggests that (1) is nearer the truth than (2).

4–7. Cf. Genesis 3:8–24.

8. *that*: The antecedent could be either the 'Word' or 'the voice of the Bard'; or both, in that the voice speaks for the Word.

9–10. Some understand the 'starry pole' as the whole starry sky, which as a result of the fall has become a restrictive circumference or 'floor', within which man is imprisoned. Stars usually have negative associations in B., especially with the restrictive father-god Urizen. Possibly there is a reference to Milton's supposition that God commanded His angels after the Fall to 'turn askance/The poles of earth twice ten degrees and more/From the sun's axle' (*Paradise Lost* X.668–70), so putting an end to the perpetual spring in which Eden had basked.

20. *giv'n*: may suggest that the mortal condition is not only a restriction, but also a grace, limiting man's fall.

Earth's Answer (p. 25). There is a discontinuity between the call of the Bard/Holy Word and Earth's answer to the 'Selfish father'. If (2) above is right, this is not surprising; Earth sees through the façade of good intentions of the Holy Word to the reality. If (1) is more nearly right, then Earth misunderstands. Though she is right to reject the jealous, Urizenic figure that she sees, it is her own fear and lack of vision that make her see God in this way.

6–10. Is B.'s syntax incorrect or subtly ambiguous? 'Prison'd' should strictly go with 'Jealousy', but one supposes that it is the 'I' who is imprisoned. Or is it both, both the jealous captor and the victim being confined, like Theotormon and Oothoon in a similar scene in *V.D.A.* 2:3–10? Cave and waves in *V.D.A.*, den, wat'ry shore and starry floor here are all symbols of the restrictions of the mortal condition. I have left these lines unpunctuated as in the original, so as to leave readers to decide how to construe 'cold and hoar'. (1) Jealousy keeps my den cold and hoar? (2) Jealousy keeps (guards) my den. Cold and hoar, I . . . ?

11–20. The rhyme scheme established in the first two stanzas breaks down.

The Clod and the Pebble (p. 26). Dramatizes two attitudes, and leaves us to evaluate them. Innocent, unselfish love and the cynical possessiveness of experience? Or are both attitudes imperfect, both products of the state of experience?

Holy Thursday (p. 26). Cf. 'Holy Thursday' in *S.I.*, and note. 'This' (1) is the same scene described so differently by the speaker of the earlier poem.

4. *usurous*: calculated to produce a profitable return, the children in the Charity Schools being conditioned to be submissive soldiers, industrial workers, servants. This speaker correctly sees through the façade of charity, but his vision is as limited as, or more limited than that of the earlier speaker. He does not really look at the children; his description is less concrete, his language more abstract and generalized.

The Little Girl Lost (p. 27). This and the following poem were originally in *S.I.* Most take the two poems to be concerned with growing up—the girl's need to become independent of the parents, her sense of guilt because of their fears (19–28), her and then the parents' acceptance of the feelings and experiences symbolized by the animals. Kathleen Raine (in *The Divine Vision*, ed. Pinto, pp. 19–49) interprets them as depicting the descent of the soul into the world of generation, using the myth of Persephone's abduction into the underworld, a story understood by neo-Platonists as symbolic of the descent into the underworld of this earthly life.

9–12. Compatible with Miss Raine's reading. Lyca's name, derived from the Greek word for light, fits with the idea that she is the soul. The 'southern clime' could be Sicily, where Persephone's abduction took place; it is a land of perpetual summer, suggestive of the light of eternity.

13. *seven*: traditionally the age when a child becomes capable of independent choice and therefore of conscious sin. In B.'s illustrations she seems older, an adolescent.

The Little Girl Found (p. 28).

30–40. The parents' discovery that the feared lion is not harmful, but 'a Spirit arm'd in gold' is difficult to reconcile with Miss Raine's idea that the mother represents Demeter, the higher consciousness which rightly resists the lapse of the daughter Persephone into a lower state. On the other hand, if the point of the poems is to show the need to accept aspects of experience that have been feared, it is odd that Lyca should remain asleep. The narrator in 'The Little Girl Lost' 2–5 foresees that the earth will arise from sleep, which at that point is clearly not thought of as a good state. Furthermore, if the ending is a happy one, why were the poems moved into *S.E.*? No single interpretation satisfies. Counter-suggestions point to counter-truths. The lapse of the soul from eternity *is* a fall; innocence can pass through dangers without harm; the feared may turn out to be beautiful.

The Chimney Sweeper (p. 30). The boy speaker exemplifies in his attitudes as well as correctly describes a state opposed to innocence. He is an embittered reasoner (understandably, we don't blame him), and has lost the compassion and power of vision of the boys in 'The Chimney Sweeper' in *S.I.*

7. *clothes of death*: the sweeps' black clothes; clothes suitable to going to a funeral—in this case their own, since their lives are living deaths.

12. *who*: Is the antecedent the Priest and King? or God also? or the parents also? One can understand (1) Priest and King (and perhaps the parents, who have sold the boy for money) live comfortably, supported by the labour of the sweeps and others like them. (2) They enjoy (a discarded version of this line was 'Who wrap themselves up in our misery') the misery of the boys, which makes them the more conscious of their comfort. (3) They (including God, as understood by these people) invent a 'heaven' afar off, in the future, and use it to excuse and so perpetuate the misery.

Nurse's Song (p. 31).

3. *days*: earlier, in the MS, 'desires'—desires which, presumably, have not been fulfilled. The lack of fulfilment in her own life has led to envy and to her repressive attitude towards the children.

The Sick Rose (p. 31). A rose is traditionally a symbol of love, and of a young girl. The rose is destroyed from within by the canker-worm, the girl's love-life by forces which enter secretly into her mind.

The Fly (p. 31). What this speaker says is similar in some ways to what innocent speakers and Blake himself say in other poems. He recognizes that he shares a common life with the fly, and that, if reality is mental, material life and death are not important; but his attitude is too abstract, rational, complacent. Like other speakers in *S.E.* he has some understanding, but lacks vision and compassion. There is a deleted second stanza in the Notebook:

> The cut worm
> Forgives the plough
> And dies in peace,
> And so do thou.

Cf. *M.H.H.* 7:6.
Stanza 4 (two shots at it) appears after stanza 5 in the Notebook, but I do not agree with Stevenson (p. 221) that this means that the 'appearance of a logical conclusion to the poem . . . is misleading'. Stanza 4 is needed to clarify the argument; but even if we read straight on from 3 to 5 the essential meaning is the same.

The Angel (p. 32). Cf. 'A Dream' in *S.I.* The dream is warning the dreamer of what her fearful, self-protective attitude may lead to.

2. *maiden Queen*: Cf. Thel.

3. *Angel*: love? a young man? Not the self-righteous 'Angel' of *M.H.H.*

4. *beguil'd*: deceived. The dreamer believes that by using her sorrow as means of dominance (5–8) she will prevent herself from being deceived into self-surrender.

The Tyger (p. 33). Consists entirely of questions; confronts us with a mystery without claiming to solve it.

7. *dare*: The creator, envisaged as a smith, creates out of existing fire which he dares to seize. Not the effortless creator of Genesis 1, he is reminiscent of Prometheus, who stole fire from heaven for men and was punished for this by Zeus. In various mythologies and philosophies (e.g. Gnosticism) the creator of the material universe is not the supreme God, but a lesser power, a demiurge, not necessarily benevolent.

12. In the draft the sentence continued 'Could fetch it from the furnace deep', and in one copy the line was amended to 'What dread hand forged thy dread feet?'; but in the end B. left the sentence

hanging, grammatically incomplete but more forcefully suggestive than the tidier versions.

17–18. Cf. Job 38.7: 'When the morning stars sang together, and all the sons of God shouted for joy.' But here the starry spirits weep. M.K. Nurmi (in 'Blake's Revisions of "The Tyger" ' in M. Bottrall's Casebook on *S.I.E.*) suggests that these lines include reference to the defeat or surrender of reactionary forces (associated with the repressive 'starry' king Urizen) in face of revolutionary energy (one meaning of the tiger).

19. Cf. Genesis 1.10: 'God saw that it was good.' But here it is left an open question whether this creation is good. The strength and beauty of the tiger, the wonderful power and daring of the creator suggest yes. The dreadfulness of the tiger and the contrast with the lamb cause doubt. Perhaps energy necessarily appears in destructive form in the fallen condition?

My Pretty Rose Tree (p. 33). To connect with B.'s life is conjectural and unnecessary. A situation is presented from the point of view of a speaker who has returned to his 'Pretty Rose-tree' having rejected another offer of love. Do we accept his point of view or think his language a bit patronizing and self-satisfied?

Ah! Sun-flower (p. 34). The sun-flower grows tall, looks like the sun and supposedly always turns its face to the sun; is an emblem of aspiration to a golden clime beyond time. The poem questions (without clearly answering the question) the rightness of such aspiration.

4. Cf. *For Children: The Gates of Paradise* 14, where 'The Traveller hasteth in the Evening'. In that context the traveller's wish to get beyond the 'grave' of mortal life to eternity seems right.

6. Stevenson (p. 221) refers to Ovid's story of the unfulfilled love of Clytie for the sun-God Hyperion and her dwindling into a sun-flower. This may have given B. the idea of connecting sun-flower and virgin; but we must attend only to what he shows in this delicately poised poem.

The Lilly (p. 34).

1. *modest*. 'Lustful' and 'envious' were adjectives tried for the rose in the MS. This modesty is a prudish-prurient rejection of love.

The Garden of Love (p. 34). The draft of this poem in the Notebook is followed by 'I saw a chapel all of gold', q.v.

The Little Vagabond (p. 35). Appropriately this speaker's language, like the Schoolboy's, is less concentrated, his rhythms less subtle than those of most speakers in *S.E.*; but, an innocent, he suggests in his naive way Blakean truths—about the hypocrisy of the outwardly pious and the 'marriage' of 'contraries', soul-body, God-Devil.

4. *will never do well*: substituted for the stronger 'makes all go to hell' in the Notebook.

London (p. 36). The illustration at the top shows an old, one supposes blind, man on crutches being led along a street by a boy. Lower down a child warms himself by a leaping flame. The speaker is to an extent the poet himself presenting a true picture of the London he knows; but the illustration perhaps connects him with the old man, whose vision is defective and needs to be complemented by that of the boy. He both marks (sees) the evils, and marks (draws) them on to the faces.

1–2. *charter'd*: originally 'dirty'. As often B. moves from mere description to the attitudes which cause what is seen. Charters confer rights, the liberty to do something; but in effect, B. suggests, extinguish liberty by regulation.

7. *ban*: curse.

13. *But most*: B. originally wrote these words at the beginning of the previous stanza, but changed them there to 'how' to emphasize the climax in the final stanza. It is especially sexual relationships that are corrupted by the false attitudes he sees behind visible evils. Notions of law and property lead to loveless marriages, which are living deaths, and to prostitution.

14. *Harlot's curse*: (1) Literally the curse the narrator hears. (2) Venereal disease. The 'plagues' which blight marriages are not confined to that, but they include that.

The Human Abstract (p. 36). Entitled 'The Human Image' in the Notebook; superseded 'A Divine Image' as the contrary to 'The Divine Image' in *S.I.* 'Human', usually in B. referring to full humanity in which the human and divine are one, here seems to mean the mortal, the fallen, distinguished from the divine.

1–4. Substantially the same lines are spoken in 'I heard an angel singing' by a devil (a really wicked devil, not the active contrary in *M.H.H.*). It is a truly devilish vision that sees like this. It has been suggested that the rest of the poem is spoken by a different speaker, who shows the consequences of the false reasoning of the speaker of

1–4. B.'s punctuation does not support this, but it is true that the poem seems to shift from the statement of a point of view to a comment upon it.

13–14. The first appearance of the tree of mystery, which is to become a regular feature of the Blakean landscape. Cf. 'A Poison Tree' and *Ahania* 3:50–76. It cannot be found in nature (21–3), is essentially illusory. It grows in the human brain, is the product, in B.'s myth, of the fallen Urizen, of intellect separated from imagination. It represents the false ideas (about God, morality, etc.) which man creates with his abstracting intellect and then feels himself subject to. Though ultimately it is illusory, the evils associated with it are real in that they are experienced.

Infant Sorrow (p. 37). Contrary of 'Infant Joy'. In the Notebook B. drafted six more stanzas in which the child grows and rebels against the father or the Priest(s) and kills him/them—a story easily interpretable in Freudian terms; he showed good judgment in choosing only the two stanzas.

A Poison Tree (p. 37). Entitled 'Christian forbearance' in the Notebook. B. first wrote after line 10: 'And I gave it to my foe'. It is subtler to make the foe be attracted by the fruit of the speaker's suppressed anger. The foe is infected with the same suppressed hatred, and is poisoned by it.

A Little Boy Lost (p. 38). Contrary of 'The Little Boy Lost' and 'Found' in *S.I.*
5. *Father*: The Priest overhears the boy addressing, presumably, God, but it could be the earthly father. (In the earlier two poems also God and the father are brought together.) The boy has been taught to obey the commandments to love his neighbour as himself, and to love God with all his heart and mind; and he innocently questions whether this is possible.

24. Symbolically children are 'killed', their lives made living deaths by cruelty and the imposition of false attitudes and beliefs; but the literal implausibility of the story and of 1–4 as the speech of a little boy makes this poem less satisfying than most of *S.E.*.

A Little Girl Lost (p. 39). Probably written as a contrary to 'The Little Girl Lost' and 'Found', though these were later transferred to *S.E.* A subtler poem than 'A Little Boy Lost' in that the young person is shown as moving out of innocence, being infected by the elder's fear, and in that the elder is a pathetic as well as mistaken figure.

34. *blossoms*: appropriately connect the father with a tree, the tree of the Knowledge of Good and Evil, under which the originally innocent in Eden became aware of sin and fear.

To Tirzah (p. 40). A late addition, probably written about 1804. Tirzah was the capital of the northern kingdom of Israel and a rival of Jerusalem; thus could be used as a symbol of the material as against the spiritual, of anything which is not part of the holy city of Jerusalem. In the illustration the words 'It is Raised a Spiritual Body' (1 Corinthians 15:44) are written on the robes of an old man offering a pitcher to a dying man. St Paul is sharply distinguishing between the natural body and the spiritual.

4. Cf. John 2:4: 'Jesus said unto her [his mother], Woman, what have I to do with thee?' Man's true being is not derived from 'mother' Earth, from the material.

5–7. In eternity male and female are parts of a single whole. The division into sexes in Adam and Eve was a fall out of this unity. Sexual life 'blow'd' (bloomed) in them in Eden until their further fall which should have led to death, if Mercy had not changed death into the 'sleep' of our ordinary mortal life. The recognition that it was Mercy that created this state is not easy to reconcile with the next two stanzas which speak of man being cruelly betrayed into mortal life. More generally it is difficult to reconcile the sharp dualism between soul and body in this poem with the emphasis elsewhere that 'Everything that lives is Holy'. Some say the poem is, like others in *S.E.*, only the statement of a point of view, perhaps that of 'The Bard' rather than of B. himself. But it is a point of view which is stated in B.'s own prophetic voice in passages in later poems, and was probably at times his own (in about 1804 more than in the early 1790s). The insertion after it in copy Z of 'The School-boy' and 'The Voice of the Ancient Bard' suggests that B. may finally have wished to remove it from the prominent final position it had occupied in some copies.

The School Boy (p. 41). Transferred from *S.I.* to *S.E.* in late copies. An illustration shows a boy sitting reading in a vine, learning natur-ally and willingly in true 'learning's bower' (14) contrasted with the 'dreary shower' (15) of the teacher's instruction.

The Voice of the Ancient Bard (p. 42). Transferred from *S.I.* to *S.E.* in late copies; probably the last written of *S.I.*, and affected by hopes roused by the French Revolution. It is addressed to a 'youth', rather than like most of *S.I.* to children, and envisages the possibility of an 'opening morn' here, not in 'new worlds' after death as in 'Night'. It illustrates how some of these poems acquire different shades of meaning from their contexts. Reading it in *S.I.* one would attend to the confident opening and think of the last six lines as referring only to a situation which is being swept away. Reading it in *S.E.* one might fear that the maze of folly is not after all going to be escaped from. Placed at the end of *S.I.E.* it makes an enigmatic conclusion to the whole series.

A Divine Image (p. 42). Etched on a copper plate and presumably intended for *S.E.* as a contrary to 'The Divine Image' in *S.I.*; rejected in favour of 'The Human Abstract'. As in the latter poem this is the 'human' (and the divine) as seen with the defective vision of experience, not the properly human in B.'s normal usage of the word.

From Blake's Notebook (p. 43). The poems in this section are taken from the part of B.'s notebook (sometimes called 'The Rossetti MS' because it once belonged to D.G. Rossetti) used for drafting some of the poems in *S.E.* They were presumably written in the same period (*c.* 1791–3). They were deliberately excluded from *S.E.* and have less authority than some later MS poems.

'*I told my love*' (p. 43). Printed without punctuation, as in the MS, to enable readers to share in the problems presented by a draft. How should one take line 3? Probably it goes with 'she'. So should one put a semicolon after 'heart'? But perhaps it goes with 'I'. It would be quite a Blakean idea that the narrator's fears should put off the beloved. There was originally a third stanza at the beginning, which most editors print but which is clearly deleted in the MS:

> Never pain to tell thy love
> Love that never told can be
> For the gentle wind does move
> Silently invisibly.

8. Substituted for 'He took her with a sigh' deleted.

'*I saw a chapel*' (p. 43). Written immediately after 'The Garden of Love' in the MS. A wrong kind of religion and of moral 'purity' causes the rejected instinctual forces, especially sex, to become destructive.

8. Substituted for 'Till he broke the pearly door'.

'*I heard an Angel*' (p. 44). At attempt at a contrary to 'The Divine Image' in *S.I.*; superseded by 'A Divine Image' and finally by 'The Human Abstract'. 'Angel' and 'Devil' seem closer to the ordinary idea of those beings than in *M.H.H.* One must decide from this poem alone how to regard them here.

A Cradle Song (p. 44). An attempt at a contrary to 'A Cradle Song' in *S.I.*

'*I fear'd the fury of my wind*' (p. 45). Cf. 'A Poison Tree'.

Motto to the Songs (p. 46). The good accept the perceptions of others and suppress their own instincts, until the resulting knavery, hypocrisy and selfishness show them how to tell the true vision of the long-sighted eagle from the limited perceptions of the night-flying owl.

7. *his*: the good man's.

The Book of Thel (p. 47). Dated on the title page 1789; probably written, though not necessarily completed in the final form, about that time; closely connected with *S.I.*, though Thel's timidity sharply differentiates her from the robust speakers of the *Songs*; the first published poem to use the seven-foot, unrhymed, mainly iambic line which was to become B.'s standard metre in his longer poems. Erdman (p. 713) says that a changed style of script shows that the Motto and Plate 6 were etched later than the rest, not earlier than 1791; but Bentley (I.689) regards his argument as inconclusive. It is not necessary for understanding to decide on this; in any case Plate 6 opens up new perspectives.

1:1. *Mne Seraphim*: probably a mistake for 'Bne Seraphim', the sons of the Seraphim, spirits associated by Cornelius Agrippa, from whom B. took other names, with the planet Venus.
1:4. *Adona*: connected with Adonis, the youth loved by Venus. This name, the sons of the Seraphim and Thel's own name, probably derived from the Greek word for 'desire', are all connected with

Venus, sometimes the goddess of 'heavenly' love but more commonly the goddess of the generative forces in nature, especially of sexual desire. The elder daughters, we may suppose, are content to remain in some remote Arcadia; Thel is moved by desire to confront experience, especially sex, but is afraid. Cf. Lyca in 'The Little Girl Lost' and 'Found', Ona in 'A Little Girl Lost', Oothoon in *V.D.A.*

1:14. Cf. Genesis 3:8. This seems to place Thel in a garden of Eden, envisaged as a state outside the ordinary world of generation, yet subject to change and death.

2:1. *Har*: In *Tiriel*, written probably not long before *Thel*, the vale of Har is inhabited by Har and Heva, who in some degree correspond to Adam and Eve. Har is not a state of positive innocence, but of sentimental, self-regarding withdrawal. Positive innocence, as celebrated in *S.I.*, is represented by Lilly, Cloud, Worm and Clod rather than by Thel.

2:4. *o'erfired*: clearly thus in B.'s hand; usually amended, probably rightly, to 'o'ertired', but perhaps one could find meaning in 'o'erfired' by referring to 2:10.

2:7. *meekin*: probably variant of 'meek'.

3:8. *Luvah*: will become an important character in B.'s mythology; here a sun-god driving the chariot of the sun across the sky.

5:14. *matron Clay*: mother Earth, the source of natural life; the mortal clay, the flesh, which those who enter the state of generation must put on; the grave, death, a necessary part of the natural cycle.

6:1. *northern bar*: Homer in *Odyssey* XIII.109–12 describes the cave of the Naiads, whose northern gate was interpreted by the neo-Platonists as the means of descent of souls into the state of generation.

6:9. *grave plot*: The whole of earthly life was treated by the neo-Platonists, and sometimes by B., as a state of sleep or death in relation to the full life of eternity. The voice from the pit speaks not of death in the ordinary sense, but of earthly life regarded as a living death. This voice, like those in *S.E.*, opens a new perspective, but does not necessarily show the way of seeing of the 'innocent' speakers to be illusory.

6:11–20. In the state of 'experience' man's apprehensions through his five senses are of pain and restriction. The sense of touch is, as often in B., associated with sex (19–20). Lines 19–20 were deleted in two copies, perhaps for prudish patrons.

6:21–2. In neo-Platonic terms Thel is the soul refusing entry into the realm of generation. More generally she may be thought of as representative of anyone at any stage of existence refusing the pain of experience and retreating into an escapist 'paradise' (Arcadia 1:1, Eden 1:14 or Har). As often B. mixes his own mythology with traditional ones, sometimes rather confusingly.

Thel's Motto: placed at the beginning in most editions, as in B.'s own earlier copies, but it is at the end in the last two copies made by B. It appropriately ends *Thel* with questions rather than answers.

1–2. Thel has refused to enter 'the pit' (6:10). Has she done rightly? The eagle, long-sighted, sees into the pit and much besides, whereas the mole is blind; but it is the mole who knows by personal experience what it is like to be in the pit. Cf. *V.D.A.* 5:40.

3–4. Repetition of a deleted line in *Tiriel* (8:18); from Tiriel's dying speech in which he, like the voice from the pit in *Thel*, questions why man should be confined within the restrictions of the mortal body.

The final illustration shows three children riding a large serpent—a reassertion, perhaps, of the vision of innocence. Unlike Thel the children can control the forces of which she is afraid?

The Marriage of Heaven and Hell (p. 52). Written probably 1790–93. The introductory poem and the concluding 'Song' look back and forward from this time of revolutionary ferment, suggesting a contemporary application for the main part of the work, which is an exuberant ironic satire on the Swedish philosopher and scientist Swedenborg (1688–1772), and a humorous exposition of some of B.'s own central ideas. B. had found many congenial ideas in Swedenborg's *Divine Love and Wisdom* (annotations in K.89–96), but had been shocked by his *Divine Providence* (annotations in K.131–3) and probably even more so by his *Heaven and Hell*. Swedenborg's presentation of heaven and hell is conventional in that he shows them as permanent states to which, as B. understood him, souls are predestined. 'Predestination after this Life is more Abominable than Calvin's . . . Cursed Folly' (K.133). *M.H.H.* is much influenced by Swedenborg both in form and content, but it can be enjoyed without reference to sources provided one is sensitive to the special ironic meanings which are being given to such words as 'heaven', 'hell', 'angel' and 'devil'. The central themes are that 'without Contraries is no progression' and that release from the cavern in which man has closed himself will come 'by an improvement of sensual enjoyment'. Reason (heaven) and energy (hell) are both necessary for human existence; they ought, the title implies, to be 'married'. To show this properly the 'Proverbs of Hell' ought to be balanced by 'Proverbs of Heaven'. But this is not a balanced work; it is written predominantly from the point of view of 'the devil' and 'hell', partly because it is written in reaction against Swedenborg and contemporary errors and partly because B.'s temperament placed him, knowingly, in 'the devil's party'. The humorous tone, without weakening the force of the satire, implicitly acknowledges this lack of balance and makes this the most enjoyable of the prophetic books. That B. later had reservations about *M.H.H.* is suggested by the fact that he did not include it in either of his lists of works for sale (*Letters*, 9 June 1818, 12 April 1827).

2:1. *Rintrah*: here a wrathful thunder-god. Later, in *E.* and *M.*, will be seen as a 'son' of Los, the eternal prophet. He is the prophet as wrathful denouncer, speaking in the 1790s through the French revolutionaries. He is presumably the speaker of 2:3–20.

2:2. *swag*: sway, or sink down.

2:3–20. Cryptic, and difficult to interpret with confidence, even if one picks up the possible references to Bunyan's Christian walking along a narrow path through the Valley of the Shadow of Death (3–5), to Moses striking water from the rock in Exodus 17:1–7 (10–11), to the dry bones in Ezekiel 37 (12), to Adam as 'red clay' (13; more dubious; perhaps it is simply the red clay of the earth) and to John the Baptist (19). Once the genuinely just and meek man (for instance, the early Christian) walked in a perilous path; but then that path was 'planted' and became no longer really perilous, and the just man's place was usurped by the hypocritically humble, the orthodox, what will later in *M.H.H.* be called the 'angel'. So the just man, for instance the modern French revolutionary, rages in the wilderness.

3. Now in 1790, thirty-three years after Swedenborg had dated the beginning of a new dispensation, renewal is coming by a revival of 'hellish' energy in the French Revolution. The possible resurrection of mankind is the same as the resurrection of Jesus, about thirty-three years after his 'advent', since all mankind is united in him. Swedenborg's writings are being discarded like Jesus's

clothes at the Resurrection (John 20:4–13). It is a pleasant coinci-
dence that B. himself was thirty-three in 1790.

Edom: the land of the descendants of Esau, enemies of the Israelites
descended from Jacob. In Isaiah 63 it appears, unexpectedly, that
salvation may be coming from Edom; so now in 1790 from France.
Esau/Adam/mankind may now be recovering the birthright of which
he was deprived. Isaiah 34 tells of God's bloody vengeance on His
enemies; Isaiah 35 of the joyful flourishing of His kingdom.

4. *Body is a portion of Soul*: Contrast the earlier 'A Little Black Boy'
   and the later 'To Tirzah'. It is possible to maintain: (1) That B. is
   trying out extreme opinions through speakers with whom he
   should not be identified. (2) That his view in the early 1790s was
   very different from earlier and later (see E.D. Hirsch, *Innocence and
   Experience*). (3) That the seemingly dualistic passages are not
   repudiating the body as properly understood, but only the notion
   of body as 'outer', 'distinct from soul'.

5–6. *Book of Job*: In Job Satan is the accuser of sin, as, in the view taken
   here, Messiah is in *Paradise Lost*. This accuser Satan is to be
   distinguished from the energetic Satan of *Paradise Lost* I and II, on
   whose side Milton is alleged unconsciously to be.
   the Gospel: John 14:16–17. As interpreted here the Holy Spirit is
   the active energy of desire. In praying for it Jesus is moving
   towards the restoration of the human wholeness, split by the
   separation of reason and energy. He is therefore after death able
   to become Jehovah, uniting fire and light. As here, Jehovah is
   usually but not always in B. a positive force, a God of mercy,
   not of vengeance. Cf. *Ghost of Abel*.

   In Milton, the Father: Milton, B. thinks, shows the Father as an
   external ruler, the Son as an abstraction, a god whose existence
   is deduced by reasoning on what is known by man's five limited
   senses; and does not show God as an indwelling spirit.

6–7. B.'s Memorable Fancies are ironical parodies of Swedenborg's
   'Memorable Relations'.
   a mighty Devil: B. himself writing on metal plates, using corro-
   sive acid and so making known his visions to the minds of
   men.

7–10. *Proverbs of Hell*: 'devilish' counterpart of the Book of Proverbs
   in the Bible.

10:7. If taken literally this is B. being even more than usually provocative. But if the nursing metaphor governs the whole sentence then the 'infant' is the unacted desire which it is better to kill before it has grown big rather than to 'nurse'.

12–13. B. is making fun of Swedenborg's claim in his 'Memorable Relations' to familiarity with heavenly spirits, and humorously displaying some of his own ideas through the dialogue of the prophets.

> *naked and barefoot*: Isaiah 20:2–5. At the time of the Assyrian occupation of part of the Israelite territory Isaiah was commanded by the Lord to go naked and barefoot.
> *Diogenes*: cynic philosopher in the 4th century B.C. Lived in extreme poverty, and flouted the conventions of decency.
> *eat dung*: Ezekiel 4:4–17. Ezekiel was commanded to lie on his left side for three hundred and ninety days, signifying the length of Israel's captivity, and on his right side for forty days, signifying Judah's captivity. He was to eat cakes baked upon dung, signifying the privations of Jerusalem during a siege.

14. *six thousand years*: Plàcing the creation, as was common in B.'s day, in 4004 B.C., the apocalypse would not be far off. B. sometimes took the revolutionary ferment of his time as a sign that the end was near. Man would return to the fullness of life from which he is now barred out—by the cherub at the tree of life (Genesis 3:24) and/or by the 'cherub that covereth' mentioned in Ezekiel 28:14. The creation as man now perceives it, finite and corrupt, would be consumed. This would not really be a destruction, but a seeing of things as they are, infinite. The 'narrow chinks of his cavern' are the physical senses as they now are, which give only very limited knowledge of reality. The cave recalls Plato's cave in *Republic* VII.514–18 in which men see only the shadows of the real.

15. Deals literally with printing-houses, including B.'s own workshop, and with how men of imagination pass on knowledge in the 'hell' of our lower world. These places are full of smoke, and occupied by energetic 'devils'. The Dragon-Man clears away rubbish from the cave's mouth, thus cleansing the doors of perception (Plate 14); he appears a 'Dragon' to the timid. One can interpret the Viper and his assistants as working against the creators, confining men within the cave and decorating it with fixed rather than fluid forms; but more probably 'Viper' is, like 'Dragon', ironical, and he also is helping, perhaps as reason

providing the necessary bound and circumference of energy. The Eagle, even within the cave, causes everything to appear, as it is, infinite. After the metal has been melted and cast into type, books are made and sent out into libraries. There may be an implication at the end that the prophet's inspired message is compromised by thus being fixed, and filed away in libraries.

16–17. It is difficult to believe that B. really thought that 'the cunning of weak and tame minds' is necessary to human existence. He has not yet developed his idea that there are 'negations', which must be destroyed, as well as active 'contraries', which must be preserved in creative tension.

Messiah or Satan or Tempter: see reference to Book of Job in 5–6 above.

17–20. Cf. Swedenborg's 'Memorable Relations' from *The True Christian Religion* quoted in Stevenson pp. 102–3.

An Angel: representative of the conventional minded to whom some of B.'s ideas would seem diabolical and who might believe that such an unorthodox person would go to hell.

stable . . . church . . . vault: Some say this succession is suggestive of the decline of Christianity as B. saw it—from the religion of the child born in a manger to the dogmatic church in whose vault Jesus is buried; but in this context the stable may suggest rather the 'horses of instruction'.

nether sky: B. imagines himself being taken by the Angel through a flat earth, from the bottom side of which roots stick out into the nether abyss. The Angel imposes upon B. his own (illusory) vision of hell.

Leviathan: in the Bible a huge sea-dragon. In Job 41 his creation is a manifestation of God's power, but in Isaiah 27:1 he is slain by the Lord, and seems to be a symbol of evil. There is a rather similar ambivalence in his treatment by B. Here he is suggestive perhaps of tremendous forces, whether in the natural world or in the deeps of the mind, which appear in terrible form to conventional persons such as the Angel. The resemblance to a tiger may suggest revolution and 'the tygers of wrath', which are 'wiser than the horses of instruction'. When the Angel leaves, the fearful apparition disappears, leaving B. in a pleasant scene.

Then B. imposes his vision upon the Angel, taking him up to the sun whereas the Angel has taken B. into an underworld.

The Angel's place is in the void between the planets and the fixed stars; his philosophy deals in abstractions which have no substantial reality. Returning to earth, dragged down by the weight of Swedenborg's volumes, they see 'seven houses of brick', the 'seven churches which are in Asia' (Revelation 1.4) and a satirical picture of the inanities and cruelties which result, according to B., when vision declines into dogmatic abstractions and thence into natural religion.

At the bottom of Plate 20 was originally written 'Opposition is true friendship'. This was obliterated in all but three early uncoloured copies. B. and the Angel have openly expressed their opposition and shown their visions to each other, and therefore can be friends. Cf. 'The Poison Tree' in *S.E.* Wisely obliterated because only sometimes true?

21–22. B. now thinks that Swedenborg, like the Angel, is complacent and unoriginal. The true seers are the great poets, Dante and Shakespeare; below these, but much above the merely conventional, are mystical philosophers such as Paracelsus (1493–1541, alchemist and doctor) and Boehme (1575–1624, writer of works on the origin of things. His ideas about God and the 'contraries' have a good deal in common with B.'s).

22–24. *Bray a fool*: Cf. Proverbs 27:22. Bray means 'beat'.
Among the passages B. was thinking of to show Jesus's disregard of the ten commandments were probably Mark 2:27, 12:12–17; John 8:2–11; Luke 22:8–11; Matthew 27:13–14, 10:14.
arose as Elijah: In 2 Kings 2:11 Elijah is taken up into heaven in a chariot of fire. The Angel by embracing the fire has become one with the prophets. This is the climax, and is perhaps reconcilable with the idea of a 'marriage', in that the Angel may be supposed to retain his own qualities in union with the fire, the prophet transcending both Angel and Devil. But then we find that the Angel has 'become a Devil'. Theoretically B. believed in a marriage; emotionally he could be friends only with a 'Devil'.
Bible of Hell: This suggests that B. had already begun to write, or at least to plan, some of the works of the next few years which are in part parodies of the Bible—*U.* (Genesis), *Ahania* (Exodus), *A.* and *E.* (prophecies).

25–27. The Song leaves Swedenborg behind and the countries of the mind in which the debate between Angel and Devil has been conducted, and celebrates changes taking place in the actual world; but it is an integral part of *M.H.H.*, found in all but a few fragmentary copies. B. sees the revolutionary ferment spreading from America and France to Spain and he hopes elsèwhere, portending possibly not just political change but the cleansing of the doors of perception written of in 14 above. The Song foreshadows scenes in *A.* and other later poems in which a female, a fiery youth and a starry king are brought together. Here the female (in *E.* Enitharmon) is the mother of the fiery youth (later revealed as Orc), whom the starry king (Urizen) tries unsuccessfully to repress. Later this scene will be treated ambivalently, but here it simply celebrates the outbreak of revolutionary energy against political, religious and moral tyranny.

26:15–16. Erdman (*Prophet Against Empire*, 192) connects with the retreat of the anti-revolutionary forces from their attempted invasion of France in September 1792. The Song was probably written 1792–3, later than most of *M.H.H.*

Visions of the Daughters of Albion (p. 66). Dated on the title page 1793, and probably written about 1791–2, when slavery and the rights of women were live issues. B.'s acquaintance with Mary Wollstonecraft, author of *A Vindication of the Rights of Woman* (1792), focused his passion for liberty specifically on the condition of women; and his reading of J.G. Stedman's *A Narrative, of a five Years' expedition, against the Revolted Negroes of Surinam* (1796), for which he engraved illustrations in 1791–3, brought the cruelties and rapes of slave-owners vividly to his mind. He uses the name and situation of 'Ossian' Macpherson's Oithona, who was forcibly abducted and hidden in a cave on an island; but rejects the conclusion, in which Oithona, resolved not to survive the loss of her honour, dies in battle.

iii:1. *Theotormon*: Erdman (*Prophet Against Empire*, 233–4) suggests that the name may be derived from Theo (God) + toremon (African word, found in Stedman, for a bird, meaning 'a talebearer, or a spy') and/or torment. He is 'God's spy' (a false God's), spying out sin and making accusations, tormenting himself and others; and/or he is one who is tormented by his God, his false conception of God.

1:1. *Albion*: England; later in B. humanity seen as one. English women are enslaved by the same attitudes as are embodied in Theotormon and Bromion; so they echo back the sighs of

Oothoon. Though they are only occasionally mentioned, the whole poem is their vision, expresses how they see and experience life.

1:5. *Marygold*: cf. Lily, Cloud and Clod of Clay in *Thel*. The plucking of a flower may symbolize sexual experience.

Leutha: no more than a name in this poem. If one brings in the reference to her in *E*. 14:9–14 one may conclude that Oothoon is being 'lured' into 'experience'; but her brave acceptance (12–15), contrasted with Thel's timidity, is admirable even if it leads to bad results for her.

1:15. *Theotormon's reign*: literally the Atlantic.

1:16. *Bromion*: associated with thunder and storms, like Urizen who appears as a sky-god above Oothoon in the title-page illustration; a slave-owner who brands his African slaves and rules them by terror (20–3).

2:3. *storms rent*: Literally Bromion's winds stir up the Atlantic waves. Symbolically the situation in the cave represents the fallen condition in which man is shut out from eternity and love is unfulfilled. Bromion and Oothoon are bound (5), whereas Theotormon is not; so it seems that it is Theotormon, with his jealousy and false ideas of religion and morality, who is the jailer. His repressed lust (10) issues in repression—of women, slaves and children sold as chimney-sweeps (8).

2:13–16. Oothoon for a time accepts Theotormon's view of her—that she is 'defiled' by what has happened to her; and allows herself to be 'torn' by his thoughts of her. But soon reasserts her purity (28).

2:23–35. Oothoon hails the coming of the dawn which, as in *S.E.* 'Introduction', could be an emblem of a reawakening of man to his full potential. But she has been told (30–4) that she is confined within the five senses; so she can see only a 'shadow' (35)—the merely natural rather than the true spiritual sun.

3:8–9. The individual characteristics of the various creatures cannot be explained by their common possession of physical senses. Therefore, it is implied, there is not 'one law for the lion and the ox'.

3:22–4:11. Theotormon does not answer Oothoon's plea to recognize her essential purity, but pursues his own vague and self-regarding train of thought.

4:13–24. Bromion wishes to believe in what the eye sees (13), in material possessions (20–1), in law (22) and in hell (23–4), but seems uneasily aware that there may be realities beyond his understanding. As usual in B. the 'bad' character is lacking in vision rather than absolutely evil.

5:3. *Urizen*: Having failed to get any answer to her pleas from her two companions Oothoon addresses the power behind both of them. In his true nature the 'Prince of Light', in the fallen condition he is reason sundered from imagination and other human faculties and seeking to tyrannize over them. He is associated with rulers, moralists, religious leaders, etc., who try to impose 'one law' on all. Though contrasted, Theotormon and Bromion are alike in displaying Urizenic attitudes. Urizen is the creator only in so far as men show these attitudes. His attempt to form men in his image is bound to fail because they are individuals, as the rambling discourse which follows is meant to demonstrate.

5:5–40. Oothoon's speech is an eloquent denunciation of such evils as landlordism (15), the tithe system (17) and the oppression of women, illogically set in an argument that there cannot be one law for all since individuals and their joys are so different, each joy 'a Love'. Does she really mean that the joys of the oppressors are to be indulged? One supposes not, though the argument seems to demand that.

7:23–7. Most commentators are happy to accept this fantasy as an expression of Oothoon's generosity, an attitude as far as possible removed from Theotormon's jealousy. But catching girls in nets and traps (especially if there is a reference to the Venus-trap or catch-fly, plants which trap and eat insects) is not an appropriate image for 'free' love. Either B. is using imagery quite unsuitable to his presumed purpose, or he is treating even Oothoon ambivalently. Just as his 'bad' characters are more 'mistaken' (5:3) than intentionally wicked, so his 'good' ones are not immune to error; they grow like what they look upon. So perhaps Oothoon's voyeurism and sadism derive from her situation in the cave? This (not the usual) reading is at odds with the tone of the poem as a whole, but sudden and unexplained transitions are characteristic of B. Are nets, traps, adamant, ever 'good' images in B.?

America (p. 75). Dated on the title page 1793. Written probably 1791–3.

1–2. The 'Preludium' sets the partly historical events of the 'Prophecy' within a larger context of myth.

1:1. *shadowy daughter of Urthona*: Urthona is here only a name, suggestive of 'earth-owner', which is consonant with his daughter being a nature goddess, 'shadowy' because physical nature is only a shadow of the real. The later revelation that he is the name in eternity of Los, the imagination as it is manifested in time, means that he is the father also of Orc (revolutionary energy the product of imagination). But this is not a theme in this poem. Orc regards Urthona simply as 'thy father'(11). For the binding of Orc by Los see *U.* 20:8–25.

Orc: The name may combine suggestions from 'orcus' (Hell) and 'cor' (the heart), and possibly from 'orc' (a sea-monster) and 'orchis' (testicle)—the fiery energy of 'hell' (as understood in *M.H.H.*), the passions of the heart which have been distorted (the order of the letters has been altered) by repression, the energies of sex (he breaks from his bonds at the age of puberty, fourteen). The illustration connects him with Prometheus, the benefactor of men by bringing them fire, punished by Zeus for rebellion. His being 'red' and hairy (11) may connect him with Esau (cf. *M.H.H.* 3).

2:7–17. The female is given a voice by her union with Orc. What she says is strangely contradictory. On the one hand, she hails him as the image of God who has fallen to give her life; on the other, 'this is eternal death'. On the one hand, human/divine energy enters into the natural world (a region of 'death' in comparison with eternity), fertilizes it and gives it life and meaning; on the other, spiritual energy may be captured, corrupted by the merely natural. The positive is stressed here, the negative in later repetitions of this incident in *F.Z.* The incident may be thought of as taking place at any time, since it is a constantly recurring situation, in the primitive past (the iron age—1:3), and in the present when revolutionary energy is bringing new life to the 'American plains' and the image of God is seen in African slaves (2:8).

2:18–21. The following additional lines were written at the bottom of the plate, separated from 1–17 by a picture of Orc emerging from the earth:

The stern Bard ceas'd, asham'd of his own song; enrag'd he swung
His harp aloft sounding, then dash'd its shining frame against
A ruin'd pillar in glittring fragments; silent he turn'd away,
And wander'd down the vales of Kent in sick & drear lamentings.

These lines were masked so as not to be printed in all but three of the copies, and of these three two may have been made after B.'s death. So B.'s predominant wish does not seem to have been to include these disillusioned lines, perhaps occasioned by events in France in 1793, as part of the poem.

3:1. *Guardian Prince*: same as 'Albion's Angel' (5:1), the repressive spirit behind the English government's actions, and George III himself. Mention first of his 'burning' may suggest that the Colonists' warlike fires are only an answer to their rulers' violence. 'Tent' may suggest, as well as war, a condition of confinement, lack of vision, being shut out from the light of eternity.

3:4. *Washington* etc.: American leaders, except for Paine (1737–1809), English radical author, whose *Common Sense and Crisis* (1776) encouraged the Colonists.

3:15. *dragon*: The English ruler appears in the form of a dragon, symbolizing the warlike spirit in which he dealt with the Colonists.

4:7–11. Orc appears as the spirit behind the Americans. Though on the American side, B. realistically acknowledges that in a war situation 'heat but not light' will be generated on both sides.

5:1. *Stone of Night*: suggestive of rigidity, law (the stone tablets on which the ten commandments were written—cf. 8:5), lack of vision. See *E*. 10:26 and note.

5:4. *Mars*: god of war. The situation in which his planet is in the centre symbolizes a state of war.

5:6. *Spectre*: Orc. Probably does not yet have the particular meanings later to be given to this word. But this paragraph, like 4:2–11, suggests an ambivalent attitude towards Orc. Cf. 'The Chapel of Gold'.

6:2. The images connect the resurrection to new life, which it is hoped is coming through revolution, with the resurrection of Jesus.

7:4. *Enitharmon*: later the consort of Los, but sometimes, as probably here, stands for women in general. From the Angel's point of view ('Angel' and 'Demon' have similar ironic meanings to 'Angel' and 'Devil' in *M.H.H.*) Orc is an Antichrist, standing ready, like various characters in mythology such as Chronos, to devour children as they issue from the womb. But perhaps it is the 'dragon-formed' (3:15) Angel who is really the Antichrist?

8:1. *the accursed tree*: the tree of the forbidden fruit in Eden. In B.'s, and some earlier, pictures Satan as serpent is sometimes represented as wreathed round this tree. Orc ironically accepts that he appears a serpent from the Angel's point of view. For readers of B.'s later works there is a double irony—that Orc really is a serpent, whose merely natural energy will not be able to bring about the desired renewal of life. But the optimistic tone of the rest of the poem probably makes it improper to bring in here the later developments of the myth.

8:15–16. Cf. Daniel 3:25 and 2:31–3. Like Shadrach, Meshach and Abednego man is able to walk unharmed in the fire; unlike the image in Nebuchadnezzar's dream he has no feet of clay.

9:1. *Angels*: seen by Albion's Angel as his, but the true guardian spirits of the colonies join the rebels (Pl. 11–12).

9:14. *rebel form*: Orc, who is being born as the revolutionary spirit animating the Americans. Orc exists at all times, and special manifestations of him may come into existence at particular times.

10:6. *Atlantean hills*: The legendary land of Atlantis, between or joining England and America, was submerged by the Atlantic, signifying for B. the barring out of fallen man from eternity by the sea of space and time, his submergence in materialism. If the revolutionary hopes were realized a new Atlantis, a new golden age might appear.

13:2. *Bernard's house*: Sir Francis Bernard was governor of Massachusetts, 1760–69. His lack of tact and insight is said to have hastened the war, even though he was recalled before it. So he is taken as exemplifying the attitudes of the governors. B. is using, but not accurately following, historical events. Boston, one of the early centres of rebellion, is in Massachusetts.

14:17–18. If the English plans had succeeded, any hope of a new Atlantis in touch with the infinite arising in America would have been lost.

14:20. *plagues recoil'd*: As shown in detail by Erdman (*Prophet Against Empire* 50–63) the English tried to subdue the Americans by starving them out, cutting off trade and sowing disunity among them as well as by military action. These 'plagues' recoiled upon England. The Americans closed ranks (14:19), but dissension about the war broke out in England, especially in London, the seat of government, and Bristol, the chief trading port with America. Revolutionary ferment caused religious and moral, especially sexual, orthodoxies to be questioned. The mental instability of

George III (15:6–8) is taken by B. as symptomatic of a loss of nerve among the rulers. The religious leaders also, the Bishops, become sick with fear (15:9–10).

15:15. *Bard of Albion*: possibly a reference to the poet laureate William Whitehead who supported the war. The poet who justifies oppression becomes less than human.

16:2. *Urizen*: The power behind the reactionary forces appears above the Atlantic as a sky god, sending down his snows and preventing for twelve years the spreading of revolutionary fires from America to Europe; but after that time the fires break out in France and then in Spain and Italy.

16:19. *five gates*: the five senses. Cf. *M.H.H.* 14. The revolution is not merely political, but is enabling man to assume his true nature. Any doubts about the efficacy of Orc as the agent of apocalyptic change seem to be swept aside in this triumphant conclusion.

Europe (p. 86). Dated on the title page 1794; written probably not long after *A*. As in *A*. the 'Prophecy' is an interpretation of historical events and the 'Preludium' opens a wider perspective. The introductory poem, found in only two copies and possibly written later, opens a wider perspective still. The Fairy sees from the point of view of eternity, and inspires B. to write (iii:25) and to show the limitations of vision of the 'cavern'd Man' (iii:1), the 'shadowy female' and Enitharmon; captured in B.'s hat, he is his inspiration.

iii:1–6. The Fairy, who can see 'all alive/The world', mocks at man for being caverned in the five limited senses, and for failing to pass out, as he could, through the sense of touch, through sex. Cf. *M.H.H.* 14, *E*. 10:10–15.

iii:20–1. Cf. the lily in *Thel* 1:23–5, and the marigold in *V.D.A.* 1:8–10.

1:1. Follows on from *A*. 'Preludium'; but now the shadowy female takes a less hopeful view of the fertility brought to her by the embrace of Orc. Her children are fallen creatures, drawn down (2:6) into the 'forests of eternal death' (i.e. into merely 'natural' life). Both she and her mother Enitharmon represent 'nature'; but she bewails the fall and retains some vision, whereas Enitharmon rejoices in 'female' dominance.

1:4. *other sons*: than Orc, who is the son of Enitharmon and Los.

1:6. *travel*: travail, child-bearing.

2:7–10. Children are in their true nature 'flames', free spirits; but on entering into the natural world they are made to take on solid, fixed forms rather than the fluid forms of fire, and are branded with a mark of ownership by Enitharmon, like the slaves in *V.D.A.* 1:21 and like flocks of sheep. In this poem Enitharmon is woman seen as dominating men by charm and sexual attractiveness; in the historical allegory perhaps Queen Marie Antoinette, whose beauty and charm were seen by radicals in the 1790s as providing a cover for tyranny. The 'female' is also used by B. as a symbol of the natural, the material, as opposed to the 'male', the spiritual.

2:12–14. She experiences joy as well as woe because she realizes that the infinite cannot for ever be bound by the restrictions which the natural world tries to impose. 'Swaddling bands' brings in the thought of Christ, and leads on to the 'Prophecy'.

3:1–4. Cf. Milton 'Nativity Ode' 29–31 and 232–6.

3:7. *Los*: the eternal prophet; the prophet acting in time and subject to error; but one can gather little about him from this poem, in which his consort Enitharmon is the chief actor.

3:9–4:14. B. does not use inverted commas. Who is/are the speaker(s)? 3:9–4:2 Los (or 3:9–14 Los, 4:1–2 narrator, but this seems unlikely in view of the comma at the end of 3:14); 4:3–9 sons of Urizen (or sons of Los); 4:10–14 Enitharmon? Or is the whole spoken by Los?

4:10–14. The speaker, either (probably) Enitharmon or a Los who is joining in her plans, addresses the new-born child as Orc, whereas at 3:1–4 the Milton echo made us think it was Christ. There is a deliberate uncertainty, a bringing together of the two. Whether the child is Christ or Orc, whether the time is the beginning of our era or the end of the eighteenth century (in effect the same to Enitharmon because the intervening period is her dream), Enitharmon sees the birth as an occasion for maintaining 'female' dominion.

5:4. *Rintrah . . . Palamabron*: sons of Los. Should be prophets, but here are false prophets. Rintrah is a king, Palamabron a priest; they join to foster a sense of guilt and belief in an unreal, distant heaven in order to maintain their power. In this situation women are able to use sex to dominate men, and mankind is subjected to the 'female' in the sense of the merely natural.

8:4. *Elynittria*: perhaps suggestive of Diana, 'Queen and huntress, chaste and fair'; of an armed chastity, which, with jealousy (Ocalythron), helps to keep men in subjection.

9:2. *Eighteen hundred years:* from the birth of Christ to the French Revolution, during which the promise inherent in the coming of Christ had not been fulfilled, men's lives had been only a sleep in comparison with the fullness of life possible to them, and Christianity had subjected them to 'female' dominance.

9:6–13:8. Events in the revolutionary era as experienced by Enitharmon in dream at the end of her eighteen hundred years' sleep.

9:8. Cf. *A*. 15.

9:11–16. Refers to the collapse of George III's attempt at personal rule and to the confused situation in the English Parliament as a result of the failure of the war with America.

10. Written throughout in B.'s seven foot lines, whereas varying lengths of line are used in other plates in the 'Prophecy'. Possibly interpolated, though present in the earliest copies? The exposition (10–23), terse and interesting in itself, is not convincing as part of Enitharmon's dream.

10:2. The 'ancient temple' is based upon the circle of standing stones at Avebury in Wiltshire, thought by some in B.'s time to have been made by the Druids and in the form of a serpent. B. moves the temple to Verulam in order to associate it with Francis Bacon. The English rulers are turning back to the origins of their false attitudes in Baconian philosophy (empiricism, materialism, denial of imagination) and in Druid religion (associated by B. with human sacrifices and priestcraft). B. envisages the whole island of Britain as being (10:3) or being dominated by (12:11) this temple, dedicated to the worship of the merely natural (serpent, 10:21–2), in which the youth of England are sacrificed as victims in war.

10:26. *Stone of Night*: Cf. *A*. 5:1. The stone in the temple on which human sacrifices may be supposed to have taken place; London stone, from which all distances were, it was thought, calculated (everything subject to measurement and limitation); associated with the 'stony roof', the human skull which shuts man out from the heavens. Commentators tell us to regard such passages about the confinement of man within his limited physical senses as attacks on a particular philosophy or way of seeing (Baconian, materialistic) rather than on the body as such; but what is conveyed does seem to be dislike of having eyes fixed in the head, nostrils, a skull, hair—in fact of being in a body at all.

11:15–20. B. is using the dismissal of Lord Chancellor (chief legal officer) Thurlow in 1792 as a symptom of the demoralization of the English Government and of the retreat of law in face of the fires of Orc. In the historical allegory Rintrah may be Pitt, the Prime Minister, and Palamabron Burke and/or Parliament. See Erdman, *Prophet Against Empire*, pp. 216–23.

12:25–31. Enitharmon sees with delight the repression which has been made worse by the laws against sedition introduced by the Pitt Government in reaction to the French Revolution.

13:1–8. The English rulers, perhaps especially Pitt ('red limb'd' because the fires of revolution are playing around him), wish to bring about a last judgment, a final condemnation of Orc and the revolutionaries. Newton is able to blow the trumpet because, for B., he represents the culmination of the materialist, rationalist philosophy which underlies all the reactionary attitudes. Instead of the hoped-for downfall of Orc it is the 'Angelic' forces that fall to the ground. There is probably a humorous reference to Newton's theory of gravitation here. Historically the blowing of the trumpet is the English declaration of war against France in 1793.

13:9. Enitharmon wakes. The situation is still the same, as she sees it, as it was in Plates 3–8. The names in her speech (13:16–14:31) are not given much substance, but a feeling of a soft, delusive sensuality used as a means of dominion is successfully conveyed.

14:35–15:11. Dawn comes, and Los appears as a Dionysian liberator in the vineyards of France. Is he going to be the true liberator, whom Enitharmon will not be able to tame as she has tamed Christ or at any rate his religion? Is this a prelude to apocalypse, the last harvest and vintage of the nations, or only a bloody war? The rhapsodic tone sweeps one along, but there are hints of doubt. Los 'in snaky thunders clad' is rather like Urizen.

The Book of Urizen (p. 96). Dated on the title page 1794. At the end of *M.H.H.* 24, B. announced his 'Bible of Hell, which the world shall have whether they will or no'. *Urizen*, originally entitled *The First Book of Urizen*, was presumably intended as the first book of this 'infernal' Bible, corresponding to Genesis. The format resembles that of some Bibles of B.'s day—short lines of text in rather cramped double columns. It is also appropriate to the theme, the 'creation' depicted being a cramping of the human spirit. The number and ordering of the plates, especially of the full-plate illustrations, differ in all surviving copies. The arrangement here is that which is now standard—that of copy D with Plate 4 added.

Urizen is an ironic parody of the Biblical and Miltonic and other creation narratives, moving from the fall of a Satan (Urizen) through the emergence of the material universe to the appearance of men and of cities and the exodus of the children of Israel from Egypt; and, by disruption of the narrative line, it shows that the fall into disunity is something which is always happening.

3:8. *divided*: Division is the central action of the poem. Urizen does not really create anything. By becoming conscious of himself as separate ('self-contemplating') he initiates the divisions between subject and object, male and female, the generations, etc.

3:36. *globes of attraction*: a reference to the Newtonian universe, governed by gravity, by mechanical forces; a universe which will come into existence, in men's minds, as a result of the fallen way of seeing.

3:37. *expanded*: Cf. *J*. 38 [34]:17–19. In eternity

> We live as One Man; for contracting our infinite senses
> We behold multitude; or expanding, we behold as one,
> As One Man all the Universal Family . . .

These are individual identities, but all are parts of a living whole. This unity, this way of seeing, Urizen's self-contemplation is destroying.

4. This plate was omitted from four of the seven known copies—perhaps because its unorthodox implications might be especially offensive to some customers?

4:10–13. The eternal life Urizen rebels against is one of intense activity, including pain, change and death (in the sense of continual self-annihilation?). Ironically it in some ways resembles traditional hells ('unconquerable burnings').

4:34–40. Urizen corresponds in the traditional story as told in *Paradise Lost* to Satan in that he rebels and is rejected by 'Eternal fury', but ironically he in some respects more resembles Milton's God. He claims 'holiness' (4:7), makes a book of laws like the stone tablets of the Law given to Moses, wishes to establish a single rule. We need not doubt his desire for peace, love, unity; his mistake is to seek these by law.

4:49–5:2. The seven deadly sins appear as a result of the attempt to impose 'one Law'; but their appearance 'in the flames of Eternal fury' makes us question the actions of the Eternals as well as those of Urizen. See note on 19:4.

5:29. Urizen's world, built 'in despair', is yet 'like a womb'—perhaps hinting that, though a consequence and symptom of the fall, it will be able to be used as a means of rebirth.

6:4. An example of the disruption of narrative sequence. We have already been seeing Los and Urizen as separate, and are now told that they split from each other. In the fragmented mind reason and imagination do not work together. This is damaging to both, especially the former. Reason becomes a cold, abstracting power (7:4–5), whereas imagination, though subject to error, retains some glimpses of Eternity and of creative force. Los's fires, though they sometimes go out, can be revived (7:8). Los at his forge is a Vulcan, a smith.

7–8. Copy C, thought to be the earliest, does not contain these plates, added in all other copies, giving two Chapters IV, numbered (a) and (b) by editors.

8:9–11. It is sometimes said that Los creates a body for Urizen, but this is not quite what we are shown. Los watches changes that are taking place, and binds them. Both Los and Urizen contribute to the new world, the new ways of seeing that are coming into existence, but neither is the traditional effortless creator.

10:9. *sodor*: solder.

10:17–18. Los creates, or is, time. Perceiving temporally is a 'bounding' of the mind, a further rending of the mind from eternity, though later (*M.*24:72) we hear that 'Time is the mercy of Eternity'.

10:31–13:19. A parody of the Genesis creation narrative. The new world is Urizen's body with its skull, skeleton, heart, nerves, senses; it is a confinement of the human spirit within the limitations of the body and its senses. Creation is fall. Psychologically the sense of the self as separate from the environment brings with it a sense of confinement. The seventh 'day' of this 'creation' is not a day of rest, but one in which Urizen begins to move painfully.

11:23. *petrified*: reference to the petrous bone, which protects the ear, a suitable symbol for the petrification of our powers of perception. As a student at the Royal Academy, an apprentice in a workshop where scientific books were engraved, and an acquaintance of the famous surgeon John Hunter, B. would be familiar with anatomical drawings. See also 11:1–9, a vivid picture of the heart and its branching veins.

13:20–3. Most commentators say that Los's activity has been mistaken, that in binding another he binds himself and therefore his creative powers decay; but here it seems that Los's fires decay because he 'shrunk from his task', implying that he should have persisted. Once the fall has taken place, the forming of some world, however restricted, is necessary, preferable to chaos?

13:50–3. Cf. 'The Human Abstract'. 'Pity would be no more/If we did not make somebody poor.' Pitying, we regard the other as separate, perhaps feel superior, wish to keep him in a dependent state. The female, pitying side of man is divided from the male, active side.

15:1–2. Corresponds to the creation of Eve out of Adam's body—an incident treated by others before B. (e.g. Boehme) as symbolic of the separation of male and female, once parts of an androgynous whole, and a stage in the fall.

19:4. *Eternals*: unfallen denizens of eternity (or an unfallen part of man's mind)? But their actions contribute to the divisions that are taking place; and their self-protectiveness contrasts with the protectiveness towards the fallen Albion of Jesus in later poems. Shuddering over the appearance of the first female (18:9) and over the beginning of sexual life (19:14), shrieking at the birth of Orc (19:41), and building a tent to protect themselves are not truly constructive actions. They are more comic than splendid.

19:9. *Science*: usually this word is used in a good sense in B., but presumably not here. The science that is based upon the observations of the restricted fallen senses is a 'tent', a barrier preventing us from seeing reality, 'the infinite in all things'.

19:15. *Man*: unexpectedly appears where we would expect 'Los'. We are not going to be told of the creation of man, since he has been present all along, Urizen, etc. all being aspects of him.

19:19–36. Shows some knowledge of embryology, of how the formation of a child in the womb recapitulates stages of evolution. Cf. 11:23 and note.

20:21–9. The bound Orc is suggestive of Prometheus, bound on a rock by Zeus, of Isaac bound by Jacob and (26–9) possibly of Jesus. The whole process—separation of male and female, beginning of sexual generation and of jealousy, birth and binding of Orc—has been treated as disastrous, as stages of division. But the voice of Orc is vitalizing. Though symptoms of the fall, sex, the senses, generation will perhaps also be means of rebirth?

20:33–9. Urizen with his mathematical instruments is, by implication, ironically compared with some traditional ideas of God as a divine geometer—a 'god afar off' designing the universe from outside. Mechanistic ideas about the universe were associated by B. with Newton, sometimes shown by him with compasses.

20:41. *garden of fruits*: presumably the garden of Eden, treated as the creation of Urizen. God's placing of the forbidden tree in the garden, His prohibition to eat the fruit, leading to disobedience and guilt, would seem to B. similar to Urizen's attempt to rule by law and his anger with his sons and daughters for failure to keep that law (23:25–6).

20:47. *globe of fire*: the light of merely natural vision. Like Swedenborg B. envisages two suns—the merely natural and that of eternity. By the lesser light Urizen (and all of us when the Urizen in us is dominant) sees only fragments (23:3–6), not wholeness; sees a condition of being which is less than human ('dens').

23:11–18. *Thiriel*, etc.: the four elements—air, water, earth, fire—of which, it was once supposed, our 'lower' world beneath the moon is made (distinguished from the perfect, heavenly bodies made of the quintessence). Hence their appearance is another symbol of the descent to a lower state of being.

25:22. *Net of Religion*: The attempt to impose 'iron laws', the impossibility of obeying them, the consequent sense of guilt lead to belief in a vengeful god who needs to be propitiated, to ritual, priestcraft, etc. The web or net is 'female' in the Blakean sense in that we make it when we perceive nature as 'outer', separated from ourselves. For relationship of this section to Hindu creation myths see essay by P. Nanavutty in *The Divine Vision*.

25:23–42. Another parody of the Genesis creation narrative; essentially the same story as the formation of a material body for Urizen in 10:35–13:17.

25:38. B. makes use of the notion that 'there were giants in the earth in those days' (Genesis 6:4). Men shrank in stature and in length of life (28:1–3) and lost sense of community (28:17–18).

28:5. *Tombs*: probably a reference to the building of pyramids in Egypt. Brings in associations of dull, enforced labour by slaves, preoccupation with death, priestcraft, the captivity of God's people.

28:9. *Fuzon*: the element of fire; a manifestation of the 'fiery boy' Orc; Moses. Historically, as Moses, he leads the children of Israel out of Egyptian bondage to, it is hoped, the liberty of the City of God, Jerusalem. In the myth he leads his followers out of Urizen's world.

The Book of Ahania (p. 112). Dated on the title page 1795. It follows on from *U.* and was intended as the second book of B.'s 'infernal' Bible, his Exodus; but the interest shifts from the biblical parallel (Fuzon–Moses) to the development of B.'s own myth about the splitting of the human psyche.

2:1. *Fuzon*: corresponds to Moses and possibly (Erdman, *Prophet Against Empire*, 314–15) to Robespierre—fiery, soon defeated, French revolutionary leader; an Orc-like figure.

2:8–9. Urizen's weapons, as sky-god, would include thunder and lightning. Fuzon is here, as later when he claims godhead (3:38), ominously like his father.

2:26–7. Fuzon's weapon, personified, remembered the arm that sent it.

2:29. Here the psychological theme begins to take over from the political and religious. The son's weapon is directed against the father's genitals, suggesting an Oedipal situation. Urizen's lust is aroused, and he begins to regard Ahania, previously the female part of himself, as an object.

2:32. *Ahania*: Cf. Athena, the Greek goddess of wisdom. She is the divine wisdom (Sophia), once united with reason, now divided from it to the detriment of both.

2:44–8. Cf. the pillar of fire which guided the Israelites through the wilderness in Exodus 13:21–2, and Los's formation of the (material, not spiritual) sun in *Book of Los* 5:27–45.

3:7. *dire Contemplations*: cf. Urizen's self-contemplations in *U.* 3, which lead to his promulgation of 'one Law' in *U.* 4:40. Here the serpent out of which Urizen forms his weapons is the product of his own mind; and the poisoned rock which he launches against Fuzon turns out to be the ten commandments, given to Moses on Mount Sinai (3:46) written on tablets of stone. Moses/Fuzon, having been a leader out of Egyptian bondage, becomes a law-giver, in effect capitulates to Urizen, and so, in his true nature, dies.

4:6. *Tree of Mystery*: the tree of false religion, growing from Urizen's brain (impeding him as much as others); the poisonous upas-tree of Java; cf. 'The Human Abstract', *F.Z.* VII:31–165. There are also perhaps suggestions of the Crucifixion. Fuzon has apparently been defeated, as Orc will be in a similar way in *F.Z.* VII:31–165; yet he is still felt to be the beautiful young victim (3:41–4 cf. Absalom), associated with sacrificial divine figures such as Balder as well as Jesus.

4:13–14. Cf. *U.* 10:21–2.

4:29–30. Cf. *U.* 8:7–8.

4:40–3. Cf. *U.* 25:23–28:10. As in *U.*, the disintegration of Urizen's mind and the materialization of his body is followed by, is really the same as, the constriction of man within his limited perceptions. Here Asia is mentioned in a corresponding place to Africa/Egypt in *U.* 28:10. After leaving Egypt, the Israelites had to struggle, not always successfully, against Asian despotisms.

4:45–5:47. Having cast out wisdom and joy, intellect has become cold, dry and unproductive; but Ahania movingly recalls what Urizen was/is in his true nature.

4:54–5. Cast out from Urizen, of whom she is part, she can have no true form (4:49–50) and exists on the verge of non-entity, like Oothoon in *V.D.A.* 7:15 and Enion in *F.Z.* III:211.

5:29–34. Urizen, as will be developed more fully in *F.Z.*, is the farmer of eternity, casting the seeds of intellectual joy on the human soul and making it fertile. 'Science' here is the 'sweet science' (*F.Z.* IX:852) of eternity, true intellectual vision, not the science based solely on the senses and reason.

5:41–3. Cf. 'Earth's Answer' 11–15 in *S.E.*

Poems from Letters (p. 120)

I. '*To My friend Butts*' (p. 120). The letter is dated 2 October 1800, about a fortnight after B. with his wife and sister arrived from London at Felpham on the Sussex coast, for a stay of three years in a cottage near the house of William Hayley, for whom he was to do some work. Butts was a friend and regular buyer of B.'s works over many years.

31. *Meteor*: then used for any atmospheric phenomenon (wind, rain, rainbow, lightning, etc.).

39. *My Shadow*: his own body, of which, as of those of his wife, sister and friend (Hayley), he is at this stage still conscious as a separate entity. This is 'Female' (37), threefold vision, the vision of Beulah, in which things are seen as in harmony, as human, but still as

separate. In fourfold vision all things are united, as 'One Man' (51). Cf. the illuminative and unitive stages of mysticism.

51. *One Man*: Jesus (cf. *J*. 38:17–21); and/or, possibly, Los. Jesus appears to Albion/Man 'in the likeness & similitude of Los my Friend' (*J*. 96:22), and Los is associated with the sun (Sol). On the other hand, 'My Fold' (69) would seem to point to Jesus, the good shepherd. In 1800 B. might be thinking of Los, the human imagination which enables us to see as one. Later the 'One Man' would definitely be Jesus, a more inclusive figure even than Los.

52. *Complacent*: disposed to please.

II. *'With happiness stretch'd'* (p. 122). Contained in a postscript to a letter to Butts written on 22 November 1802. B. says he is afraid he may have bored Butts with such a long letter, and goes on: 'But I will bore you more with some Verses which My Wife desires me to Copy out & send you with her kind love & Respect. They were Composed above a twelve-month ago while Walking from Felpham to Levant to meet my Sister.'

7–8. William Hayley (1745–1820) was a minor poet, whose fussy, well-intentioned patronage was increasingly irritating to B., who did not admire his verses and would have difficulty in not letting his tongue speak what his heart felt.

13–15. B.'s father died in 1784, his favourite brother Robert in 1787, and John, who, according to B.'s friend Tatham, after leaving his apprenticeship with a baker 'sought bread at the door of William', 'lived a few reckless days, Enlisted as a Soldier & died', must have been dead by 1802. Their appearance brings to mind B.'s lack of worldly success, and interrupts his happiness in the scenery.

31–40. If he goes back to his work as poet-prophet his devotion to Los will leave him in poverty, working in a room made black and gloomy by the smoke of his trade as engraver.

47–8. Cf. Letter to Butts, 10 Jan. 1802: 'I find on all hands great objections to my doing anything but the meer drudgery of business . . . . This from Johnson & Fuseli brought me down here & this from Mr H. will bring me back again, for that I cannot live without doing my duty to lay up treasures in heaven is Certain & Determined.'

77–80. B.'s refusal to give way to discouraging thoughts leads to an experience of 'fourfold vision', in which Los is no longer manifested as the external, natural sun (which 'stood trembling in heaven'), but as the spiritual sun and as one with B. (hot with the bows of *my* Mind). Cf. *M*. 22:4–14.

83–8. Single vision (Ulro) sees with the corporeal eye only, all things as external and dead; twofold vision (Generation) sees the contraries; threefold vision (Beulah) sees the 'marriage' of the contraries in a state of harmony; fourfold vision (Eden) sees union.

From Blake's Notebook (p. 125). These three poems were drafted in the Notebook probably about 1802–4. Punctuation is editorial.

'*My Spectre around me*' (p. 125). Primarily concerned with relationships between different elements in the self—male Spectre and female Emanation; but can be thought of also as a dialogue between a man and a woman. Absence of punctuation leaves the reader to decide who the speakers are. 1–11 is presumably spoken by the narrator, of whom Spectre and Emanation are both parts. 12–32 might be spoken by the Spectre, as he follows the Emanation, seeking to get her to return; but this speaker is hardly a 'wild beast' (2). So is this part still spoken by the narrator (Blake himself? Los? Albion?), one who represents the whole man or at least retains some conception of wholeness? 33–40 are clearly spoken by the Emanation, here representing the 'female will', seeking to maintain separation and attain dominance. 41–56 are presumably spoken by the same speaker as 12–32. If this is the narrator, he seems to surrender to his spectrous aspect in 45–8 but to attain to true vision in the end. Or one might imagine 49–56 to be spoken by both contestants together? The poem can best be appreciated as a fascinatingly suggestive draft; it is not an achieved whole. Cf. *J*. 17:1–28, and see Adams, *Shorter Poems* 101–20.

17–28. In B.'s number symbolism, four is the number of wholeness, complete humanity, Eden; three of the sexual, Beulah; seven, combining the two, of the cycles of history. The passage may suggest that the speaker is, potentially at least, an Albion, universal man, capable of drawing the cycles into unity by the multiplier four, if he were not impeded by the jealousy of the Emanation.

49–50. *Love*: presumably 'Female' (41), sexual love, which tends to be jealous and possessive.

'*Mock on, Mock on . . .*' (p. 126). Voltaire (1694–1778), Rousseau (1712–78) and Newton, who wrote about the composition of light, though differing from each other, are all regarded by B. as protagonists of Natural Religion (see *There Is No Natural Religion*). He treats them and the ancient Greek philosopher Democritus, originator of the atomic theory, as materialists, believing in an external reality made up of particles of dead matter, in opposition to the true prophets, such as those of Israel, who see that reality is spiritual. To B. each grain of sand and particle of light is 'distinct' and 'human form'd' ('To my friend Butts' 17, 22).

Morning (p. 127).
1. *Western path*: the gate into Eden, now 'walled up until time of renovation' (*J*. 12:52).

From the Pickering MS (p. 127). In this MS, named after a nineteenth-century owner, B. wrote fair copies, without punctuation, of ten poems. The poems were probably written between 1801 and 1805.

The Mental Traveller (p. 127). The 'Mental Traveller' is someone with enough vision to be able to see our mental world from the outside, and so to see the horror of the exploitative relationships between man and nature, men and women, in a way that those who are used to the situation do not.

11–14. The images connect the babe with Prometheus (on a rock), Jesus, and B.'s Orc; but he is any child, whose energies are subdued by the 'female'—possessive mother, wife or mistress or the whole natural order (Vala).

23–4. Cf. *A*. 'Preludium'; but now it is clearer that this Orc's union with the female, though fertile, is disastrous. He treats her with the same cruelty that has been shown to him as a child; he does not transform, but is subdued to, nature; becomes an 'Aged Shadow' (29); is driven out, becomes young again, is reborn as a more terrible Orc (93–6), but is again nailed down by the female (103–4). The cycle continues.

44. *female babe*: The second half of the poem concentrates mainly on the cycle of the female. She is, in B.'s mythology, Vala, seen in her most fallen forms as the seducer Rahab (69–80) and the restrictive Tirzah (103–4) cf. 'To Tirzah' in *S.E.*.

64–5. When we see the earth as a ball in a scientific diagram, and stars, moon and sun as separate, distant balls, this is, for B., a false, abstract way of perceiving. Cf. *J*. 70:32: 'The Starry Heavens all were fled from the mighty limbs of Albion.'

88. Reverses what happened in 65. Seems to hint at the possibility, not to be realized in this poem, of a break-out from the cycle.

The Crystal Cabinet (p. 131). Another ambivalent poem about sexual love. Cf. 'Song: "How sweet I roam'd"' in *P.S.*, 'My Spectre around me' and 'The Mental Traveller'. The speaker starts in a state of innocence ('dancing merrily'); enters the state of threefold vision or Beulah, treated both as entrapment and as offering expansion of vision; fails to move on to fourfold vision or Eden, and falls back into 'experience'.

21–2. Perhaps he is too much the male spectre here and should heed 'My Spectre around me' 41–52.

Auguries of Innocence (p. 132). Some editors (see Erdman 484–6) have proposed rearrangements of the couplets to make a more logical sequence; but perhaps B. deliberately interweaves the themes. It does not much matter in what order you look at the particulars, for infinity is to be found in all of them. To put 59–62 before 55–8 seems a definite improvement, however.

13–14. Cruelty to the hare damages our own brains, our capacity to perceive.

25–8. The unbeliever chooses to live, like bat and owl, in darkness.

35. *Chafer*: a kind of beetle. The tormentor builds for himself a confined, visionless dwelling-place.

42. *Polar Bar*: the barrier between eternity and the realm of generation. Cf. *Thel* 6:1, but here it is the passage upward that is in question.

125–6. Cf. last sentence of *V.L.J.*: 'I question not my corporeal or vegetative eye, any more than I would question a window concerning a sight. I look through it, and not with it.'

129–32. To see God as light is to see Him as shining into the darkness from some distant heaven and as non-human.

The Four Zoas (p. 135). About 1795 B. began a long poem, originally called *Vala, Or The Death and Judgment of the Ancient Man, A Dream of Nine Nights*. In it the nightmare of man's fragmented condition is shown more subtly and comprehensively than in the shorter poems. Instead of two-sided confrontations we have four Zoas (Urizen, Luvah, Los and Tharmas—roughly, too simply, intellect, emotion, imagination and instinct or body), their female counterparts or Emanations (Ahania, Vala, Enitharmon, Enion), sons and daughters of these, spectres, shadows, etc. Emphasis is now placed on Vala rather than Urizen as the prime cause of the fall, on man's surrender to the feminine part of himself and/or to the natural world regarded as external; but really the contentions and splittings of the different 'characters' are all aspects of a single, continuing process, which takes place in history and in each individual. The poem was added to and revised over a long period. The title was changed to *The Four Zoas*; the Ancient or Eternal Man was given a name, Albion (though Albion continued sometimes to stand for England as well as for universal man); the part of Los as the keeper of the Divine Vision in time of trouble was much enhanced; and the Christian element was strength-ened. By about 1805 the MS had got into such a jumble that it was abandoned. It was not printed until 1893. No attempt is here made to represent this work comprehensively. A few passages are chosen to show developments in B.'s mythology between the Lambeth books and *Milton*, especially passages concerning Urizen and Orc which continue the themes of the earlier works. After the Night/line num-bers as in Keynes, the page/line numbers as in Erdman are given in brackets.

I:9–20 [3:4–4:4]. These lines are written over earlier ones erased, and are late.

I:9. Against this line is written 'John XVII 21–3', which reads: 'That they all may be one; as thou, Father, art in me, and I in thee, that they also may be one in us: that the world may believe that thou hast sent me. And the glory which thou gavest me I have given them; that they may be one, even as we are one: I in them, and thou in me, that they may be made perfect in one; and that the world may know that thou hast sent me, and hast loved them, as thou hast loved me.'

I:10–11. Against these lines is written 'John I 14', which reads: 'And the Word was made flesh, and dwelt among us, (and we beheld his glory, the glory as of the only begotten of the Father,) full of grace and truth.'

I:12. *Living Creatures*: The Zoas correspond among other things to the four beasts before the throne of God in Revelation 4:6–9.

I:17–19. Urthona, the unfallen Los, propagated through the ear (his rightful station) of universal man. His imaginative productions (poems, etc.) were later corrupted into theological systems.

I:19–20. B. is beginning to treat Urthona/Los almost as if he were universal man rather than one of four equally important Zoas.

I:260–4 [10:9–13]. Spoken by Enitharmon. This incident is often repeated, with many variations, in *F.Z.* The 'death' of Albion is here shown as resulting from his seduction, during the sleep of reason, by Vala, the Emanation of Luvah, the Zoa of passion. Luvah and Vala rise from their proper station, here the heart though elsewhere the loins, into the brain. Albion gets 'sex in the head', and the place of reason is usurped by passion—a very different emphasis from that in earlier works.

I:264. Uses the story of Phaethon being allowed, with disastrous results, to take his father Helios' place as driver of the chariot of the sun.

II:397–418 [35:11–36:13]. Spoken by Enion, the rejected feminine portion of Tharmas, speaking, like Ahania in a similar situation in *Ahania* 4:52–5:47, from 'the dark deep', 'the verge of non-entity'.

III:41–65 [39:12–40:18]. Another account, this time by Ahania speaking to Urizen, of Vala's seduction of Albion and of its consequences. Smitten by inner divisions Man projects a delusive self-image, and worships it as God.

VI:87–99, 115–46 [70:5–17, 70:30–71:14]. In a long expansion of *U.* 20:46–25:14 Urizen 'explores his dens', his ruin'd, less than human world. This 'Abyss' has a good deal in common with the Chaos explored by Satan in *Paradise Lost* II.890–1033. It is the chaotic, subhuman world which the abstracting intellect divorced from imagination makes for itself by its way of perceiving. Yet Urizen is part of humanity; he is ourselves, suffering from failure to communicate with the natural world and other men, suffering all the more because it is our own fault.

VI:141. *curse*: In VI:35–46 Urizen cursed his sons and daughters, in a scene in some ways resembling the encounter between Satan and his offspring Sin and Death in *Paradise Lost* II.629–735.

VII:109–65 [80:1–81:6]. There are two seventh Nights. Some editors call this VII(a). Urizen is sitting on a rock with his books around him, above the caves where the bound Orc is raging. This is the final, and most impressive, encounter between the two, though the end of the story is at IX:187, when Urizen renounces the wish to curb Orc.

VII:110–34. Urizen instructs his daughters (who are not given any distinct character, so one might say females in general) how to obtain dominion by using morality and sexual attractiveness. The passage combines B.'s myth (Urizen's desire to subjugate Los by using Enitharmon) with contemporary, and wider, history (the ruling classes' subjugation of the poor and damping down of discontent in a revolutionary time).

VII:113. *wondrous tree*: Urizen's tree of Mystery, which is also in this Night the tree of the knowledge of good and evil in Genesis 2:17. Under this tree Enitharmon (Eve) is brought to a repetition of the 'fall' later in this Night (210–400).

VII:120–2. Perhaps a reference to Thomas Malthus's theories in his *Essay on the Principle of Population* (1798), which were used as excuses for failure to relieve poverty.

VII:143. Urizen has succeeded in weakening Orc's 'divided Spirit' (137). The human in him still rages against all that Urizen represents; but partly he has become a 'worm' or 'serpent' which will ascend Urizen's tree.

VII:147–50. Orc reveals himself as a manifestation of Luvah, the Zoa of passion, who in I:264 stole Urizen's light.

VII:152–6. In taking on a serpent body, turning 'thought into abstraction' and rising into the heavens as a 'dark devourer' Orc is becoming like Urizen. Politically the 'affection' that was present in the early years of the French Revolution turns into fury in the Terror (1793), leading on to a new tyranny under Napoleon. But that which is human in Orc is still undefeated. Cf. Fuzon in *Ahania*.

VII:162–5. This seems to be Urizen's victory. He has perverted the revolutionary forces to serve him, e.g. in Napoleon's empire. But his tree is associated not only with the tree of the knowledge of good and evil, but also with the Cross. Orc, as bright young victim god, is associated with Jesus. Lines 164–5 recall Jesus's sayings: 'And as Moses lifted up the serpent in the wilderness, even so must the Son of man be lifted up' (John 3:14) and 'And I, if I be lifted up from the earth, will draw all men unto me' (John 12:32). The voluntary climbing of the tree by Jesus in Luvah's robes is the defeat of Urizen's empire and 'the dread result' he does not know.

IX:162–93 [121:1–32]. Night IX is B.'s 'Last Judgment', based to some extent on Revelation. Los pulls the sun and moon out of the sky, destroying the old world—or the old way of perceiving. The fires of eternity burn up Urizen's books, Orc in his serpent form and all tyrannies. Albion wakes and calls upon Urizen to 'Come forth from slumbers of thy cold abstraction', and resume his proper station.

IX:165. *futurity*: B. first wrote 'the past'; and in 180, 181, 182, 183, 'remembrance'. Brooding on past and future both prevent the vision of eternity in the present.

IX:184–7. At 142–3 Albion said in his call to Urizen:

Let Luvah rage in the dark deep even to Consummation,
For if thou feedest not his rage, it will subside in peace.

Milton (p. 143). Dated 1804 on the title page; written probably 1800–4, with revisions up to about 1808. B. revered Milton as England's last great poet-prophet, but thought his work and his life, and therefore his great influence on eighteenth-century England, flawed. Milton created a school divine God in a distant heaven from which the energetic Satan was expelled, symbolizing for B. inner divisions within the poet himself, in England and in mankind in general, which needed to be healed. B. envisages Milton descending into time to redeem his Emanation Ololon and to loose Satan 'from my Hells'—to heal the divisions within himself and to repair the mistakes in his work. All poets, and all of us so far as imagination lives in us, are 'sons' of Los, the eternal prophet; and all of us are parts of Albion, universal man. So Milton, Blake, Los merge; and Milton's action causes the sleeping Albion (England, mankind) to stir on his couch, and brings us to the brink of the apocalypse, in which mankind will fully waken into eternal life.

1. *'And did those feet . . . ?'* B. uses notions, current in his day, about Jesus having come to England with Joseph of Arimathea and about London having been 'The Primitive Seat of the Patriarchal Religion' (J. 27), Jerusalem. These are only starting-points for his imaginative picture of a state of being in which Jesus, the divine humanity, dwells in Albion (both Man and place), in England not in some distant heaven.

1:7. *Jerusalem*: the Holy City; the Bride of the Lamb (as in Revelation 21:2–27); freedom; a state of being in which the divine and the human, the material and the spiritual are one.

1:8. *Mills*: primarily the mental mills, mechanical ways of thinking and feeling which cause our vision to be 'clouded'; but the mills of industrial England, enslaving men in routine (cf. *J.* 65:12–28), could be included.

2:1. *Beulah*: 'married', in the Bible the name given to Zion when restored to God's favour. 'The Lord delighteth in thee, and thy land shall be married . . . as the bridegroom rejoiceth over the bride, so shall thy God rejoice over thee' (Isaiah 62:4–5). In *Pilgrim's Progress* the last country the pilgrims pass through before entering the eternal City. In B. a state of being in which the contraries (male and female, etc.) are in harmony, 'married'. For the eternals entry into Beulah is a descent, into a 'land of shadows' (11), a realm where shines only the moon, a reflection of the sun of eternity, where there is repose after the strenuous activity of eternity. For those in the realm of Generation entry to it is an ascent; to them inspiration comes down from Beulah, the divine voice is heard in the songs of Beulah (*M.* 33:1). So the daughters are muses, channels of inspiration. Cf. *M.* 30:1–14.

2:10. *False Tongue*: In the fallen condition the tongue becomes an accuser of sin, demanding sacrifice. From B.'s point of view it is the false tongue, not divine justice, which demands 'atonement' and so brought about the Crucifixion.

2:17. *One hundred years*: from his death (1674) to the time when, through B., he re-enters the world of Generation.

2:19. *Sixfold Emanation*: Ololon; on one level Milton's three wives and three daughters.

2:22. *Bard's prophetic Song*: deals with contentions between Los and his 'sons', among whom Satan in this context is one; makes Milton conscious of his errors, of how in his Selfhood he has become Satan.

14:14. *Eternal Death*: (1) Fallen life in time which is 'death' from the point of view of eternity. (2) Annihilation of the Selfhood, which is a continuing process. Milton may be thinking of this as a destruction of the self, but it is really the means towards renewal of the true self.

14:15. *Gods of Priam*: the belligerent gods of Greek mythology who caused the Trojan wars. The attitudes which cause wars to continue had been strengthened, B. thinks and his Milton has been brought to realize, by defects in Milton's own writings.

14:30. *Satan*: in the later works usually equated with the Selfhood, the selfish, dominating, self-righteous, accusing part of Milton's (or anyone's) self, sometimes the same as the Spectre; but the earlier energetic rebel Satan is not wholly discarded, which causes confusion. The energetic Satan needs to be loosed from the hells into which Milton consigned him; the Selfhood needs to be annihilated.

21:4–11. It is through B. that Milton's errors are being corrected. B. and Milton and all men are parts of universal Man; so what is done in one is felt imaginatively by all, even if not understood.

21:12. *left Foot*: Left is associated in B. with the material as compared to the spiritual right, and sometimes has 'sinister' connotations. But here the material is to be redeemed. This Vegetable World, seen imaginatively, helps us to walk through eternity, and is carried by us into eternity.

22:9. *Udan-Adan*: the lake on which Los built his city of Art, Golgonooza (*F.Z.* V:76). Water is suggestive of flux, lack of form. Los, and artists inspired by him, operate in a world which seems chaotic, and must strive to give it form.

22:15. *Six Thousand Years*: the whole of time—from the supposed date of creation about 4000 BC to the expected apocalypse. Los is returning from his fallen condition as a 'Shadowy Prophet' to his right position in the divine humanity.

24:76. *Zoa*: 'And round about the throne were the four beasts [Zoa; properly plural, used as singular by B.] full of eyes before and behind' (Revelation 4:6).

25:66. This is the beginning of a long passage (to 29:65) celebrating the activities of Los and his sons. Los has seen in Milton's descent a sign that 'the Last Vintage now approaches' (24:42), and has called 'his sons around him to the Harvest & the Vintage' (25:65). At first one might take what follows as a speech by Los to his sons; but when one gets into it, it seems more natural to take it as addressed by B. (the spokesman for Los, who has entered into him) to the reader. The speech celebrates the physical world seen imaginatively as the creation of Los rather than of Urizen. The stars, usually associated with Urizen, and the ocean, often associated with Tharmas and chaotic flux, are seen differently from usual in B.

26:33. *Bowlahoola & Allamanda*: Golgonooza is a city, the collective 'body' of society. In relation to this Allamanda is the cultivated area round the city. Golgonooza is also the individual body. In relation to this Bowlahoola is the stomach (sometimes other motive organs, the heart and lungs), Allamanda the nervous system and Cathedron the womb. In Golgonooza Los and Enithar-mon mercifully give form to the Spectres (38), sometimes called Spectres of the Dead, ghostly unformed portions of spirit which have descended into Ulro, the lowest region man enters, that in which vision is most restricted. Los gives different forms to these Spectres in accordance with their natures. It is the spiritual cause which is the determining factor.

28:62–3. By inspiration, with the help of a daughter of Beulah, eternity may be entered at any moment, which is then equal in value to the whole of time.

29:4–14. What is real is space as we actually experience it, 'an order'd Space' (9) given form by the Los in us.

29:11. *valves*: halves of a folding door. The whole earth is envisaged as the halves of a door which can open to reveal eternity.

29:16. *Globe*: A scientific model, such as the Newtonian, of the earth and solar system is merely an abstraction.

29:25–6. The circulatory system (heart, lungs, stomach) and the nervous system regulate the vital motions in the body.

31:28–62. This is a 'lamentation' in that Ololon is descending from Eden through Beulah to a 'lower' state of being, and a celebration in that her descent opens a road to eternity. See 35:42–36:12 and note on 35:46.

31:49. *Og & Anak*: Og, King of Bashan, and the sons of Anak, giants, in comparison with whom the Israelites seemed to be 'as grass-hoppers' (Numbers 13:33), were obstacles to the Israelites' entry into the promised land. They symbolize forces in the mind which inhibit us from seeing visions of eternity, which seem strong and yet can be circumvented.

32:1–43. This plate, not in the two earliest copies, was inserted to explain some of B.'s ideas rather than to advance the action; so can be appreciated on its own.

32:2. *Seven Angels of the Presence*: Cf. Revelation 5:6—'seven eyes, which are the seven Spirits of God sent forth into all the earth'. In this context 'Angel' does not carry the ironic connotation of the word in *M.H.H.* Entering into time Angels are capable of error, but express the divine guardianship of and presence with man in the seven ages of history. Completed by the addition of Milton the eight (twice four, which is the number of wholeness) become Jesus, the One Man.

32:4. *Spectre*: Cf. 'My Spectre around me' 1–12. The personality is fragmented, as was Milton's universe, with its exclusive heaven builded on cruel rationality.

32:8. *Hillel*: Hebrew name for Lucifer, the light-bringer, the morning star. The first of the seven, he speaks for them all.

32:11. *Druids*: B. uses current notions about Druidism having been an ancient wisdom which spread from England over the world and then became corrupted into a religion of cruel rituals in which human beings were sacrificed. So, B. thinks, religious vision always tends to harden into systems, rituals, laws, symbolized as 'rocks' (17), and ultimately into materialism.

Annandale: whose iron-age hill fort, rocking stone and oak groves might be regarded by B. and his contemporaries as Druidical.

32:22. *States*: Cf. *J*. 49:70–5:

> . . . the Evil is Created into a State, that Men
> May be deliver'd time after time, evermore. Amen.
> Learn therefore . . . to distinguish the Eternal Human
> . . . from those States or Worlds in which the Spirit travels.
> This is the only means to Forgiveness of Enemies.

Satan is a 'dunce' because he cannot distinguish 'the Garment from the Man' (*Gates of Paradise*). States are both successive historical eras and states of being through which individuals pass.

32:25. *Satan and Adam*: God does not permit man to fall further than into the state Satan, the limit of opacity, of lack of vision, and the state Adam, the limit of contraction.

Twenty-seven Churches: states of religious error through which men have passed from the time of Adam to the present; erroneous, yet giving form and limit to error. Cf. 35:60–5.

32:26. *about to be Created*: given form in the material world.

32:40. *Death's Door*: the mortal condition.

32:42. *Linen Clothes*: the linen clothes left lying in the empty tomb after the Resurrection, symbolizing our mortal bodies discarded when we awake into eternity.

35:46. *Ololon*: has appeared as a river in Eden, 'multitudes', sixfold, and will soon be manifested as 'a Virgin of twelve years'; is the feminine in Milton and the women in his life; in some degree foreshadows Jerusalem in *J*., the Emanation of Albion, the feminine in general (multitudes). Believing herself guilty of having driven Milton from heaven, she resolved to descend also and give herself 'to death in Ulro among the Transgressors' (21:45).

Her descent opened a 'wide road' to eternity (35:35). Such timeless moments are not perceptible to those who think nothing exists but what can be measured (35:42–3). In such moments communication is open 'downwards' from eternity, and also 'upwards' out of time and space. The latter movement is expressed in images of the lark's ascent and of the rising of the scent of the thyme to meet the rays of the sun at dawn. Ololon's descent 'to Los & Enitharmon' is in another aspect her descent to William and Catherine Blake in their cottage garden at Felpham (36:19–20).

35:50. *streams*: in the timeless moment a road is opened between Eternity and Ulro. The streams also connect the different realms. Though in one metaphor Eternity is imagined as above, and Milton and Ololon 'descend' through Beulah to Ulro, another way of looking at it is that Eden is the centre, surrounded by Beulah, with Ulro at the furthest remove. Los's city is built in Ulro; so a stream from it through Beulah to Eden connects the circumference to the centre.

35:59–60. Cf. the women at the tomb of Jesus, who died 'in Luvah's robes'.

35:65. *Twenty-seven Heavens*: Returning to the vertical metaphor we imagine these as successive layers of space round the earth through which the larks ascend. They correspond to the twenty-seven 'Churches', from Adam to the present, periods of history in which various dogmatic systems of belief (false, dividing man from Eternity, needing to be superseded, yet attempts, however imperfect, to give form to chaos and as such the creations of Los) have been dominant. Now the seven 'Eyes' are being completed by Milton, the eighth, and the twenty-seven larks, churches, heavens by the twenty-eighth, 'sexual' threes ($3 + 4$, $3 \times 3 \times 3$) giving way to numbers of wholeness (4×2, 4×7).

36:13. *Polypus*: sea creatures such as the jellyfish and sea anemone; often having poisonous tentacles; sometimes 'colonial', reproducing new individuals by putting out branches. An image of the 'vegetable world' seen merely from a materialist point of view—meaningless proliferation.

36:30. *affliction*: B. had written a great deal during his three years at Felpham, but in the service of the Muse had suffered much—for instance, from the fussy patronage of Hayley, who wanted him to give more time to money-making projects. His wife had suffered from ill health and from worry over the disturbed relationship with Hayley, who probably tried to get her to help in persuading B. to be more 'sensible'.

37:8–12. At the moment before redemption the evil in Milton is seen more clearly than before, is given a form that it may be cast out.

37:8. *Covering Cherub*: See the prophet's denunciation of the Prince of Tyre, 'the anointed cherub that covereth', in Ezekiel 28:1–19—in him great wisdom and beauty have been corrupted by pride; and the Cherubim in Genesis 3:24, who keep men from entering Eden.

37:9. *Rahab*: in Revelation 17:3–5 the scarlet woman, 'Mystery, Babylon the Great, the Mother of Harlots and Abominations of the Earth'. In B. the most corrupted form of Vala.

37:11. *Wicker Man*. See Caesar, *Gallic Wars* VI:16, about Druid methods of human sacrifice. They 'use huge figures, whose wicker limbs they fill with living men and set on fire'. B. sees wars, in which human beings are sacrificed, as resulting from false beliefs and attitudes which Milton through his works in their worst aspects had helped to perpetuate.

37:17–18. In Milton's mistaken theology B. sees both all the pagan idols and false gods (the double twelve) and all the perverted forms of Christianity, the twenty-seven churches.

38:6. *Paved work*: See Exodus 24:10. The law-giving God of Israel is seen by Moses and the elders; 'and there was under his feet as it were a paved work of a sapphire stone'. The black-clothed puritan Milton is associated with the law-giving God; but yet he is now for the first time in human form, portending that his sleeping humanity will awake and release itself from false coverings.

38:14. Cf. 39:16–20. Spectre and Satan are here the same. The Spectre is a split-off portion of humanity; so this Spectre cannot devour Milton without destroying himself.

38:30–2. If one fights against an evil seen as external, one may appear to defeat it, but in fact only provide a cover for it still to work, e.g. Napoleon's tyranny succeeding that of the kings. What is to be annihilated is one's own selfishness.

38:36. *other's good*: B.'s shifting conceptions of Satan cause difficulty. Can he both be the Selfhood, which must be annihilated, and an 'other', for whom good can be done? One must be willing to annihilate oneself for an 'other' who is in the state Satan, but the state Satan itself is to be destroyed.

38:50–7. Biblical language ironically used. Satan presents himself as God. To B. the conception of God as wrathful judge is a Satanic delusion.

39:3–9. A dramatic reversal of Satan's expectations. He thought the Seven Angels his, messengers like those in Revelation 16:1, who 'pour out the vials of the wrath of God upon the earth'; but when they appear they send forth 'Forms Human'.

39:11. *the lake*: Cf. Revelation 20:10: 'the devil . . . was cast into the lake of fire'. But here the Spectre will be purified in the fire of Los rather than destroyed.

39:22–31, 59–61. The final appearances of Satan. He is seen as God, but this is only a delusory imitation, the true God being human. One might expect some dramatic conflict at this climax; but the victory is to be won by 'mental fight'.

39:32. *Albion*: in one aspect Britain. There seem to be no specific meanings in the connection between parts of his body and the places mentioned.

39:35. *Legions*: Caerleon in Wales.

39:53–4. *Urizen*: In 18:51–19:14 Milton encounters Urizen 'on the shores of Arnon'. Urizen pours icy fluid on to his brain, while he creates new flesh, a human form for Urizen.

39:55–9. All the actions of the poem—the descent of Milton, his striving with Urizen and confrontation with Satan, his appearance to B. etc. – are aspects of one action, and take place in a moment, a pulsation of an artery.

39:60–1. To fourfold, complete vision the world is part of Albion, of man, is human. When in the state Satan we see fallaciously our selfhoods as separate, and the world as 'outside'.

40:6–8. The four Zoas exist separately only in the fallen condition; so, seeking unity, Milton strives against them all.

40:12. *Voltaire*, etc.: Eighteenth-century intellectuals, who in different ways opposed orthodox religion but who, B. thinks, promoted it in its worst form, deism or natural religion. Cf. *J.* 52.

40:14. *the cause*: Cf. 22:39–45, where Rintrah and Palamabron say:

'Milton's Religion is the cause: there is no end of destruction.
Seeing the Churches at their Period in terror & despair,
Rahab created Voltaire, Tirzah created Rousseau,
Asserting the Self-righteousness against the Universal Saviour. . . .
To perpetuate War & Glory, to perpetuate the Laws of Sin.'

As in *E.* 6:2–9 and many other places the 'female' obtains dominion by use of false religion and moral laws. In this situation there is an outward appearance of virility, in war, the pursuit of power, etc.; but the inner attitudes are, in B.'s terms, 'female'. So we have Rahab in Satan's bosom, the 'Female hidden in a Male, Religion hidden in War' (20). Rahab is Babylon (17), the city of this world opposed to the holy city Jerusalem, seen by John (22) in Revelation 17–18.

40:24–6. The seven kingdoms (Hittites, Girgashites, Amorites, Canaanites, Perizzites, Hivites, Jebusites) and five Baalim (Gaza, Ashdod, Ashkelon, Gath, Ekron) make twelve 'nations', opposed to and yet corresponding to the twelve tribes of Israel. As often in B. the fallen thing is a caricature, distortion, enemy, but yet in some degree an image, of the real.

41:26–8. At the Crucifixion the veil of the Temple, where the stone tablets of the law were kept in the Ark behind curtains, was rent; symbolizing for B. the passing of the old order.

42:3–6. That in Ololon which caused her to regard herself as a 'virgin' separate from Milton drops off, and the true Ololon is then able to be united to Milton.

42:7. *Moony Ark*: an ark in the shape of a moon. The ark is descending into the fires of intellect, where it will be burnt up—in eternity the female does not exist in separation from the male. Ark suggests protection (Noah's ark), the female's protective function during mankind's passage through time. See Raine, *Blake and Tradition* I.231–5.

42:12. *Garment*: The separations between men and between the sexes are coming to an end, and Jesus, in whom all are as One Man, appears. He has suffered with men throughout the six thousand years of history. His wearing as a garment the 'Clouds of Ololon' (she was originally 'multitudes') has much the same meaning as his appearance in several passages in *F.Z.* 'in Luvah's robes of blood'.

42:16–18. *Twenty-four . . . four*: See Revelation 4:4–10, where twenty-four elders and four beasts surround the throne of God, and the four living creatures and four wheels in Ezekiel I:4–25. The Cities are named in *J.*, where they are called 'The Friends of Albion'. They are the Cathedral Cities, in which, however imperfectly, the Divine Family can be seen (*J.* 40:45).

42:19. *Jesus wept*: John 11:35. Jesus wept over the death of Lazarus whom he then brought back to life, as the 'dead' Albion is presumably soon to be revived.

42:25–35. B.'s soul returns into its mortal state, to find his wife at his side and the lark and the scent of the thyme rising as at 35:48. The intervening visions have been in a pulsation of an artery. We are now back in the mortal condition where the cry of the poor rises from London to Los. The last judgment seems at hand, but we are left on the brink.

42:31–43:1. The final harvest is described in Revelation 14:14–20 and in *F. Z.* IX:576–852. The winepresses ('on the Rhine' in 25:3), in which blood is made into wine for the harvest feast, may include reference to the contemporary European wars; but mainly suggest the annihilation of individual Selfhoods.

Jerusalem (p. 164). The title page is dated 1804, but this may mean no more than that the poem had been conceived by then. In 1807 a friend recorded that B. had engraved 60 plates of a new Prophecy, presumably *J.* Revision and the addition of new plates continued at least for the next few years, perhaps until 1820, before which no complete extant copy was printed. In *J.* the fragmentation of Man is expressed mainly: (1) Through the separation of Albion from Jerusalem. In relation to him as an individual she is the soul—in this aspect she is the bride of the Lamb (not of Albion, whose bride is Vala); in relation to him as universal man she is the city of God, as in Revelation 21:10–27, sometimes the historical Jerusalem, to which in England London corresponds, the city being the embodiment of the collective life of society. She is also liberty, in that, united through her with each other and with Jesus, men would be free. (2) Through the separation of Albion from his twelve Sons and twelve Daughters. They are, like the Zoas, aspects of himself; they should be part of him, but are 'self exiled from his bosom' (48:61). In one aspect they are simply the people of England (twelve Sons corresponding to the twelve tribes of Israel), who damage the country and themselves by selfishness and lack of vision. During Albion's 'sleep' Los struggles to preserve the divine vision; he has to contend against internal (the splitting from him of his Emanation and his Spectre) as well as external difficulties. The poem is not a story, but a showing from various perspectives of the fallen condition of Man and of the redemptive forces that might, and in the end do, awaken him to his true nature.

4:16–17. On the title page Jerusalem is depicted as a butterfly, thus connecting her with the Greek legend of Psyche (butterfly, soul, girl loved by Eros God of Love). She is the bride of the Lamb, but Albion jealously hides (32–3) his own soul from fruitful relationship with the divine lover.

4:22. After this line was originally written: 'Saying: We are not One: we are Many, thou most simulative.' This was deleted from the copper, indicating B.'s firm intention; but it is printed by Keynes and included in his numeration, which I follow.

5:24. *Entuthon*: forest of error, containing the lake Udan-Adan: opposed to Golgonooza in which art, form, truth are found.

5:25–6. The Sons of Albion are given names of, or suggestive of, contemporaries of B., who impeded him in his prophetic mission—by attacking his art (Hand, the Hunt brothers who ridiculed him in their periodical *The Examiner*), by fussy patronage and incomprehension (Hyle, Hayley), by having him tried for sedition after he had put a soldier out of his garden (Coban, etc.). In small incidents in his life B. sees the forces that are always opposed to the light.

6:15. *Locke*: philosopher, whose *Essay Concerning Human Understanding* (1690) had much influence in the eighteenth century. Against his doctrine that all our knowledge derives from experience B. asserts that 'Man is Born Like a Garden ready Planted & Sown. This World is too poor to provide one Seed' (*Anno. Reynolds*).

6:16. *Newton*: author of a mechanistic view of the external universe as Locke is of the internal. Together they weave a covering shutting men from vision of eternity.

6:18. *Wheels*: The wheels which move each other by compulsion refer primarily to inhuman systems—in religion, philosophy, science, morality or social organization; but also suggest the machines of industrialism which reduce men to a machine-like existence. The wheels that revolve in freedom probably derive from the four wheels of the chariot of God in Ezekiel 1:20, where 'the spirit of the living creature was in the wheels' (the impulse is within them) and perhaps from the older, Ptolemaic, model of the universe, in which the spheres revolve harmoniously, guided by Intelligences. B. likes to use the same image in bad and good senses (cf. war), suggesting that things seen in the fallen condition are corrupt imitations of the realities of Eden.

27:1–88. From the Preface to Chapter II of *J*., addressed to the Jews. In the prose before the poem, B. brings together his own Albion with the Jewish tradition in the *Cabala* of a cosmic Man, who 'contain'd in his mighty limbs all things in Heaven & Earth'. Albion/Man's ancient wisdom spread over the earth as Druidism, and was corrupted. Britons and Jews have only to go back to the origins of their best traditions to recover a common vision. Israel and England were originally one. London was, and still potentially is, Jerusalem, the holy city. B. takes over contemporary notions about the Druids and British Israelites, cranky if taken literally but usable to good imaginative effect.

27:1–20. The change of tense after the first two stanzas moves us from a past golden age to the vision of innocence which is always present, as in B.'s own *S.I.* and the experiences behind them when as a boy he could walk out from the much smaller London of those days to the inns, the Jews-harp-house and the Green Man, and to Willan's farm, all on the north in what is now Regent's Park.

27:25–6. The 'golden builders' are Los's 'Sons', who are always building Golgonooza, and the builders who in B.'s day were making new houses in the slum area of Paddington.

27:33–4. London Stone and Tyburn were places of execution in ancient and modern (Tyburn) times, symbolizing the decline of the patriarchal wisdom into a religion which practised human sacrifice.

27:37–43. The fall of Albion (29) is a self-division. There split from him his Spectre, Satan, associated with the corruption of sexuality (37), war and false religion; and his Emanation, Jerusalem, who ceases to be part of him (in Lambeth) and falls away across the sea to Israel.

27:65–6. Self-righteous pride is in B. and all of us; so all are guilty of slaying the Lamb. Even the Satanic Selfhood is to be reclaimed (75).

27:77–80. Again applies to all, but perhaps especially to the Jews with their strong family feeling and claim to be the chosen people.

27:85. *Exchanges*: Cf. *J*. 24:42–3

In the Exchanges of London every Nation walk'd,
And London walk'd in every Nation, mutual in love & harmony.

This includes reference to London as a great commercial centre. Even financial Exchanges may image mutual dependence and help, but the emphasis on 'my . . . mine' marks the contrast between the exchanges the prophet wants and the merely commercial.

31:2–42. 45:2–42 in Erdman, following B.'s arrangement in some copies.

31:7. *Minute Particulars*: a phrase which occurs several times in J., never before in B. His stress on universal man is complemented by stress on the individuality of men, animals, works of art, lines in works of art, etc. Cf. 91:20–22. Here the Particulars are primarily the people of London, but also perhaps the particulars of the natural environment, which are also degraded in the great city. The attitudes producing this degradation are hidden within, in people's minds.

31:9–12. Natural ingredients are used to make bricks, and these are made into great structures, such as the pyramids, a metaphor for the sacrifice of individual souls for some inhuman purpose.

31:12. *Heber & Terah*: ancestor and father of Abram; perhaps associated by B. with the building of the tower of Babel, described in Exodus 11:1–9 immediately before the geneaology of Abram.

31:14–25. Los's walk is from Highgate, north of London, through satellite villages on the north-east to the Isle of Dogs on the Thames on the east; then west to the Tower and London Bridge; then to the Bethlehem (Bedlam) Hospital for the insane in Moorfields north of the bridge (or, less likely, to the post-1815 site of the Hospital in Lambeth).

31:16. *Leutha's*: Cf. the 'lureing' Leutha of E. 14:9–14; suggestive of the degradation of sex, here especially of prostitution in the dock area of east London.

31:17–18. The particulars here are London's children running down the open sewers (kennels).

31:23–5. It is ironical that the Tower, a place of imprisonment, should be built by Luvah, the 'lover', 'the mildest Zoa'. Cf. *F.Z.* I:260–4 where Luvah and Vala are the cause of Man giving the sceptre to Urizen..

31:25. *Bethlehem*: means house of bread; housed lunatics who were often ill-treated.

31:37–8. This includes Los/Blake's wish that the English should not take vengeance against the French, their enemies in the Napoleonic wars.

31:39–42. Travelling west (the gate to Eden is in the west; cf. 'Morning') Los sees beneath appearances to the holy city which London still potentially is. Vala, who first appeared in *A*. as 'the Shadowy

Female', is now the shadow of Jerusalem. External nature is only a shadow of the real.

38:7–26. 34:7–26 in Erdman.

38:7. *he*: Albion. Cf. *U*. 3–5, where Urizen, 'petrific' (3:26) and 'cold' (3:27), turns away from the warmth of Eden, asking 'why live in unquenchable burnings' (4:13). In *U*. the 'Eternals' separate themselves from Urizen, but here the Saviour follows the fallen Albion, pleading with him to recognize that the intellectual wars of eternity are wars of life, and that living as One Man does not submerge individual identity.

52:1–28. From the Preface to Chapter III, addressed to the deists. In the preceding prose B. has argued that deism is 'the Worship of the God of this World'. Believing in natural virtue and finding men evil deists can 'never be Forgivers of Sin'; and therefore they become causers of war. 'The Glory of Christianity is, To Conquer by Forgiveness. All the Destruction therefore in Christian Europe has arisen from Deism, which is Natural Religion.' The poem is derived from a draft in the Notebook, from which 'The Grey Monk' in the Pickering MS is also derived.

52:17–20. Satan, the Selfhood, abstracts moral law from the Gospel, becomes an accuser of sin, and so in the Pharisees murders Jesus. The monk is a Christ-like figure (13–14).

52:21–2. Titus, Roman Emperor, defeated the Jews and destroyed the Temple in Jerusalem in AD 70; Constantine, Roman Emperor, having been converted to Christianity in 313, made the Empire officially Christian, thus corrupting religion by associating it with power—a process continued, as B. would see it, by Charlemagne, Frankish King, becoming Emperor of the Holy Roman Empire in 800 and fighting 'religious' wars.

52:25–8. In the Pickering MS poem this is part of a speech by the monk in which he deprecates his relations gathering to avenge him:

> vain the sword, and vain the bow;
> They never can work war's overthrow.

60:50. *Jerusalem*: In an action reminiscent of that of Ololon in *M*. in descending to join Milton in Ulro Jerusalem has, after the fall of Albion, forsaken 'Beulah's pleasant lovely shadowy Universe' (48:19) and descended to become 'an Aged pensive Woman' (48:28) suffering in the mortal condition. As Kathleen Raine has shown she is in one aspect Psyche, the soul, suffering at the hands of the cruel Aphrodite (Vala) before she can be reunited with the divine lover (Jesus). Though fallen and subject to doubt, she retains something of the divine vision.

60:69. *Brother*: recalling the story of Lazarus in John 11:1–46.

61. This plate is an interpolated one, quite relevantly introducing an account of a particular act of forgiveness into the colloquy between Jerusalem and Jesus, which continues in 62.

61:3–13. B. is interested in meanings rather than facts. At times he accepts the Virgin Birth (*F.Z.* VIII:241) as a symbol of his rejection of the merely natural; but here he makes Mary really an adulteress in order to give more reality to Joseph's forgiveness.

61:31–4. Euphrates, Gihon, Hiddekel and Pison are the four rivers of Eden (Genesis 2:10–14); Arnon and Jordan are in Palestine. The rivers fertilizing the dry lands are like the divine and human forgiveness.

61:38–40. See Ezekiel 16:4–6: 'In the day thou wast born thy navel was not cut, neither wast thou washed in water . . . but thou was cast out in the open field. . . . And when I passed by thee, and saw thee polluted in thine own blood, I said unto thee when thou wast in thy blood, Live.' In 36–46 B. makes use of this whole chapter from Ezekiel on the continuing love of God for Jerusalem in spite of her 'whoredoms'; but the tone is different.

61:48–51. Jerusalem as city sees the events of Jesus's life. Those who crucified Him accepted the attitudes B. associates with Druids, deists, Romans, kings. Cf. 'I saw a monk' *J.* 52:17–24.

61:52. Cf. 'For the Sexes: The Gates of Paradise' 61–4.

62:2–29. Continues the colloquy between Jerusalem and Jesus from Pl. 60 without taking account of the insights given in interpolated Pl. 61.

62:7–13. Not much particular meaning can be seen in these twelve wives and mothers, stretching from Cainah, 'wife of Cain', not mentioned in the Bible, down to Mary. Most were of dubious reputation—either in themselves or through their husbands or sons. B. is concocting as unrespectable a genealogy for Jesus as he can. Jesus will be born in the natural process of generation, of Vala, with the danger that he will, like Orc in *E*. 'Preludium', become subject to the 'female'. But unlike Orc he will be able to take on 'the Body of death' without being subjected.

62:16. See Job 19.26.

62:20. *Luvah*: Luvah and Vala must be given material form in order that they may be redeemed. In several passages in *F.Z.* Jesus appears 'in Luvah's robes of blood', and in *M.* he appears 'in clouds of Ololon', human suffering throughout history being borne by Jesus. Luvah (e.g. in *J.* 65–6) and in earlier works Orc are sometimes shown as victims, and by the imagery are associated with Jesus, but they are not able to redeem the sufferings by forgiveness.

62:25–9. Recalls God's care for the Israelites in their journey through the wilderness in Exodus 13–18.

62:36–42. The prophet at any time divided from those who should support him and losing his inspiration; and B. himself isolated and unheard in England, at times at odds with his wife. Yet Los/Blake continues with his task.

65:12–28. In the preceding passage, on the crucifixion of Luvah by the Sons and Daughters of Albion, the general theme of man's repression of his own affections and desires has been given a contemporary reference by identifying Luvah as France; in warring against France, England tried to repress the movement towards liberty which the French Revolution had stood for. So here the general theme of the ill effects of abstract reasoning is given contemporary reference to the Industrial Revolution.

65:14. *Cheviot*: being near the border, associated with fighting between England and Scotland, and so with war in general.

65:15. *Annandale*: associated by B. with the Druids. Cf. *M.* 32:11.

90:67. The poem is moving towards the climax. In the preceding plates the negative forces have been seen consolidating—into the Covering Cherub (89:9) and One Great Satan (90:43). In 91–3 Los defines his positive vision, and subdues his Spectre, and the Female Will in Enitharmon.

91:7–10. Cf. *M.H.H.* 22–3.

91:32–3. Cf. Psalm 104:2. These are mental constructs, such as the Newtonian model of the universe. The Spectre (of Los or of Urthona) makes a final attempt to impose a rationalist system on Los.

91:34. *Smaragdine Table*: a set of thirteen propositions attributed to 'thrice-great' Hermes, sometimes identified with the Egyptian god Thoth, and thought by the Alchemists to provide the key to the universe; regarded by B. as another attempt to impose a rigid system on reality.

91:36. Los pays attention to the particulars; the Spectre makes an abstract model.

91:38–41. Cf. two pictures exhibited by B. in 1809—'The Spiritual Form of Nelson Guiding Leviathan' and 'The Spiritual Form of Pitt Guiding Behemoth', symbolizing the sea and land wars waged by these leaders and in general the psychic depths from which the impulse to war arises.

91:44–6. In smiting the Spectre Los is subduing a part of himself and 'unbinding' the eye and ear so that they will be able to see and hear truly.

91:47–8. *grains of sand*: Los is restoring the vision which enables man to 'see a world in a grain of sand', in each minute particular.

91:49. *moth*: recalls the title page illustration in which Jerusalem appears as a moth or butterfly, and the connection through the Greek word 'Psyche' of moth and soul. Spiritual vision and the reunion of Albion with his Emanation are being made possible by the subduing of the Spectre.

92:1–6. The capacity of the English to unite different peoples into one nation, even if still a sinful one, is an emblem of the coming realization of the unity of all in Albion/Jesus. The union of the ancient enemies, Hebrew and Canaanite, is a similar emblem.

92:7–20. Continues the quarrel of Los and Enitharmon from Plates 87–88. In 87:12–18 she said:

> 'No! I will seize thy Fibres & weave
> Them, not as thou wilt, but as I will; for I will Create
> A round Womb beneath my bosom, lest I also be overwoven
> With Love; be thou assured I never will be thy slave.
> Let Man's delight be love, but Woman's delight be Pride.
> In Eden our loves were the same; here they are opposite.
> I have Loves of my own; I will weave them in Albion's Spectre.'

Now she fears that a power greater than she can control is appearing, Albion will awaken and her separate existence come to an end.

92:15–20. In Eden the division between male and female and the contentions of sexuality will only be remembered (and forgiven) as warnings of what is to be avoided. In 88:3–7 Los had acknowledged that in Eternity the Emanations would still have a role:

> When in Eternity Man converses with Man, they enter
> Into each others Bosom (which are Universes of delight)

In mutual interchange; and first their Emanations meet
Surrounded by their Children; if they embrace & comingle
The Human Four-fold Forms mingle also in thunders of Intellect.

94:1–17. Los has seen in the consolidation of error in Satan/the Cover-
ing Cherub and in the taking on of 'this Waking Death' (93:18) by
Jesus and by himself the 'Signal of the Morning' (93:26). But
Albion still lies on his rock, his fallen state symbolized by the
isolation of Britain, as an island, from other nations (14), and by
the land being covered by fog and clouds, which constitute 'a
Female Shadow' obscuring the light of eternity.

94:20. *England*: Though in the preceding passage England was an
obscuring shadow, she wakes first in response to the breath
divine, repents, and wakes Albion. This gives a positive role to the
female at this climax. 'England' in relation to Albion as England is
much the same as Vala in relation to Albion as universal Man—
'Shadowy Female' in the fallen state, true bride in eternity.

94:20. *Brittannia*: At 36:28 'England, who is Brittannia, divided into
Jerusalem & Vala'. This division is now healed.

94:22. *Dream*: Cf. *E*. 9:5, where eighteen hundred years were 'a
female dream' of Enitharmon.

95:16–18. Albion compels the other three Zoas to their proper tasks,
whereas he sees Urthona doing what he should be.

95:19–20. Seems to identify Los here as 'Urthona's Spectre'. Los, the
imagination in time, is only a spectrous form of Urthona, imagi-
nation in eternity.

96:1–2. Probably Plate 95 was rewritten, and these lines, after being
used in it, should have been deleted.

96:9. *Sinai*: It is man's Selfhood, proud in the possession of the moral
law, that has crucified Jesus.

96:17. *Covering Cherub*: See *M*. 37:8 and note.

97:1–4. It is rather surprising to find Jerusalem only now being called
on to awake. During 'the Night of Death' she (as the soul) has been
more awake than Albion, retaining some vision of Jesus. But only
now are all things to be revealed in their Human Forms (99:1), and
Jerusalem as their Emanation to be seen in her universal aspect.

98:6–7. Albion's Spectre, the self-righteous, judging aspect of him-
self, is annihilated by the arrows of Intellect or of Love (97:12).
This is much the same as Satan, Selfhood, Covering Cherub. All
these are sometimes, as here, presented as 'Negations'—things
which are essentially illusory and vanish in eternity; more com-

monly the Spectre seems to be a split-off part of the self, which should be 'alter'd' (91:50), reintegrated rather than annihilated.

98:9. *B.* brings in his opponents as well as the more congenial poets. If (the syntax is not clear) we understand these writers to be the chariots, they are 'Threefold' chariots, i.e. each in his writings has conveyed something of the truth, but imperfectly. Now each will become 'Fourfold', complete.

98:46. *Heathen*: all those, including the orthodox religions, who do not accept Christianity as understood by B.; those who believe in moral law which leads to war—as in the Classical civilizations, among the Druids and in the British Empire.

98:52. *Gog-Magog*: 'Gog, the land of Magog', enemy of Israel is denounced in Ezekiel 38–39; Gog and Magog are allies of Satan, destroyed by fire from heaven, in Revelation 20:8–9. There are statues of Gog and Magog outside the Guildhall in London, the centre of England's commercial empire.

98:56. *Thirty-two Nations*: Listed in 72:38–42.

99:2–4. Even now there is still alternation between the full life of eternity and a lesser state in which time and space is experienced.

99:5. *I heard*: Cf. 4:4–5. The whole poem has been dictated to B., has been heard by him.

For the Sexes: The Gates of Paradise (p. 189). In 1793 B. produced a small emblem book *For Children: The Gates of Paradise*, consisting of a series of designs with cryptic titles. Much later, perhaps about 1818, he changed the heading to *For the Sexes*, and added greatly to the text, including the addition of the prologue and epilogue here printed.

The Gates of Paradise (p. 189)

3. *the Accuser*: Satan, as in the next poem and in *Job*. What this Satan would object to would not be the writing of the law, but God's penitence and withdrawal of it.

7–10. The dead corpse of the law given on Mount Sinai was buried by Jesus, but has been resurrected by the Christians.

To the Accuser (p. 190). Cf. *M.* 32:22–9. Satan is unable to distinguish States, through which Individuals pass, from Individual Identities, which 'never change nor cease'. He himself, though now worshipped as the God of this world, is in his true nature Lucifer, son of the morning, the morning star. As Satan he is an illusion in the mind of

Man, who is lost like travellers in traditional tales transported to a land of faerie and losing years in sleep and dream.

The Everlasting Gospel (p. 190). Twelve fragments, one (d) headed 'The Everlasting Gospel', of an unfinished poem are written in the Notebook and on a separate sheet of paper watermarked 1818. Probably all the fragments were written in or soon after 1818. Using Keynes's and Erdman's lettering I print fragment (d), the longest and perhaps the last written (it is a second draft, though still clearly imperfect), and fragment (j), probably intended as a prologue. See Erdman's edition 791–6 and his 'Uprose Terrible Blake' in *From Sensibility to Romanticism* (O.U.P., 1965).

The title is derived from Revelation 14:6: 'And I saw another angel fly in the midst of heaven having the everlasting gospel to preach unto them that dwell on the earth'. Ideas about the everlasting gospel descended from the medieval mystic Joachim of Flora to various religious sects in the sixteenth and seventeenth centuries. It was supposed that the ages of the Father, of fear and servitude, and of the Son, of filial obedience, would be succeeded by the age of the Holy Spirit, of complete liberty in which the unity of God and man would be fully accomplished. See A.L. Morton, *The Everlasting Gospel* (Lawrence and Wishart, 1958). B.'s stress on human–divine unity and on liberty links with this tradition, but he is expressing his own visions and includes no suggestion of a third age, succeeding that of the Son.

9–10. See Luke 2:49 and Matthew 12:46–50.

14. See John 3:1–7.

18. See Matthew 11:28–9.

41. Scientists, by banishing God to a distant heaven, helped to hand over this world to the rule of 'Caesar'.

66. *ancient Elf*: presumably the Devil.

78–84. One cannot imagine that B. intends to endorse this speaker's apparent advocacy of hypocrisy and revenge. Are we to suppose that this is a false 'God' speaking (unlikely in view of the Blakean content of 73–7?)? or that God is stimulating Jesus into a combative answer (which He gets—'thunders hurl'd')? or that what He says does not mean what it seems to? After 84 was originally written

All corporeal life's a fiction
And is made up of contradiction

It is only the illusory which is to be destroyed, not pardoned.

83. Luke 23:34:'Father, forgive them; for they know not what they do.'

86. John 17:9: 'I pray not for the world, but for them which thou hast given me; for they are thine.'

87. Presumably refers to Jesus's prayer that 'if it be possible, let this cup pass from me' (Matthew 26:39). In a moment of weakness He wished for 'a Bodily Pardon', but repudiated this. This world, that 'was born in a night to perish in a night', is not to be pardoned, but to be burned up so that eternity may appear. But this does not mean revenge.

89–96. This sentence peters out without a verb, showing the imperfect state of the draft. The conclusion would presumably have shown that 'that which was of woman born' being only a 'dark fiction', would perish. Cf. 'To Tirzah' 1–3.

101–6. Cf. Auguries of Innocence' 125–8.

Against the last line is written:

I'm sure This Jesus will not do
Either for Englishman or Jew.

Index of First Lines

chimney Sweepes - Chimney Sweeper
Holy Thursday - Holy Thursday
Nurse's song - Nurse's song
Introduction - Introduction + Earth's answer
Infant joy - Infant sorrow
The Lamb - The Tyger
Divine Image - Divine Image and Human Abstract
On Another's sorrow - The Clod and the Pebble.
Blossom - The sick Rose, The Lily.
A Dream - The Angel; The Fly
The Echoing Green - The Garden of Love
Little Boys and Girls Lost and Found.
The little Black Boy - The Little Vagabond.